Swansea Girl

BARBARA HARDY

Swansea Girl

A Memoir

seren

Seren is the book imprint of
Poetry Wales Press Ltd
Nolton Street, Bridgend, Wales
www.seren-books.com

First published by Peter Owen, 1994
This edition 2004

ISBN 1-85411-381-X

A CIP record for this title is available from
the British Library.

The publisher works with the financial assistance
of the Welsh Books Council.

'Sweets' and 'In No Named Place' from
Severn Bridge: New and Collected Poems,
Barbara Hardy (Shoestring, 2001)

Printed by CPD (Wales), Ebbw Vale

Contents

List of Illustrations

Sweets

I walked again the way we went to school
from 22 Cradock Street up Carlton Terrace
where every day I counted cracks in walls
played Daddy Daddy Can I Cross the Water
and the Big Ship Sailed on the Ally Ally O
to Heathfield up the stone steps by the Green
where I picked bitter wormwood and blanched barley
near the corner house where Valerie Williams lived
whose parents talked fast Welsh in front of the children
past the quarry where we dared Alpine climbs
and Peggy Petters told me the facts of life
while I gaped and gasped no-one would do it
near steep Primrose Hill whose iron rails remain
a bit bent now where we hung like wobbly bats
telling tall tales about the gory stain
and my tightroping brother cracked his new front tooth
just across from the Spanish chestnut tree
felled long ago but the grassy slope we searched
for skeleton leaves and tender nuts still green
by Cromwell Street where Glenys James told me
boys liked big breasts and her old grandfather
recited all Poe's *Raven* in deep solemn tones
as we listened rapt and nearly died laughing
then Norfolk Street where the school's still standing
Terrace Road School with its weathervane veering
gold glitter on a tower above the playgrounds
high flights of steep sharp steps we jumped
where bold as a heroine from the Abbey school
I punched a rude boy teasing Valerie
as we played orphans and cruel guardians
and I sulked when Miss Clements sent me out for talking
saying I couldn't be a fairy in her Christmas play
where we had singing games with Loopy Loo
ran out to icecream carts and raspberry vinegar
or an old hunched man swopping rags for goldfish
near the twin sweetshops on opposite streetcorners
Mrs Davies for the boys and for us Mrs Lily
yellow sherbetsuckers and cocobutternuts
pied peardrops flinty mints and lucky packets
windows filled with everlasting sweets.

Chapter 1
Be Good, Sweet Maid

Children hate their parents to be sad. I was furious when my mother's eyes filled with tears because someone was singing 'In My Solitude' on the wireless and when she choked up reading an Ella Wheeler Wilcox poem about living 'in the shade of a dark brown eye'. I loved it when she sang silly songs, like my favourite,

> I love our Sarah, she lives at the farm,
> And long as she's true to me I'll do her no harm.
> Tol rol de rol ray, tol rol de rol dare,
> Like the buttercups and daisies that grow in the air.

I took it as gorgeous nonsense until I came to understand it was a ruthless rural ditty about a village idiot. Mother sang sad songs more often than funny ones, 'Loch Lomond', 'My Bonnie Lies Over the Ocean', 'For Those in Peril on the Sea', and 'Oft in the Stilly Night'. She used to sing two ditties, which I sang to my children and grandchildren. They must be by the same forgotten lyricist of childhood sweethearts. One is a girl's invitation, the other a boy's, but the genders could be changed. I can hear her singing them in her high sweet voice, very seriously:

> Come round on Sunday, come round to tea
> I shall expect you when the clock strikes three,
> You are the best boy I've ever found,
> I've an extra lump of sugar for your tea,
> So do come round.

and

> Come on over the garden wall, little girl, to me,
> I've been waiting a long, long time,
> And the wall's not hard to climb.
> Just jump up and then just jump down,
> I won't let you fall.
> We'll play at sweethearts, going to be married,
> Come over the garden wall!

They are the first love-songs I remember.

I was born in 1924, at 7 Hall Terrace, Swansea. There were two brief spells when my parents had a home of their own, one in rooms over their shop in High Street, one a house in Brockley. After 1929 my mother, my brother and I went to live with my grandparents and their unmarried son, Ron, in 22 Cradock Street, Swansea. It was a narrow, rambling house, with three bedrooms, an attic, an outside lavatory and no bathroom. It was lovely bathing in the zinc washing-tub, in front of the roaring fire on Friday nights. I remember holding the flannel – a real bit of Welsh flannel – to my eyes when my hair was being washed with Evans Williams Camomile Shampoo, to keep it fair. I remember my mother drying me, telling me you must always wipe under your arms because there were 'glands' there, and gently pressing down the ticklish half-moons of my toe-nails. She eventually persuaded my grandmother to have a bath and geyser installed in the back kitchen, but that was chilly compared with the old baths on the kitchen hearth.

The bedroom my mother, brother and I shared had three paintings. There were two flower prints, one on each side of the chest of drawers, which had a tip-mirror. There was red and blue in each, but one was a thick, clumpy bunch of sweet-williams and the other a more spread-out arrangement of fragile sweet peas. Over my mother's big bed, shared with one or other child at different ages, was a big rectangular painting by my father. It showed a sailing-ship, black masts and rigging, but little or no sail, on a stormy sea. There were green shadows and bright white wave-edges on a dark-grey water. In the fore-ground on the right was a large buoy, perhaps too large, though I can't be sure in the dimness of memory. I didn't see the painting after we moved to the Uplands in 1941, though I didn't miss it for years. My mother told me, when asked, that she'd thrown it away because she thought nobody valued it except herself. One of her maddeningly spontaneous and improvised explanations that made me want to scream. My father's neat, slopy initials, M.N., were in the corner. There was a wedding group, with Gladys and her bridesmaid, Leah, looking hand-some and rather severe, my father looking very young, and a second cousin, Betty Jones, resplendent as the little bridesmaid. And there was a photograph of my mother in Wren's uniform.

Mother told me proudly about Father's courage in the war. She was inclined to be jingoistic and look down on men who could have fought and didn't, in both wars. She confessed that she and a friend had proffered white feathers to men in civvies. 'Why?' I asked, in amazement. 'Because I was daft, and didn't know any better,' she answered drily.

On the chest of drawers was her beautiful ivory manicure set, and a dressing-case of my father's, with glass and silver bottles, relics from another time. I used to gaze at myself in the small mirror, less in admiration than in meditation. You could tilt the swing-mirror back and see yourself at funny angles. When I was very young I found that if you went on staring at an object, a picture, a vase, a clock, a face, it would become unreal. If you tried this with your own face it was frightening. And if you stood with your back to the mirror, tipped your head back, with the mirror at the correct angle, your face would not only look unreal but thin, high cheek-boned and crazy, with staring eyes. I knew that if I went on looking madly at my face I'd really go mad. I always stopped just in time, but not before I'd thoroughly frightened myself. I'd undress quickly and dash into bed. Sometimes I'd change the game and persuade myself that my upside-down bony face looked like Marlene Dietrich's. Downstairs was the family, loud, loving, teasing, quarrelling and gossiping. Upstairs was the secret life.

I spent a lot of time in that room, lying on the big bed, or the little one, both specially hand made of plain oak bars. At the very end of the top piece of wood in my bed there was – and still is – a tiny wedge, which I would pretend was a door, with a corridor inside, an entrance for the imagination, thrilling or chilling. I liked to put pillows on the window-seat, drawing the curtains and making a small one-window-sided room, to read or day-dream. The room shut off, I could look out at the small garden, with its tired old privet tree which I wanted to grow so that I could swing in it from a hammock. I would try to improvise a hammock with an old red table-cloth, but the tree was so low that I touched the ground. When I was small the window-ledge fitted like a womb, but when I outgrew it I'd lie on my mother's bed, pulling feathers out of its blue silk corner. This was forbidden. Sometimes too many feathers would come out and I'd be discovered. I usually wanted only four or five, white for women (fairies or queens or princesses), black or brown for men (kings or princes). There was a cream-coloured blind, and one night I pulled it so hard that it tore. I fell asleep and woke up in guilt. There was another occasion when I fell asleep in guilty fear for something worse. My father had gone on an Antarctic expedition, as chief steward on a ship bound for South Georgia. One of the explorers, Scout Morse, had given him a New Testament as a souvenir. I developed a longing for the little leather book, and decided that I'd make it mine by tearing out and tearing up the flyleaf with the names of the donor and my father. My mother was angry, as she seldom was, and looking back I am astonished at what I did. Nobody in the family was ever very cross with children, and we were overfed, loved and indulged. Religion was strict and repressive but the family was not.

But I felt sorry for myself and my brother Bill because we didn't seem to have a father. He was so far away, home so seldom, and in the end, never, that he might as well have been nowhere. He was away at sea, and his ships always came in to Liverpool or Birkenhead, never to any of the South Wales ports. I accepted this as a reason for our never seeing him, until one or two of my friends' mothers asked awkward questions. After a while the words came glibly off my tongue because I said them so often, 'My father's a sailor and his ship never comes to Swansea but Liverpool, and it doesn't stay long there, so we don't often see him.'

One friend of mine called Jean Williams, a plump, clever girl with a beautiful voice, had a mother whose maiden name was Rhodda. My mother always referred to her coldly as Netta Rhodda. She was a real Nosy Parker, and in the art of extracting information Uriah Heep's mother had nothing to teach her. Every time I went to have tea with Jean, as I was carelessly munching a sandwich or pastry, she would pounce, 'And when did you see your father last? It must be difficult for Gladys.' One day I heard myself telling the Liverpool story, saw Netta Rhodda's pop-eyes, and stopped believing in it.

In the early years I repeated every night what my mother told me to say and what I felt: 'Please send Daddy home, and keep him safe.' I used to write to him, too, always ending 'I love you, I miss you. Please come home.' Later, I didn't believe he would ever come back. I didn't think about him much. My friend Glenys James once came up to play in the bedroom, and pounced on a photograph of my father, in evening dress, with a bow-tie, in the middle of the mantelpiece, balancing a thirties' silver-grey, half-moon clock Mother had won in a British Legion whist drive. 'Who is that dissipated-looking man?' Glenys asked, and I suddenly saw that he did look dissipated. I had a vague but sufficient grasp of the word, and Glenys's smile was full of meaning, half-disapproving and half-admiring. I had a sudden recognition that my father, absent from our lives, was somewhere living his life.

I still have some of his letters, written in the early thirties, with funny drawings of little people, all ending 'I love you all the blinking world.' My mother never talked about him except when we were alone. She kept him alive and present. She'd tell me how he 'idolized' me, and how she hoped we'd all be together again some day. One night she dreamt he was shipwrecked, and some weeks later she got a letter saying he'd been in a bad storm, with waves mountain high. After that, I used to look at the waves in Swansea Bay and the Mumbles and they seemed very small. I didn't see how waves could be as big as mountains, but I believed my mother and father. Moving from real waves to imaginary ones was as bad as trying to think about God.

God and Jesus were nearly as present as Mother and Father. My best friend in Terrace Road Infants School, Glenys Dodson, shared my infantile interest in religion. We had long discussions after school about heaven, immortality and God. Jesus was no problem. He was very human, and his miracles were no different from the magic in fairy-tales. But believing in God was another matter. He was human in the Old Testament stories that we knew so well from Sunday School, but also harsh and violent and tyrannical. I went to Sunday School from the age of four to seventeen. They told us in Sunday School that old men like Methuselah weren't quite as old as they seemed, because the way people measured time was different then and years were more like months. That made the Old Testament patriarchs easier to accept but didn't help with God. He was like a human being and yet all-powerful and immortal. Then of course we didn't really die either, or at least we lived after death. That was hard to believe too, especially when you looked at dead flies and goldfish, which seemed so very dead. Worst of all was eternity. Glenys agreed with me that it was the big teaser. It was impossible to imagine living for ever, but it was also impossible to imagine coming to an end. There are times when I feel the same as I did at five or six, teased by thought out of thought. When I was sixteen or seventeen I had long religious arguments with a theological student called Idris, who amazed me by believing as little as I did but wanting to call his lack of belief, and mine, versions of Christianity.

My mother used to tell stories of her childhood and girl-hood, and gradually the pieces fitted together. My grandfather was the village baker in two Pembrokeshire villages, Carew and Milton. My mother wasn't born in the country but in Swansea, and wasn't keen on village life, or the village school. As the eld-est child, and a girl, she had to help in the house and serve in the shop. They sold my grandfather's bread and cakes, and everything else too. One day she saw two grinning boys looking at her through the window and nudging each other. She prepared herself. They came in, trying to keep straight faces, and one of them, who had a bad stammer, asked, 'P... p... please for a p... p... penn'orth of p... p... pigeon's milk?' Gladys looked at them, considered, and answered briefly, 'Just a minute.' She went round the back, out of sight, got a bottle of HP sauce and emptied about an egg-cupful into a twisted sweet bag. Handing it over, she said politely, 'That'll be one penny, thank you.' The boys paid up and retreated without a word. Her reactions were always lightning quick, up to the age of ninety-eight. A couple of weeks before she died, I was visiting her in Singleton Hospital, and explained that I was going back to London for a few days because of the election. 'Are you standing?' she asked wryly. Once she was supposed to look after her little sister, but got lost in a book, and came to the end of a chapter to find Leah was missing. She looked in the house and the garden, but there was no sign of the child. She had to tell her parents, and everyone went out to search all over the village. The two-year-old Leah was missing for hours, and was found at last in the house of an old blind woman whose cottage door always stood open. Leah had called in, found a dish of butter, eaten it all, and fallen asleep under the table. Her hostess had assumed she'd gone home. We loved this story because of Leah's feast of butter. Her little sister and five brothers were the bliss and bane of Gladys Emily Ann Abraham's life. She was a competent but reluctant little mother and the chicks weren't easily kept under her young wing. Arthur once went off with his friend Tommy Galvin and set fire to a neighbour's rick, and Arnold distinguished himself by screwing the necks of twenty ducklings. This was epic naughtiness, beyond our towny imagination.

Gladys was afraid of one thing in her childhood, the big wall outside their house in Milton, which blocked the view from her bedroom window. She was afraid that when the end of the world came, the wall would fall on them. So the end of the world became for her, and then for me, a tottering wall. She had other anxieties, more tangible. She desperately wanted to go to college and be a teacher, but there was no question of that. With a mother always pregnant, and all those little brothers and sisters, she was needed at home. She told me her serial story, repeatedly and piecemeal, over many years.

When she had to leave school at twelve, it broke her heart. The schoolmaster, Dominie Something, met her one day looking very sad, crossing a field. Leaning on the stile, she told him her troubles, and he smiled, put his hand on her shoulder and recited Charles Kingsley's 'Be good, sweet maid, and let who will be clever; / Do lovely things, not dream them, all day long'. My mother recited the line movingly, and I was comforted to know they had comforted her. They moved me too. But this was a story that changed, and after a time I was furious with the schoolmaster for soothing a clever girl by promoting virtue over brains. And another day came when the distinction between dreaming and doing seemed not only false, but nothing to do with the poet's argument. Even later, when I read *Alton Locke*, that wonderfully sympathetic story of an education-deprived working man, and learnt about Kingsley's concern for adult education, I was even angrier, on behalf of women and my mother. Some ignorant man who should have known better once asked me if I had ever met anyone who was really educationally deprived because of gender. The world is full of examples, I said, but I grew up hand in hand with one. I hated the consoler for his consolation, but my mother had been consoled. For the moment.

I don't know if it was the same schoolmaster or another who hit my mother. She was about ten or eleven, and I've forgotten what she had done, probably talked or been inattentive during a lesson. He called her out to his desk, told her to hold out her hand, and struck her palm with the cat-o'-nine-tails. 'What's that?' 'A horrible old whip with tails. Called "the cat" for short.' I shuddered, feeling the smart in flesh and pride. She forgave him as she remembered, 'Oh well, he had a lot to put up with.' She had gone straight to her father with the story, and William John went back to school with her after dinner. They went up to the schoolmaster's desk together, and before her father could speak, Gladys said, 'Hit me now my father's here', a challenge that achieved the status of family myth and proverb. Her father quietly told the master never to hit his daughter again, and he never did.

I envied her as she told us her story. They had a horse, a fat little full-bellied pony that drew the baker's trap. He was called Don, and when he had to be put down they were all broken-hearted. Once she was given a lamb whose mother had died, to bring up by hand and feed with a baby's bottle. And she had what she'd never let me have because I was too careless – a bike. It didn't seem fair, I thought when I was sixteen. Everyone had a bike, even my little brother. And she had told me so often how she used to ride with her hands behind her back and go like the wind down a hill near their village, so fast that a bee going the other way had landed in her ear, not stinging but vibrating and roaring. She told it so that you felt the bang and the buzz. She had been a reckless rider, but I didn't get a bike till I was twenty, and bought one for three pounds from my husband-to-be's landlady's daughter, Alice. My first ride was a glorious sixty miles round the Bethesda Loop in Snowdonia. And my mother was wrong. I was a careful, nervous rider, perhaps because I came to it late. I was taught to ride when I was fifteen or six-teen, by my boyfriend Rob Sumner. On my first ride, swerving madly to the right of the road, I was shouted at by a driver, and chivalrously defended by Rob, who called out, 'It's her first time.' I did only one silly thing on a bike, and that was to ride through the traffic-lights by Swansea Station, telling the police-man who stopped me, with stupid truthfulness, that I didn't think they applied to cyclists. Luckily he had a sense of humour.

There is a family group, sepia, studio-posed and elaborately dressed, of my grandparents and the first three children in their Sunday best. The mother, daughter and infant son, Arthur, wear lace-trimmed dresses, and Nana has her anxious young look, with a frown just gone or about to come. Grandpa had a waxed, curled moustache, a smart suit, and his watch and chain. Elvert, the second child and eldest son, is in a frilly shirt. They are all beautiful. My mother is wearing a dress with yards of material gathered into the skirt, lace collar and velvet trimmings. She has slanting eyes, under a long, silky fringe, and looks like a sadly puzzled Alice in Wonderland. All my life I wanted to tell her how much I loved that child, staring into the camera, the future, and the unimagined eyes of her own children. She told me she looked sad because her father was drinking heavily, coming home late and upsetting her mother. Gladys hardly ever touched drink until my husband and I introduced her to the pleasures of wine, and she took to burgundy. Right up to ninety-eight she could tell a good wine from plonk, and had a tendency to ask for Macon, one of my husband's favourites because our Earls Court grocer used to buy it. In our childhood, she used to say now and then, 'I need a good tonic', and would either ask Dr Scurlock for one, or buy a bottle of Wincarnis or Sanatogen, which she swore did her good – 'It's the iron.' Sometimes my grandfather would present her with a bottle. I never saw anyone in the family the worse for drink. The Rechabites, who frequently converted my grandfather to repentance, didn't come round in my day, though we did once hear a temperance lecture at school, welcomed as a change from routine. It was the first time I consciously heard the work 'lecture', and I wondered what it would be. It was a gripping account of the physiological effects of alcohol, with an exemplary tale of miners trapped by a fall of coal and deprived of oxygen. Their red blood cells, the lecturer said, were in exactly the same state – just before they were rescued in the nick of time – as those of a drinker. There was an introduction about the Three Essential Bs, Blood, Beef and Bread. I still have the certificate we were all given for excellently reproducing the lecture.

When my father lost his job in 1929 and my mother went home to her mother in Swansea, with her two children, I was five and Bill just over one. My grandfather was a struggling yeast merchant, a term that sounded grand in my ears but didn't mean a lot. Mother needed the family nest, and her mother was glad of her help and some extra money. I used to go down with her to the GPO which she called 'The General', in Wind Street, to cash the money order from the shipping line my father worked for. The money didn't go far. We always bought clothes on a credit system known as 'the Club'. Clothing firms let you have what you wanted, and you paid 'a bob down and a bob for life'. We got most of our clothes, including school uniforms when we went to secondary school, from a shop called Sidney Heath's, and a soft-spoken gentlemanly man called Mr Charles used to call for the money every week, striking off the payments in mother's club-book. I thought that was how everybody bought their clothes. I remember coming in to tell my mother I'd passed the Scholarship. She was on her knees scrubbing the bedroom lino, which had a pattern of red and brown circles on a green background, ice to the feet on winter mornings. She started to cry. I sentimentally thought they were tears of joy, which I'd read about in novels. In fact she was crying because she was afraid she wouldn't be able to afford the uniform for the next seven years. She did so by never buying any clothes for herself.

When I was about eight she had a lovely coat with a fur collar, from the better-off days. I would stroke the fur in affection and sensuous delight. The photographs – which she called snaps and I snobbishly corrected – of her and her friends and sister in the twenties, display some dashing coats and hats. All the time I was at school she hardly ever went out in the evening, except once a week, on Tuesdays, to the British Legion whist drive, and to the meeting of the Legion Executive Committee, 'The Exec', which sounded important. She wore out her old clothes and never came to the school functions, like the plays and the annual hobbies exhibition, which all the parents attended. Every penny went on clothes and food. Like most children, I knew nothing about money, and used to make unreasonable demands. Once, I signed up for a school trip to Cardiff, which cost a pound. When I put my name on the list, Nansi Evans, our form mistress, said: 'You must be one of the affluent ones.' I mused on this new word, but came down to earth when my mother said she couldn't afford it, and I should have asked her.

I sulked and said I couldn't cancel the acceptance. The problem was solved, to my relief, because for some reason the trip had to be cancelled.

Even when my mother went to work, first for the General Electric Company, and then as a barrister's clerk, she spent as little as possible on clothes. After the war, when the man she'd replaced came back, she was offered a job in the smart dress shop run by a friend of one of the barristers. She said they'd given her a couple of dresses, observing, to my chagrin but not to hers, that they'd obviously been discussing her clothes. She was calm, never self-pitying. She didn't like the shop, but was fascinated by the clothes. She asked me what *haute couture* meant, and though I'd done Higher School Certificate French and was living in London, I didn't know. She told me how mystified she was that they took off the designers' labels. She loved coming shopping with me, and choosing my dresses, suits and hats. Many of my dresses were made by Aunt Renee, and some by a little dressmaker who lived in a steep little street off Walter Road. I remember one pink-and-white striped dress with deep pockets where the stripes ran counter to the ones on the skirt, which was really original, as I can see from a photograph taken by my boy-friend Rob when I was sixteen. I remember going with her to buy a new dress for herself, once. It was very plain and 'elephant grey'. 'Madam is short-waisted,' the salesgirl assistant said, and I was pleased that she looked so smart. When she wore her shabby black skirt and cardigan, or an old navy-blue jumper suit with red pointed buttons, one of them still in the family button-box, I didn't want her to come to school functions. When she said 'I'd let you down', I made no protest.

The First World War gave my mother her chance. She joined the Wrens, and was given training in telephony and commercial skills. She worked as a telephone operator. She also went to an evening institute called the Greg School, where she took cookery classes and did some shorthand and typing too. The Second World War also gave her a chance. She left her clerical job in the General Electric Company and became clerk to a brilliant Swansea barrister, Morris Morgan. She loved the work and it

professionalized her. A great Welsh gossip, she always refused
to discuss her clients. She might say a little about the personality of people but only ever specified one case, soon after she
went to Angel Chambers, in Salubrious Passage, a corner of old
Swansea where Jaggers and Wemmick might easily turn up. She
told me about a divorce case in which the husband had taken a
bottle of gin to bed along with the bride. I thought that sounded fun, but Gladys was deeply shocked by this and other details
she didn't specify. 'I didn't know how much I didn't know,' she
said. I've heard relations and friends ask her about so-and-so
who was involved in some case, and a shutter of professional
discretion would come down at once. Her thinking changed
too, at least in one professional pocket of her mind. She was
infuriatingly superstitious and irrational in many ways, lacking
science, but the educated part of her brain could take over
when she discussed politics and people, as well as the law. She
briefly admired Thatcher, but was always a staunch socialist.
She had welcomed Neville Chamberlain's 'Peace in Our Time',
but patriotically supported the war while hating and doubting
the uses of violence. She grew, or perhaps always was, tolerant
and permissive. As an adolescent I couldn't have imagined
watching television bed scenes with her, or discussing Aids, as
I did when she was in her seventies and eighties. She had excellent judgement and general knowledge, was always better on
geography than I was, and not bad on history. But she could be
wild or silly in ways that education doesn't permit. We had violent arguments about the depth of Blue Pool, a wonderful
round, big rock-pool in a little cove in the limestone cliffs
between Broughton and Rhossilli, which the locals used to
believe was bottomless. 'There's no such thing as a bottomless
pool,' I would say. 'But Olwen says so.' Olwen was a friend
who'd been brought up in Rhossilli. 'That's idiotic,' I'd say
rudely. Mother would ask vaguely, when I came up from the
sea, 'Tide out, I suppose?' or 'Tide in, I suppose?', as if tides
were irregular and erratic. She was good on flowers, and my
first interest in botany came from walking with her in Gower
lanes, or in Hendrefoilan Road in Tycoch, now totally and hor-

ribly developed. Or the parks, where I remember learning to recognize bugloss and bird's-foot trefoil, which she called fisherman's basket. She taught me bird's-eye speedwell, cowslip and foxglove. Buttercups and daisies came before you could walk. She loved gardening and accepted my dislike of weeding and watering with regret and surprise. When she stopped going out and came to live in my cottage, I would bring her violets and meadowsweet and honeysuckle. She loved strong-scented flowers. On her chest of drawers there were little bottles of scent, California poppy, Parma violets, and 4711 eau-de-Cologne. She was determined that her children should go to secondary school and college, to get the education she had been denied. It was marvellous to have support and ambition, special even in the anti-Philistine Welsh environment which values and promotes culture and education, but it was a burden too. 'Your mother makes great sacrifices for you,' my grandmother and aunts used to say. They were all pained when my school reports regularly criticized me for being careless and talkative. Waiting for them to land in the passage at the end of term was agony.

Until I was about thirteen we were very close. I used to cuddle up to her warmth, more frequently than would be usual because of the space in her bed. I loved being 'comfy by the wall', feeling the coolness of the wallpaper on one side and Mother's protective warmth on the other. When the alienations began I was horrified and guilty. I no longer wanted my mother's warm body. I used to say, 'I love our smell.' But the family smell, familial, erotic, maternal, a bit foxy, became obnoxious. I began to bath more often, hold aloof, offer my cheek instead of kissing. I stopped saying lyrically, 'If all the leaves on all the trees were tongues, they couldn't tell how much I love you.' I didn't love her any more. But she must never find out.

A refrain from my grandmother's domestic litany was: 'And perhaps I can sit down now.' The women never sat down for long, but jumped up and down from the table waiting on the men and the children. When my mother started to work, she still did all the housework. Though I hated Ron for never doing a hand's turn, having to be begged even to chop a few sticks for the fire, I didn't help either. Only my grandfather did. My mother developed a habit of putting her hand on her left breast when she sat down. I'd heard about cancer of the breast because Mother's girlhood friend, Sally, had died of it when a young woman. And since Nana had died of cancer, and I'd read it was hereditary, I began to hatch the horror that Mother had a lump in her breast. 'Your mother works too hard,' they would say. At a Brownies' Hallowe'en party where we ducked for apples in a tub and told ghost stories, our Brown Owl, a sturdy, red-haired, freckle-faced woman whom I liked very much, suddenly said, 'Your mother isn't strong, is she?' It was out in the open. 'No,' I said quietly, and went home to worry and watch. I wanted to say 'Don't' or 'Have you got a pain?' but didn't dare. The anxiety wasn't unselfish. Of course I didn't want my mother to suffer, have a terrible operation and die, but I also didn't want to leave school and work in a shop. 'Your mother's making sacrifices for you, but if you don't work hard you'll have to leave and go to work in Woolworths,' they said. Going to Woolworths where everything was under sixpence was a treat, but I began to look at the pale, common girls behind the counter and see myself in their place. 'Please God, keep Mother well and alive,' I'd pray, with an unspoken sub-text, 'till I've got Higher', and later, 'till I've finished college'. So deep was my fear that when I passed my Higher School Certificate and got my degree, underlying pride and pleasure was the thought, I made it. She's still alive. She lived fifty-five years after that first fear, and after a while she stopped putting her hand to her breast. Afterwards I told her all about it, and she laughed. The bad news at Hallowe'en came from nowhere.

So I grew away from her, and the soft intimacy of the big bed. I remember my father in it once or twice. I was close to him, looking at the blue tattoo on his hairy arm, an anchor and perhaps a dragon, as I lay next to the wall where we made shadow animals with our hands, dogs and rabbits and big bad wolves. I have one memory or dream of him jumping out of a small cupboard in the middle room at Cradock Street, where we all lived before the move to London. Between 1923 and

1929 my father had a good shore job managing the Mackworth Hotel in Swansea, owned by the catering firm of R.E. Jones. He was transferred to London, to headquarters or perhaps their hotel in Tottenham Court Road, and we went to live in Bratham Road, Brockley. I can't find it in the *A to Z*. Perhaps it was bombed. I remember going to St Paul's, and riding on a red, open-topped London bus which stopped by a pub called the Brockley Jack. The conductor once mocked a woman who didn't want to go upstairs in the rain. 'Why, you ain't made of sugar.' Another legend and family saying that grew by repetition. I remember Father bringing Mother a bunch of specially grown green tulips – or were they black? When they bought the house my father told me there was an apple tree in the garden. But we moved in winter, and in case I was disappointed, he tied red apples on the branches with string. I remember his reading me the Grimms fairy-tale, 'The Robber Bridegroom', deciding too late it was too grim and violent, and terrifying me because he refused to go on to the end, leaving that to my trembling imagination. I was frightened by his face, frightened for me.

I was a nervy child, they said. That was partly Uncle Ron's fault. My parents were careful with their children, but the world was full of rough, rude, working-class teases and tales. One that I loved was not a story but a drama, played with Ron. You never knew when he'd start it. You might be reading a book by the fire or walking through the kitchen where he shaved, and he would suddenly turn and stop you, asking fiercely, 'Will you be the bride of a pirate bold?' I would pipe up, 'No, never.' He would roll his eyes terribly, coming closer, 'Then over the blinking cliff you go.' I would cast my eyes round, surprised and contemptuous, protesting, 'But there is no cliff.' He would say, very loudly, in climax, 'Then I'll chalk one... out.' I'd end, 'What about my poor baby?' I have no idea where this great fragment came from, nor why it ended so oddly, nor why we thought it so hilarious. But I played it, with increasing proficiency, from the age of two to ten, or later. That was fun, but Ron terrified me out of my wits with his rendering of *Red Riding Hood*. He would tell it, wild eye glaring and mouth agape with teeth, relishing the final dialogue of Red Riding Hood and the wolf, until I would implore him to stop. In the end, he wouldn't need to do more than say 'Once upon a time' and I would shriek, run, or burst into tears. This ordeal by story-telling had started when I was very young because Ron used to say the opening ritual in baby-talk, 'One upon a time.' After we moved to Brockley my mother decided that I was so nervous and highly strung that she would take me to a doctor. I vaguely remember a young man, who prescribed white, sugary, horrible medicine. After the first spoonful, I lifted the bottle and poured its contents over my little fair head. I can still feel the crisp stickiness of the drying sugar.

I remember my grandmother coming to stay, bringing me a huge, dark-haired china doll which I dropped on the deep-crimson carpeted stairs, and broke. I remember some friends of my father's visiting, with a little boy about my age, bringing a blue-green gas balloon which floated up to a corner of the front-room ceiling. It eventually escaped into the garden and vanished. My mother or father told me there'd been a bit in the paper about its travels, and I was impressed. I remember sitting in the little light kitchenette while my mother tried to persuade me to drink my soup. A fairy was watching. My mother slipped the spoon in my mouth as I was turning my head to catch a glimpse, 'Look, just over there. The sunlight's on its wings. Can't you see it? Drink up, and we'll have a good look.'

I can't remember departure. The Wall Street crash broke up the Brinkley semi-detached house before the apple tree bore fruit. The managing director of R.E. Jones, Howard Jones, after whom Bill was named, blew his brains out, Mother said. There were no more jobs on land, and my father went back to sea. 'A dog's life,' he said. I have his Seaman's Continuous Certificate, showing voyages to Africa, China, Japan, Java, the Spanish Main, South Georgia and the Canaries. And his ships – I remember the *Woodville*, on which he made his last voyage in 1923. Then there is a gap for the early family years, until 8 November 1929, when he sailed for China in the *Hector*.

My mother used to say it was a big mistake, they should

have stayed together. A separation of twenty-five years began. For a year or two Father came home when his ship came in, but things were difficult. My Aunt Leah was still at home, and slept with my mother, and there was no room for the young married couple. I remember one visit when my father stayed up all night, listening to a boxing match – perhaps it was the Tommy Farr/Joe Louis fight – relayed from America, or playing cards with my uncles. I was aware that this was somehow not quite right. Many years later, when I was married, my mother said they'd had nowhere to go, and Father said he'd never come back till her parents were dead. History was shaping the passions. The war brought my parents together, the Depression tore them apart.

Once Mother decided to make an attempt at reconciliation and went off to Liverpool, where Father's ship embarked and returned, and where Father's parents and brothers lived. She bought a pair of blue-green linen pajamas, which eventually I inherited, and came back saying little, looking miserable. Her brother-in-law, Gersh, had been very kind to her. I guessed nothing. Father sent me dolls, including a wonderful brown Italian doll whom I called Bingo, and my daughter Julia, who had him on long lease in her childhood, called 'Baby'. He was the family favourite, kept in a drawer but shown to visiting cousins as a treat. During Julia's fetishistic possession of him, his face began to wear under the fervor of her kisses, so my father, who had come back, gave him a new velvet face, a new head of hair, and freshly painted scarlet lips. Father was a magician, making pennies pass through a solid oak table. He was a ventriloquist, delighting my children by summoning the place-changing voice of Mr. Eynon, a local pastry-cook famous for Eynon's pies, who called himself in Father's game 'Mr. Hynon' from here, there and everywhere. He made marquetry trays and jewel-boxes. He mended toys. He was an excellent cook, whose own digestion, he said, had been ruined by good eating but who loved to cook special dishes – one was partridge with tiny game chips, all very *haute cuisine*, for my husband Ernest and me. When he first ran away to sea, after his father remarried and he couldn't get on with his stepmother, he'd been a cabin-boy. He never related his adventures at sea but did say he was taught by an old Chinese cook who used to scorch his spices in a dry pan to start his curries. He taught me how to make mayonnaise, pouring the high-held oil in the thinnest, steadiest gold stream into the egg. He told me never to keep cooked potatoes and onions more than a day. He taught us to play poker.

All this was when Father came back, after twenty-five years, for a family reunion. At first, after going back to sea, he sent my mother a decent proportion of his pay, but at some point, for some reason, he stopped. She struggled for a time on national assistance, till they advised her to try to get in touch with her husband. The payments started again and continued during the war, when Father was in the Merchant Navy, as was my father-in-law, who was reported missing in one of the Atlantic convoys. When in the Army in the First World War, Father was gassed. He died of emphysema, perhaps as a result. He was said to have been awarded the Military Cross, for bravery in action, and told his officer not to make the recommendation but to stick it where the monkey stuck his peanuts. The story probably had some grain of truth, as Mother's stories usually did, but he couldn't have won the Military Cross as a private. Mother had more than one 'boy' during the war, including a Scot called Willie Steele, who gave her a copy of Burns with relevant lines from 'O my Luve's like a red, red rose' inscribed on the flyleaf, with heavy lines under: 'And I will come again my Luve, / Though 'twere ten thousand mile.' She had also been engaged to a teacher called Ivor Jenkins, Jinks for short. They had separated because of his jealousy. Once or twice she said, 'I must have been daft. I should have married Jinks.' They had been childhood sweethearts in Pembrokeshire. She had also been engaged to a captain in the Army, Cliff Martin. During the war she wrote to several boys, and it seemed to get a bit out of hand.

But she married Maurice Nathan. They must have met in the summer of 1914, when his ship, the *Myrmidon*, docked at Swansea between trips to China. On the night before their wedding he said he had something to tell her, which might make her not want to marry him. 'I'm not a Christian,' he said. It was his way of saying he was a Jew. My mother loved him and was no racist, but she didn't tell me the story till some time after I was married and lecturing in Birkbeck. Elated by the news, I told my friends, the historian Eric Hobsbawm, and a rat psychologist Harry Hurwitz, in the college refectory. They grinned: 'Of course. We always knew.'

Mother said my paternal grandfather, whom I met only once, came from Russia – 'or was it Poland?' He settled in Liverpool, started a tobacconist business, and married an Irish trapeze artiste called Rose, who left him, with three or four children. He married a second wife, Gertrude, or Gertie, disliked by my father though liked by my mother. I think there may have been another child by this marriage, but I've forgotten Mother's history of the Liverpool uncles and aunts. I never asked my father about his travels or our relations. One day I'll look them all up, in the records and perhaps in the flesh. We once went to visit my paternal grandfather and step-grandmother in Liverpool. I remember my white-bearded grandfather, Nathaniel Nathan (he changed his surname but I don't know from what). We had dinner in a big, dark underground kitchen, and I was at the end of a long table. He said, 'Put more light on. It's dark for the child.' This impressed me. My Swansea grandfather was always trying to economize and one of his refrains was 'Put that light out', as uncles or grandchildren left on the landing or the passage lights. There is a flickering image or two from a fun-fair at New Brighton, visited with Father and Mother and Uncle Gersh. I remember a clown in red and orange.

Some time in the early fifties Mother and Father resumed their correspondence. She had left Angel Chambers when the clerk she replaced came back from the war, but he'd been no good, and she was delighted to go back, staying until she retired at seventy-six, though the barristers didn't know her age. Father was the joint owner of a café in Manchester. Mother had told him about the birth of Julia, my first child, in 1955, and he asked her if he could come down for the weekend and meet us all. My grandfather had died a couple of years before, so he kept his vow, knowing or unknowing.

My husband, brother, baby and I came down from London. My mother was calm, and went off in a taxi to meet the train. My brother and I were edgy. Ernest was amused. I had my first really expensive dress, long, narrow and tweed, from Peter Jones. I'd bought it when Joyce Cary invited me to have lunch with him in Oxford, having liked an essay I wrote about his novels. Now I wore it to celebrate meeting my long-lost father. I pulled on the dress. Was the chicken over-cooking? My zip stuck and Ernest advised me to relax. We heard the front door open. Father looked familiar, and I loved him at once. It must have been more difficult for Bill, who had no memory of him. Father and Mother laughed and were easy. I decided to call him Father. He loved the meal, and he liked Ernest. And the baby was about a year and a half, all winning ways and prattle. After the first evening, my mother said to me, 'He loved it when you called him clever-sticks.' His face was the face in my memory and the photograph. In a week or two he wrote to me and Bill, both in London, to ask us to meet him for a quick drink some-where. We met the Manchester train at Euston and went to a pub, where he gave Bill a diamond ring and me his gold ciga-rette-case because I was the smoker. I had it expensively converted to a powder-box, with a mirror, and afterwards it was stolen from me in a hotel at Bari, where I was lecturing.

A month or two later, Mother wrote to say Father had asked if he could come home. She said yes. So for seven years, until his death in 1962, he had a wife again and children and grand-children. They seemed to get on easily and happily, and were a good couple. I loved him, and found it easier to be with Mother when he was there too. He tidied and organized the kitchen and scullery, laid carpets and papered walls, 'improving your prop-erty' he'd say to me, because I had bought Mother's house when her landlord – a man she said never looked you in the eye – wanted her to go or buy.

Father came in for a share of family joys. He loved Julia and my second daughter, Kate. They remember his conjuring tricks, and how he always called Kate 'Mike'. I dedicated my first book, on George Eliot, to him and my mother, and he said to her 'Look at that.' He helped us to fill the Christmas stockings and decorate the tree. I gave him Mahler's 'Song of the Earth' and a Kathleen Ferrier record. He made a ring of clowns that danced on an old gramophone turntable to the tune of 'The Day That the Circus Left Town'. His story had a happy ending.

Chapter 2
Between Golden Gates

One story my mother told me was about her mother's prize-winning ugly face. She had gone in for a competition at the annual Sunday School treat and won half a crown, big money. It wasn't for having an ugly face but for making one, and it made my grandmother seem young and human. I cross-questioned her about the victory. 'It wasn't all that ugly,' she recalled, 'but I was quick.' 'What was it like? Go on, show us.' But she wouldn't. Even when I prompted her by bundling one of my cheeks into a knot, squinting till my eyes disappeared behind my nose and putting out my tongue till the roots ached, she did not oblige. She didn't encourage imitation. 'You watch out,' she warned. 'The wind might change and you'd be stuck with that old face for good.' I rapidly relaxed into my ordinary features.

Daily life was stiff with superstition. You had to eat all your crusts to make your hair curl. Curly hair was an essential component of female beauty, though there were always perms. I didn't object to crusts, as such, but I loathed bread and butter, which you had to eat with everything. Quite recently, at a French restaurant in Bloomsbury, I was offered 'bread and butter' and longed to ask them to say 'rolls' not bread. You were given bread and butter with fresh and with tinned pears, apricots, peaches and fruit salad, adding its cloggy substance to fruit, apples, oranges and bananas to flatten textures and tastes. I could never get rid of it quickly in a good swallow, unless the bread was toasted. I remember chewing one obligatory slice, thin and white and everlasting, for hours, and in the end surreptitiously spitting it

31

into a handkerchief for future disposal. It was a poor people's fill-up, like pasta, but not so nice. You had to eat it as a kind of penance, I thought. At least you could cheer up at the thought of those curls you'd wake up to find one morning. If you put too much vinegar on your food – I loved it on eggs as well as fish and chips – it would thin your blood. Too much salt would dry it up. If you ate too much of anything, you would die of eating diabetes. If you fidgeted or shuffled in your chair at meals, you had worms or St Vitus's dance. If you woke somebody up when they were sleep-walking, or if somebody woke you up when you were sleep-walking, the result was death. I never met anyone who walked in their sleep but my grandfather told me about a distant relation, some Willy or Billy, who fell into a bucket of water someone had put at the bottom of the stairs, and died of chill or shock. So when I offered up my nightly prayer that I should not see a ghost or the Devil or have bad dreams, I added the petition that I should not walk in my sleep. Once I dreamt that I woke up downstairs in the passage, having sleep-walked. It was cold and dark and lonely. I was relieved to wake up again in my bed, but troubled. Had I only dreamt that I walked in my sleep, or had I walked in my sleep and gone back to bed?

You must never bring pink hawthorn into the house. I picked a bunch for my grandmother, who was so horrified that the tree became unholy at once. My mother objected to white hawthorn as well, but less vehemently than Nana, who would have crossed herself in another culture. (When someone told me that Catholics crossed themselves, I knew they were joking.) You had to take down the Christmas decorations before the New Year, not on Twelfth Night. Spring was a dangerous time, because the blood was supposed to grow impure then, and children were dosed with brimstone and treacle, a dreaded remedy. I developed a taste for it once I had shaken off a horror of the name. I especially liked the mashed lumps of sulphur in the treacle – really Tate & Lyle's golden syrup. When I eat treacle tart I remember standing by the window in the Cradock Street kitchen watching my mother spoon out the thick, gritty mixture, and thinking that the brimstone aspect of a hellish diet wouldn't be too bad. Children were vulnerable all the year round, especially if they were thin, fat, nervy or pale. My grandmother would look at my naturally pale cheeks and say: 'That child needs a good dose.' It might be Californian syrup of figs, incredibly sweet but preferable to that most loathsome of all our fearfully-named opening medicines, senna. I drew the line at senna, shutting my mouth and shaking my head. An aunt encouraged me, 'Go on, it tastes just like tea', not knowing that I detested tea. Tea was given to children from a tender age, first in spoons and saucers, diluted with milk but starting off lifetime addictions. My mother had to have tea at two-hour intervals throughout her life, and when she stopped asking for it I realized that she was going to die. But I was a mutant. The thought of tea made that khaki brew of senna pods even more disgusting. Its sickly bitter taste comes into my mouth as I write. 'Hold her nose,' the gentle, child-loving elders would advise, but the only time they tried, I spat a mouthful all over my mother. They were obsessed with the dangers of childhood constipation, I don't know why. As far as I know, we were never constipated, and nobody ever asked if we'd done Number Two, or caca. My brother was a delicate child so he had extra patent medicines, Virol and Scott's Emulsion, both of which were delicious. I used to steal spoonfuls on the sly.

My grandmother was a great one for wise saws and folk imagery. Rejecting some suggestion or remedy, she'd spit out in contempt: 'As much good as a sore behind to a tailor.' She had been what was always called a tailoress, with emphasis on the 'ess', but I think the analogy was an old family saying, not a professional one. If somebody had a red face it was compared to 'a farmer's behind on a frosty morning'. Imagism from Pembrokeshire and Swansea tended to be rude, in every sense of the word. There was – and still is – a firm of solicitors or accountants called Ashmole and Somebody, which my grandmother would render as 'arsehole', with one of her rare laughs. If you looked glum your face was a yard of pumpwater or you were like the man who killed his father. There were Welsh wellerisms like our family version of *de gustibus*, which ran: 'Everyone to their own taste, as the old woman said when she kissed the cow.' An exclamation of universal application was 'My Gawd, Mary Ellen!', said fast, the words run together.

Nana had many familiar forms of address for her daughters and granddaughters, all or any of whom might be called 'Sarah Jane', or 'Jane Ann', whatever their real names. If you looked untidy, or exotic, you were called names which I presume derived from famous old local whores, 'Anna Banana' and 'Flossie Fourpence'. Put on a little weight and it was 'Twice round the gasworks once round Nellie', or 'She's a bladder of lard'. It was the females who were so addressed, by females, usually with as much fondness as criticism. Nana's younger daughter Leah was the only one of the family to carry on such forms, and when she referred to Sarah it might be any of her three daughters, none of whom was a Sarah. There were of course religious superstitions and taboos. We were a card-playing family, but not even my grandfather would take out a pack of cards on a Sunday. Deaths were organized by the common traditions. After my grandfather's death, when his coffin stood in the middle room, I got into trouble for absent-mindedly pulling up the front-room blinds, forgetting the house must be darkened, and my brother was asked to stop playing the piano. But such strictness was for funerals and holy days. Weekdays were free and easy enough, and though you never heard a woman or a child swear, my uncles and grandfather would say 'Damn', 'bloody', 'hell' and occasionally 'Christ' or 'Jesus Christ', though my grandmother and mother would protest at the last two. There were no sexual swear-words or innuendoes, ever. Children were sometimes little buggers, but I'd never heard of buggery. When I went to High School I learnt to swear, with pleasure and a sense of freedom, but never at home. That was unthinkable.

My grandmother was a wonderful cook, and we had hot dinner every day at one o'clock. My uncles often dropped in to have dinner at home, as they always called their parents' house. Meals were cooked by Nana and my mother in big, black, cast-iron saucepans on the kitchen fire, until the gas stove was installed in the back kitchen or scullery. Even then, some of the vegetables would be put on the hob. Nana was always on the move, her lips pressed together and her forehead puckered. She cooked ham and hake with parsley sauce, hake stuffed with thyme and breadcrumbs, sewn up and roasted in butter, like a chicken, thick potato slices in batter, called scallops, tasting quite unlike any other potatoes. She made a deep dish beef pie, with thick suet pastry, the lower half in the gravy, a delicious dumpling consistency, the upper crust short and brown and crisp. There was boiled bacon with cabbage and dried peas, and cawl, lamb broth with parsley which my mother made for me right into her middle nineties. The puddings were plum-duff or spotted Dick, slow-cooked rice pudding with currants and a brown, spicy skin, pancakes with currants, and that great working-class delicacy, bread pudding, divine hot and diviner cold. My grandfather made the Christmas cake, and my mother most of the other cakes, her specialities being walnut cake and Australian walnut loaf, fatless, cut thin and buttered. The local delicacies, laverbread, faggots and cockles, I detested until I grew up, though I liked watching the cockles hopping in the bacon fat. Our vegetables tended to be overcooked, and the pastry was on the heavy side. My grandmother never knew how her big custard tarts would turn out, and called them upside-down tarts because the pastry, made with self-raising flour, tended to rise up above the filling and merge with it. But it tasted all right. These pre-war dinners were marvellous, but I wasn't keen on the things we usually had for tea, cheese and salad and piles of bread and butter. Children were expected to be faddy and I had a long list of foods I wouldn't touch. We had spam and dried egg and no bananas in the war, but memory prefers the rich diet of childhood.

My grandfather was a baker, so his cake and bread were professional. He taught me how to make French pastries from puff paste rolled up, turned sideways, sliced, twisted and filled with jam, cream slices, made with flaky pastry and confectioner's custard, and doughnuts. Every stage in doughnut-making was thrilling, from the raising of the first dough, the shaping and proving of the little balls that at first seemed too small, to the frying in the big chip-pan. Bill and I would gobble them hot from the pan. That was after watching them cook on one side and turn over, sometimes nudged by the ladle, then lobbed out, dark and crisp, stabbed with scissors and filled with jam. They hardly ever got as far as plates, let alone the table. I can't eat shop doughnuts to this day.

Cooking with my mother was an interesting lesson. She showed me how to clean a chicken, turning the gizzard inside out and scraping away its contents, putting grated orange in the stuffing, and cleaning fish, which I didn't take to. But cooking with Grandpa was a game. He taught all his daughters, daughters-in-law and me to make puff pastry, starting by beating the water out of the butter and softening it with a rolling-pin. Some of the aunts would drop in for a refresher course in mince pies before Christmas. Christmas pudding is the only thing I have a clear memory of seeing Nana actually make. We all had to give it a stir and the mixture was so stiff that a child's wrist could scarcely manage it, though the task grew lighter as the years passed. Best of all was the making of the cake, or rather its icing. I only liked the icing. I loved the ritual of making the little greaseproof-paper bags for the icing cones. No pumps or pipes but the twists and turns of a cunning old hand. Pink-and-white flowers would bloom from Grandpa's finger-tips and he could make criss-cross tracery as good as that on a Gothic revival plaster ceiling. The cake slowly metamorphosed from mere cake, brown and fragrant with peel and spice and fruit, better to smell than eat, I thought, to a mound of golden marzipan smoothness, and lastly to a fairy palace. My mother would complain about the mess, but for me it was enchantment, and Christmas.

As he worked and I watched, licking the spoons and knives and cones, he would first tell me how to do it, then how he used to do it in the bakehouse in Pembrokeshire. He used to make a cake every Christmas for the squire, in Carew or Milton, where he was the baker. 'Horrible old thing he was, too,' my mother would interject. 'When we moved down from Swansea I hated having to curtsey to him.' 'Well,' Grandpa would go on, 'he used to send down a glass of good brandy to the bakehouse every year.' 'To drink his health?' 'No, no, for the cake, of course.' I had never heard of alcohol going into food. Nor did it. 'No, no, I would drink it, see. Then I'd breathe hard into the cake mixture.' That was my first encounter with a cook's finesse.

Grandpa's stories were legion. There was one, told when I was almost too young for stories, about a little boy in the sands who gets lost down a hole, is in danger of drowning, and is dug out and rescued by a dog. The last one he told me was a childhood memory he marvelled at as it returned, highly coloured while his recall of last week was dim. He was three, and they told him not to eat the red berries at the bottom of the garden, because they were poisonous. Lying runs in our family, and the forbidden fruit was red currants. He remembered looking at them in fear: 'Eighty years ago, and I can see their colour now.' There were stories about the Devil, and many ghost stories, one about a lady in white at the market cross. One of my favourites was the story of mad Tommy Rogers of Watershill. He wasn't all there, but he was harmless except at full moon, when you had to watch out. One evening my grandfather was driving back from his rounds in the trap. Tommy suddenly came out of the wood and asked for a lift. After a mile or two he started to threaten Grandpa: 'I'm going to get you, baker.' Grandpa said nothing but drove on. At some point he reined in Don, the little fat white pony my mother loved, and pointed with his whip across the road: 'Look over there, Tommy. What's that?' The lune-turned Tommy looked round, 'And if he did, I tipped him into the road, drove off quick, singing out, "Remember the baker".'

One bizarre story was authenticated by my mother. There were a couple of young boys who used to work for my grandfather in the bakehouse. After work, illiterate, short of cash, and apparently strangers in the community, they had nothing to do. They would shout to their boss to come up to their room over the outhouse. He would take off his belt – called a kaffir belt – and they would take off their trousers, to be whipped till they stopped laughing and screamed to him to stop. 'Yes, they loved it, they were so fed up.' The story frightened me, and I never asked him to tell it.

As Grandpa grew older, the rheumatism he'd suffered since middle age grew worse. He slowed up, walking with the roll and waddle of the arthritic. He would never stop for traffic but walk on to the pedestrian crossing waving his stick at the cars with a smile as he swayed across the road. He went out to do a bit of shopping for a paper or a packet of tobacco at Fergie's (Ferguson's), the corner shop. For years he went daily to a group of pensioners, all men, called 'The Cheery Boys'. They used to meet in the shelter in St James's Park, quite a step for him, but giving him that old pub company he'd once enjoyed as a baker and later on his pedestrian yeast round. He also became the family cook, as my mother went out to work, and though Gladys and Ron often complained about his overcooked vegetables, the meals weren't bad. I can remember his sharpening the kitchen knife on the back-kitchen doorstep. He gave me lessons in sharpening and carving. When I came home from college I started to help him. Sometimes he would stop and say, 'Babs, it's like toothache in the legs', in a tone of detachment. When I started to work I would bring him a half-bottle of whisky on each visit, which he would receive with a smile and a sincere 'just for when I'm feeling really bad'. His sons also brought him the odd bottle, but his drinking days were long behind him. What always strikes me when I look at the early family groups with my grandparents and their first two or three children, is the extreme youth of that rigidly posed, formally clad couple, Nana with elaborate high-piled black hair, Grandpa with waxed moustaches. They stand together or behind their starched and beautifully dressed children, all in their Sunday best, and look at the camera with an innocence and young vulnerability that breaks my heart.

My relationship with Grandpa was loving and easy. When I was a child it was one of play, and when I grew up I didn't have to live with his irrationality and rudeness, exhibited and dramatized to irritate the children on whom he grew dependent. He was relaxed about his demands. 'Cut my toe-nails, Babs' and 'Do my boots'. I would kneel down, tightening the laces, left loose but ready laced, then wind them round the little pegs at the top, leaving the very top one unlaced. 'Not too tight, Babs.' I did it willingly, but my mother had to do it every day. She and her father argued and grumbled at each other, but he once told a visitor, 'She is the flower of the flock.'

Grandparents are easier to help than ageing parents. My affection for Grandpa was a continuation of childhood. He was a wonderful grandparent because he loved playing with us and was never too busy to play, except when he was doing his football coupons. I used to help him mark off the results as they came through on the wireless on Saturday nights, and I loved the roll-call of those familiar, strange, metaphorical names, Spurs, Arsenal, Queens Park Rangers, Everton. He loved giving away the fortune he might win, and would tell us excitedly about our share of the thousands other people won. When he won, Ten Results, Three Aways or Four Draws, thousands of others did too, so the pickings were small. But it was part of the week's ritual, and I posted many a coupon for him in the Uplands post office where Peter, one of my early boyfriends, used to live. I hate the macho-pride and violence of football – and most sports – but in childhood even soccer had its romantic aspects.

He taught Bill chess, and Bill learnt to infuriate him with Fool's Mate. But I never liked the combination of visual calculation and forward planning. I was put off when he taught me the knight's move which seemed too geometrically complicated to perform, let alone anticipate and combine with other moves. I preferred draughts, from the first simple exercise of Fox and Geese, which he usually won, to the interesting draught games when he let me win and the even more interesting times when he tried to win and almost always did. He would play endless games of rummy and knock-out whist, all for love, or for buttons out of Nana's brass shell-case button-box, which I still have, with ancient strata of buttons. He would play 'Tip-it' when we were very small, only now and then refusing with the mysterious formula 'No, not now, I've got a bone in my leg', which it took me years to understand. Even his refusal to play was playful. The only game he detested was Monopoly, which he christened 'Monotony'. I don't know why he disliked it, perhaps because it displaced the traditional games, and went on too long. Perhaps it was sound instinct, because Monopoly turned us all into ruthless, bloody-minded capitalists. When we played it, first, after I was given the newly issued game for Christmas, we went on till the small hours. 'My God, you're mortgaging Park Lane,' said Ron in horror and admiration, and I replied: 'I'd mortgage my mother if necessary.' None of Grandpa's games, even nap, pontoon, and solo, played for money with the boys, led to hostile arguments about what was fair or unfair, and there was never any cheating at the bank, or flouncings-out in a tantrum. 'Monotony' was an enemy, like the Nasties. Grandpa called them that too, quite independently of Churchill. He was a dab hand at offensive pronunciation.

Grandpa was a great provider of sweets, glassy (glacier) mints, mintoes, and hard boils – 'Please, is there a pear-drop?' He would hand them over with the warning: 'Now don't cranch them or you'll break your teeth.' When we were old enough to smoke he would produce a cigarette for Bill or me: 'I told them I'll put it behind my ear for later on.'

He was 'Gramp' or 'Grampa' to us, 'William John' in the dialogue from the Grandma legends about his mother, 'Father' to my mother, 'Dad' to his sons, and 'Will' to his wife. My mother told me how jealous he was in his early married life in Pembrokeshire. The gamekeeper fancied my black-haired, green-eyed, white-skinned grandmother. They used to dance together in the village-hall dances while Grandpa played the fiddle with mounting passion. Once or twice I recall his flying into a hot rage, at my mother or Ron or me, but these fits were very few and far between. After his wife died, in his early sixties, he seemed to grow milder and more passive. My mother would tell him off for his bad table manners, as he would say, especially when we had guests, 'Don't put on the cloth, news-paper'll do for me' or 'It tastes better like that', as he slopped tea into a saucer. He would deliberately make a noise drinking his soup, and Mother and Ron would giggle, mimic or shout, depending on their mood. When I visited Japan, and was told by my friend and guide, Yuichi Maekawa, expert on late-nine-teenth-century English dandyism, that it was good manners to slurp your soup, it took me right back to Grandpa in his big chair, pretending that his Greenhill or Tontine Street manners were even worse than they were, with Gladys or Ron exclaim-ing '*Ach (uch) a fi*' or '*Gudge a fi*'. In the family group my mother is gazing with a gravity beyond her seven or eight years, her almond eyes confronting the studio camera. 'Yes, I'm looking sad. That's because my father used to come in drunk every night.' Like Housman's drunkard he was always swearing repentance, not always soberly, and joined the Rechabites, wearing their blue ribbon, on more than one occasion. I never saw him drunk, and through most of my childhood and after I grew up he never had enough money to spend on anything more than tobacco. But he always gave us presents, asking my mother to get them. When I left home he used to give me two pairs of Marks & Spencer's pants, 'drawers', for Christmas. I was surprised when I heard that he used to play the fiddle and sing, because he only showed his talents to us when reciting and telling stories. Once he gave a rendering of his village-hall con-cert repertoire, a song about a father of twins, which was sung with two imitation babies, a bundle on each arm. My mother would say: 'Oh, I was ashamed of him up there singing. Everyone was laughing and clapping but I wanted the ground to swallow me up.'

He was in his element in those country villages in Pembrokeshire, getting up in the small hours for the baking, leaving the shop and the children and the house behind, doing the rounds in the pony and trap, gossiping and drinking and coming in when he felt like it. But my grandmother, forced to marry at eighteen, having a baby every year, pined for the bright lights of Swansea and at last persuaded him to go back.

He never prospered after that. He went into business with his younger brother, also a baker, Uncle Albert Ystradgynlais, who became so rich he bought a chapel and converted it into houses for his children. Grandpa had given Albert a job and taught him his trade, but they quarrelled, and Grandpa felt some resentment, for reasons which were never made quite clear to us. He took up his yeast round, selling from the house, delivering it to the bakers by hand, or getting his daughter and sons and grandchildren to deliver it, in cloth-covered, seven-pound bags. The small business dwindled over the years till he had only one customer, Manny (Emmanuel) Thomas, who gave us free crates of pop. Mother persuaded him to give it up, because it wasn't worth it, and he did, with great reluctance. He'd often give you a taste: 'Eat a bit of yeast regularly and you'll never get boils.'

He left me his big oak carver chair, and the eight-day clock which hung on the wall in 22 Cradock Street, 28 The Grove, and my cottage in Llanmadoc, after my mother moved there. It was stolen three years ago, the burglar breaking in and letting himself out with my clock while my deaf mother slept. It was mine but I'd never taken it from my mother's possession. Bill and I learnt to tell the time from it. I gazed at its face, doing what Gerard Hopkins calls looking at an object till it begins to look at you, many a time. I stared at it when I was expecting my first official boy-friend, Rob, on Wednesdays and Saturday nights. We looked at it when the German planes dropped bombs and smashed the centre of Swansea in February 1941. Its chime sounded through the days and nights of my childhood. Grandpa used it in his one-sided dialogues with his grown-up son. Ron was in his thirties, early forties even, but at breakfast Grandpa would say: 'Well, what time can you say you got in last night? I heard the clock strike twelve, then one, then two, and it must have been nearly three when I dropped off and I hadn't heard you come in. Where were you till then?' Ron would chant one of the time-honoured formulas, more or less local, 'Ashore for a loaf', 'To Skewen for six eggs', and 'To see a man about a dog'. The first phrase I was familiar with before

I could separate the words, hearing it as an abracadabra, and for years I believed firmly in the authenticity of each explanation.

One night I was saying my prayers in Mother's bed, either so young that I slept with her, or a bit older but not too old to come in to say my prayers or for a cuddle. 'Say a special prayer for Nana,' she instructed gravely, 'and her poor broken body.' I didn't know what she meant, stopped praying to ask, and was told that she had 'something like a plum' growing 'down there'. It was 'a growth'. My grandparents were members of the 'panel', but in those pre-war days medical treatment was expensive. It was decided to tell the family, and Ron paid for a consultation with a gynecological 'specialist' called something like Lloyd Davies, who diagnosed cervical cancer, long neglected. The consultation cost three guineas, which seemed, and was, a vast sum. Nana went into Swansea Hospital, then at the end of St Helen's Road, and I remember or imagine visting her, her white skin even whiter on the hospital pillow.

Nana came home, and the operation was pronounced a success. She had to make regular visits to hospital for follow-up radiation treatment, but after a while she stopped going. My mother told me she couldn't bear exposing her private parts to the men. After about a year I could tell from my mother's night crying and daytime sadness that the growth had come back. My grandmother took to her bed. As my grandparents' room was next to ours, I could hear her groan in the night, and eventually in the day too. In the beginning the groans were irregular and spaced out. Then they came with every breath, muted but clear through the bedroom wall. Auntie Leah came over every day to help my mother, and they nursed Nana, unaided, till her death. I saw the bloody towels they washed in the kitchen boiler. About a week before they knew she hadn't got much longer, I was sent to stay with Uncle Arnold and Auntie Renee. I had my first bath in a proper bathroom, and my first all-over puff-and-pat with talcum powder. Renee, who was also to die of cancer, of the liver, gave me a big hug and said: 'You smell lovely and wuffly.' And a day or two after that Arnold told me Nana was dead. He held me tight.

Everything fell apart. My mother said: 'It was a bleeding cancer. The neck of the womb.' Ron said he wasn't a tough guy after all, and wept. Grandpa developed phlebitis (or was it kidney-stone?) and took to his bed for a time. I felt the pride of bereavement when I told my friends at school, and guilt at feeling pride. It was my first death.

I loved going shopping with Nana on Saturday nights, especially to the market, though I blushed with shame when she asked the butcher for a pound and a half of belly-pork. Once she asked me to go and get it and I inquired: 'Couldn't I say "stomach-pork"?' I was offended when she laughed. She criticized my friends, said I was a snob and didn't help my mother. True enough. As Nana said, I didn't do a hand's turn, nor ever thought of helping. The only times I remember my mother speaking angrily to her mother was on this subject, 'I'm not having her grow up a skivvy like me', or 'One skivvy's enough in the family.' When I was very young, we had a series of real skivvies, young girls, to do the scrubbing. One was Cilla, famous for her reply to Mother's question about whether she was quick at her work, 'Sometimes I'm quick and sometimes I'm slow', which became another family proverb, trotted out in truth or irony. There were many of these. My mother read me the story of *The Three Little Pigs* in a version that made much of the clever pig's triumph when the wolf turned up to have apple pie with him, and the early-rising survivor gloated: 'I've finished making it and cooking it and eating it long ago. Can't you see the peelings behind the door?' If you turned up offering to help after the job was done, out it would come with a wry smile: 'Can't you see the peelings?' There was my special line, 'I've got my tangerine.' I had spoken up and reminded them of my woolly orange suit when told I had nothing warm to wear and couldn't go out. Another usefully adaptable image. More obscure was 'Our Peter had an egg for breakfast and he took the spoon', which had been said by a poor relation in the Hafod by way of apology for the absence of a spoon to stir the tea. My closest and warmest memories of Nana are of being in bed with her when my mother had her only serious illness, pneumonia, some time in her thirties. I must have been about three or four, and sent to sleep in my grandparents' front bedroom. It always smelt strongly of Sloane's Liniment and Thermogene rub, for Grandpa's rheumatism. My grandparents had a double bed with brass bed-posts, and I had a little brass bed put next to it. All the posts and knobs and rails gleamed like gold, so as I walked to bed I said I was going between the golden gates. It was another phrase passing into family currency, a radiant image of love and comfort and play. Perhaps my brother wasn't born, because he doesn't figure in this memory. I used to climb into the big bed in the morning, and I remember looking close-ly at Nana's white skin. On her cheek was a tiny black spot. I stared at it and asked her what it was and quick as a flash she said, looking serious, 'That's where I was shot.' 'Go on, you weren't really.' She persisted, so I believed.

Many of my memories of Nana, like most of her photo-graphs, see her in pain. She is serious, resigned and bitter. She is waiting on her husband and sons. In those early posed pho-tographs, with Grandpa and the first children, she is a beautiful girl with grave eyes. She had been a bright girl, top of her class, and in retrospect I appreciate her vivid phrases and sharp wit. She was famous for her sneeze, a real aria beginning 'Asha'. In later years, she often ate before or after the family because she had a nervous throat and used to choke over her food. I remember her eating on her own, Grandpa and the boys out. She would have nice little special suppers on a cloth laid over a corner of the table, with a cup of tea or a glass of stout, bread and butter cut very thin, a Marie biscuit or sponge-finger, plump crispy biscuits, like rice-cakes or Energen bread, with a dab of butter in the hollowed-out centre. I would be given a bit to taste, but these were her treats. I don't remember her having many friends outside the family, though there was one called Cilla, whom I found fascinating because I was told she was a spiritualist, and told Nana how she'd gone to a seance where the dead had spoken. Nana used to read the tea-leaves and point to the stranger flapping on the grate.

She loved her daughters, who loved her, and nursed her

devotedly. Leah said, 'Your mother always comes first.' Ron was her baby, spoilt from start to finish, my mother said. But what I thought were special treats for him were the meat meals for the manual worker, like steak and onions with mashed potato. We'd get tastes of this too, though the steak was often hard and a bit gristly, not in my kitchen paradise. I preferred Nana's 'ash' or hash, sliced cold meat reheated slowly in good gravy, an almost forgotten taste. In Cradock Street, we always ate at her old deal table, which I've recently had sanded and repaired. I remember it covered with greeny-brown oilcloth, which was stuck over with dried old translucent fish-scales from Uncle Gilbert's fish. It was amusing and compulsive to pick them off, as the grown-ups talked or we listened to the news or a comedy programme. Nana always said to us, as she served a cutlet of fine hake or a piece of coarse flounder: 'Now eat up that fish. Fish makes brains.' One of her daughters-in-law complained of her husband's attentions in early married days and Nana spoke to him severely, saying, 'That's lust, not love.'

She once took me to an exotic magic show at Ben Evans store, promoting the sale of oriental carpets. There was a levitation trick that amazed us both, and terrified me. It opened a new door into the undesirable supernatural world, and I dared not ask Nana if she believed it was only a trick. I held her hand tight. And it was with her that I first had a meal in a restaurant, actually the café in High Street Woolworths. I remember the immense sense of social novelty and luxury, especially when Nana said I could go and get our second course. I've forgotten if she said 'a sweet' or 'dessert' or 'afters' but I know I went to the self-service counter, proud and grand, and asked for banana fritters, fourpence 'a portion'. I rolled the word 'portion' over my tongue after our love-feast.

She died when she was sixty-one, and I was puzzled when my mother said 'She was a young woman when she died', but of course I know better now. She'd say, 'A son's a son till he gets him a wife. But a daughter's your daughter all your life.' Born in May, she could wear emeralds, she said, and had green glass necklaces and earrings. Her pierced ears amazed me. She wrote in my autograph album, in her beautiful sloping writing: '*Make new friends but keep the old, They are richer far than gold*' Her terms of abuse were 'snobby' or 'brazen'. And every Sunday dinner-time she would ask Grandpa, to whom she was 'Flo', to say grace. It was the only time we ever had grace at that noisy, newsy, fast-eating table. Grandpa would shut his eyes, and say, gruffly and reverently, 'Be present at our table, Lord, / Be there and everywhere adored', then after a line I've forgotten 'And grant that we, / May feast in paradise with thee'. When I first heard it I was too young to know the meaning of 'adored', or 'paradise', and listened only to their sounds. I remember the last time that grace was said. It was one of the rare occasions when we had a cold dinner, much to Grandpa's disgust. Bill and I waited for grace, which sometimes used to make us get the giggles, but instead Grandpa said angrily, with a scornful look at that sacrilegious object, a cold Sunday joint, 'Doesn't seem worth saying grace for cold dinner.' 'Right,' said Gladys, colder than the joint, 'then we'll never say grace here again.' That was after my grandmother's death. I heard a new tone in my mother's voice. She was in the ascendant. There was a new head of the household. And we never said grace at dinner-time again.

Chapter 3

The Man Who Broke the Bank at Monte Carlo

There were always songs. Everybody sang at the top of their voice, up and down the house, up and down the stairs, attic to cellar. There were soprano love-songs and ballads warbled by my mother and grandmother as they scrubbed, dusted, swept, made the beds and put the washing on the line. 'The Lily of Laguna' and 'Annie Laurie' were Nana's favourites. They didn't actually do the washing, which was done every Monday by Mrs Gray, the washerwoman. She scrubbed on the copper washing-board in the zinc tub (also the children's bath), boiled the whites in the big black kitchen boiler, and did the mangling out-side the back door. The kitchen was usually draped with airing sheets and shirts, hanging on the fireguard and the chairs. Mrs Gray was plump, neatly dressed, and had fine black bobbed hair, with a fringe. My mother told me she had such dreadful headaches she could never wash her hair, 'She uses a dry shampoo and it's every bit as clean as yours and mine.' Mrs Gray gave my mother our first cookery book, which I still have. It is wonderfully random in its ordering, moving through the alphabet in unpredictable fashion, putting under D, not Doughnuts, but Delicious Apple Pie, or under P, not Pancakes, but Popular Beef Stew. Fine, once you know its funny ways.

My uncles did most of the singing, picking up songs from the wireless, the gramophone and the dances they went to in the Patti Pavilion in Victoria Park, a conservatory given to Swansea by Madam Patti, used as a dance-hall and for concerts and magic shows. I once saw a conjuror there fail at the same trick three times running, pouring 'Water from the Orient' out of a jug, then claiming to stop the flow. We thought it was the usual gimmick, pretending to fail before succeeding but it was real, and funnier than success. My uncles – always called the boys – sang as they washed in the kitchen after their hard, dirty work as joiner and electrician, or shaved, emerging from the back kitchen, the washing-place in our Cradock Street house, with shiny pink faces or in masks of soap, jolly white minstrels roaring their heads off or plaintively wailing. One of the earliest songs must have been Uncle Arnold's singing of 'The Man Who Broke the Bank at Monte Carlo', because I was small enough not only to be danced up and down in his arms as he sang but tossed in the air, high up, nearly touching the ceiling, at the song's last chorus and conclusion. I screamed with pleasure and whenever he came in would ask for 'Carlo'. He became the song. As I became more articulate, he was 'Carlo' and 'Uncle Carlo', until I grew up and called him 'Uncle Arn', as I still do. Always my favourite uncle, he played with us because he loved playing and loved us. He was close to my mother and looks a lot like her, with an aquiline nose, hair that never goes white, dry humour, sharp eyes and a keen intelligence. He looks at my grandchildren, Rhiannon and Simon, as he used to look at us, fond and enjoying. He got married and left my grandparents' house when we were still very young, so my brother and I never had the fights and quarrels with Arnold that we inevitably had with Ron, not quite a sibling or a superior, though at times he tried to be both. When Arnold sang me his song, I had no idea what breaking a bank meant. Last year I was at a Beckett conference in Monaco, and sent Arnold a postcard from Monte Carlo, for old times' sake.

Arnold was like a father. In his young days he was a socialist, like Ron, but after the 1945 election moved to the Right, in an unfortunately common reaction to continuing austerity and increasing regulation. And as a man becomes a master, moving into another class and new prosperity. I remember my uncles' tea-cans, containing tea-leaves and condensed milk, prepared by Nana or my mother. And I remember their affluence and partnership after the boss, Mr Nicholls, died. My history is landmarked by Arnold's kindness and support. He told me of that first death, his mother's and my grandmother's. Years later, when my father died and my mother asked me to go to the funeral with the men, against the grain of local custom, I was pleased, as daughter and feminist. I'd always detested the exclusion of the women, left behind to weep and make the tea. There had been a scandal in a teacup when my grandfather's only remaining sister, Auntie Beaty, had turned up at his funeral, amongst the male mourners. Everyone was shocked, and I was jealous. Arnold, always a traditionalist, told me he disapproved of my attendance but he'd support my mother's wish. At the graveside he told me where to go and what to do. I went forward with him to drop the handful of earth on the coffin, and gaze down for the last look into the grave. In May 1992 I held his hand by the same grave, in Oystermouth Cemetery, by the sea, at my mother's funeral. Once more he disapproved, as he told me, this time because we were only having a graveside ceremony, less convenient for gathering mourners than a cemetery chapel. But I looked round and he stood by my side, holding my hand tight, later on pulling me forward to follow his example and throw a flower on the coffin. I took a lily of the valley, drooping and drying, which I'd stuck in the buttonhole of my black linen jacket. I'd forgotten about that look into the grave, until he set the example once again. The sun shone, birds sang, and everyone was there, my brother and I, our children, Arnold, her nieces, nephews, great-nieces, great-nephews, the barristers from Angel Chambers, friends from the village, and the Rector of Llanmadoc who said everything we asked him to say, in a loud voice. Arnold is rather deaf now, and when I asked him if he could hear everything, hoping there was nothing he objected to in the brief obituary, he grinned and said, 'No, didn't hear much but I did hear "The Lord is my shepherd", and remembered her teaching it to me.' The psalm had been a lucky choice.

I also loved his wife Renee, clever, pretty, affectionate, dog-breeder, brilliant international bridge player and gifted dress-maker who made me so many lovely things (my crinoline, a frilled pink dress, a blue one with gold spots), and their children, Norma and Jill, though Jill was born too late for our chief generation of cousins. Their comfortable house in a cul-de-sac in Tycoch was another middle-class refuge and a step up in social education. There I learnt about luxuries, though the luxuries were today's necessaries, fitted carpet, bathroom, fridge and indoor sanitation. But not central heating, because Renee thought the pipes and radiators too ugly.

In their dining-room, the main sitting-room, there was a big reproduction of Millais's *Bubbles*, which I took for granted was an original, and much admired. (In autumn 1992 Arnold gave it to my daughter Kate.) Arnold and Renee lived there with Renee's mother, Granny Rickard, who had a butcher's shop in the market. *Bubbles* came from her house in Lyon Street, was dumped in the basement of the new house and rescued by Arnold. Granny Rickard was the only woman I've known who really was a sweet old lady, with shining, snow-white curls, rosy cheeks, sparkling eyes, and a beneficence beamed at everyone. Like Nana, she had the folk in her speech. 'She's full of her skin,' she would say of the adored baby, Norma, who was 'into everything', and 'She's full of her shoes'. I loved visiting them, and the first talcum powder, like the pricey chocolate eclairs on their tea-table, was a comfort, a sacred object in the rites of love and kinship.

Granny Rickard, like my grandmother, favoured the old ways of cooking. She told my mother, less modern in the kitchen than the young Renee, that she was forbidden to put soda in with the peas – to soften them or keep them green – but always popped some in when Renee's back was turned, and would laugh up her sleeve when Renee pointed triumphantly to the tender bright peas cooked without that old soda.

Arnold was a joiner by trade. I have an old work-box, a chessboard and a letter-rack, which he made when he was an apprentice to Nicholls the builder, whom I never met but was aware of as Arnold's and Ron's boss. When they eventually bought his business, on his retirement, it seemed a huge promotion. Arnold and his older brother Gilbert went to painting classes, and a painting by each of them hung on the kitchen wall in Cradock Street. All that remains in my memory is dark, thick oil paint, grey and brown and green, landscape or seascape. Arnold went back to painting in later life, and I have a painting by him of my Llanmadoc cottage, beating Grandma Moses hollow. He's also given me one of Dylan Thomas and a copy of a big Italian papal scene, but I like the cottage best.

When he was eleven or twelve, he went to chaperone his sister Gladys on a visit she paid to her fiancé, Maurice, whose ship came in to Barry Island. Her mother wouldn't let her go without Arnold, who didn't know 'what a chaperone was'. They spent a night or two in the ship – 'I don't know where Glad and Maur slept' – and Arnold was impressed by the Armenian cook, who had his motto up in the galley: *Take life as you find it, but don't leave it like that.* He gave me love, with occasional severity, so he was a father-figure after all. My grandfather was, or became, too easy-going and indulgent, Ron was too much like a quarrelsome brother, and the other uncles had less time for us, though Gilbert was close and kind. When my father came back home, for his few last years, I was over thirty and we'd been apart for more than twenty-five years, so though I was surprised and delighted by the ease with which we slipped into love and familiarity, we were extremely polite to each other. Politeness didn't put a chill on our attachment, but kept it more self-conscious and controlled than family relationships, especially Welsh and lower-middle-class ones, usually are. On one half-forgotten occasion he said or did something to annoy me, or I said or did something to annoy him. It's no doubt significant that the details have vanished, while more trivial ones have stayed. I remember an impulse to shout in anger, and a look on his face as if he had a similar impulse. Then there was brief silence, withdrawal, a smile, an unspoken graceful decision, taken mutually, to calm down and say nothing. That silence held the ghost of all the rows and rages we might have had if we'd known each other and lived together for all those missing years. I'd be a different person, and so would he have been, and my mother and brother. My marriage and children might have been different too. Better or worse, but not the same.

But there were the uncles, to spoil, play, boss, tip, tease and love. The two shadowy ones were Uncle Arthur and Elvert or Bill. Arthur was the uncle least known and least liked. He was first a fireman and then an engine-driver on the GWR. He and Olive, his wife, seemed more aloof than the other uncles and aunts, more so as we all grew up and older. As children do, we sensed that they didn't like us much, so we didn't like them. Arthur was very like my grandfather, only shorter, with fair hair, blue eyes and ruddy skin. He had a rough manner and the rapid speech of one of our great-uncles, Ernie, and Ron. They talked impetuously and amusingly, but the speed and rush were frightening to a child's ear. The last time I saw Arthur was at my grandfather's funeral, where my mother was cold to him, eventually speaking her mind as she had to walk near or hand a cup: 'Not much point in coming to see him now he's dead, since you never came when he was alive.' I wished she hadn't spoken, though I liked her style. I think there was some family quarrel, dimly sensed by the children, involving my mother and Olive. But someone told me that later on Olive said she couldn't feel hostile to my mother after she was told how devotedly Gladys had nursed her dying mother. What the row was about I don't know, but after a certain time we stopped exchanging visits and Christmas presents, though John and I met at school and Joyce and I at Sunday School. Olive was a bit like her name, dark, lean and pungent. She was very tall and thin, sharp and talkative. When I read *The Mill on the Floss,* which I borrowed from her, I associated her with Maggie's aunts. She was tight-lipped like Aunt Deane, well-dressed like Aunt Poyser, disapproving like Aunt Glegg. She was said to be touchy, and had a sharp tongue. The last time I met her, at a family birthday about twenty years ago, she said, 'I knew your mother when I saw her the other day, but I'd never have known you', and the put-down took me straight back to childhood. I am almost certainly reflecting my mother's feelings, which may have been the tip of some iceberg. Olive made a local reputation as a poet, on the chapel circuit, where she gave successful readings. She published a volume, which my mother bought and read, and her love-poems to Uncle Arthur made me see clearly how small my image of them had been.

Handsome Uncle Elvert was friendly enough, and my mother was devoted to him, as her nearest brother, but he often seemed anxious and preoccupied. We saw more of his friendly, happy wife, Auntie Marjorie or Marge. Auntie Marge was always smiling. I remember her greeting us once with her hands deep in Christmas cake mixture, once when she was lovingly but anxiously showing us her new baby, Bob, born with a hare-lip and cleft palate, and a last time in hospital just before she died, whispering a wry little joke. I associate her with a snatch of song, 'Dear little jammy-face, I loved your mammy, long ago, because her face was jammy.' Her baby, Bob, died in 1991, the first of our cousin kin to die. He was a quiet, sensitive man, occasionally seen at family funerals, and much mourned by his sisters, Maureen and Carole.

Elvert bred dogs, first Sealyhams, then Corgis. Our childhood dog, a loving and lovable shaggy Sealyham bitch called Nippy, came from his first kennels when he and Marge lived in a bungalow called Killkenny. I remember this un-Welsh name partly because it was a kennel name used for his dogs, and partly because it sprang into family legend one Guy Fawkes' night. We were strict about keeping the dog and cat indoors because they were terrified of bangs, and Nippy was always shut in the 'middle room'. But by some mischance the door was opened, and then someone opened the front door, so Nippy dashed out in a panic, to disappear into the dark night of bangers and whizz-bangs and jumping jacks. We cried ourselves to sleep. But the morning was happy. Nippy had fled not into the unknown, but all the way, several miles, to the old house Kilkenny, whose owner thought she might be known to the Abraham family, and took her back to their house. She hadn't been there since she was a few weeks old, and had never ever gone there or from there except in a car, so it did seem like the wonder of nature it was. 'Wonderful thing, an animal's instinct,' Grandpa said.

Uncle Elvert came down on Saturday nights to play cards with his brothers and father. As card-players, the Sketty lot were said to be very keen. They were famous for their whist. Every family had its card-playing habits and to this day, if anyone plays a court-card, then follows with the higher card, ace after king, or king after queen, someone will say 'Sketty play'. Elvert was my father's generation, and the other man of the family to be visibly and badly hit by the Depression. He and my father were the only out-of-work men I knew. Father went back to sea and his first hated work, to be separated for most of his life from his wife and children. Elvert was no doubt also scarred, by loss of job, anxiety and humiliation, but he stayed at home. They weren't badly off, because Marjorie's aunt, Auntie Bessie, lived with them, and she was said to have pots of money. I remember being told that Elvert had lost his job. 'Poor Uncle Bill's on the dole.' He was 'a traveller', or commercial traveller, which I thought very high up. Perhaps he visited his parents more often because he was at a loose end, looking for work or going to collect the dole. He would often come to midday dinner, bringing cigarette cards for us, like the other uncles. There was a terrible ring about the Depression phrases, 'out of work', 'on the dole', 'means test'. I associated 'He's had to go on the dole' with dolefulness, and the means test, which I barely understood, with meanness. I remember seeing a dole queue. Everyone was smoking, as everyone did in those days, and all the people in the queue were men. After the thirties such misery seemed part of the past, for South Wales and the rest of Britain. Nobody imagined the return of poverty in the ugly eighties and uglier nineties.

I would get a penny for going down to the tobacconist's to buy Woodbines or Players for my uncles, strong black pipe tobacco for Grandpa. There was the big thrill of cigarette cards. I got the genuine collector's frisson when they let me open the packet, to discover if the card was one I didn't have, a shiny clean Jean Harlow or a Claudette Colbert, a William Powell or a Claude Hulbert. We went to the pictures once a week, so the faces were all familiar. I collected kings and queens of England, too, but only Richard III's dark, keen face has stayed vivid. We collected stamps, and I think it was Uncle Gilbert who gave me his album. We also collected little enamel figures, called Cococubs, from some brand of cocoa. Anything would do, but cigarette cards of film stars were the best of all.

Gilbert was a clerk in the Consolidated Fisheries. He brought us fish several times a week, in a big straw fish-frail. He and Arnold and Ron probably looked happier than Uncle Bill because they had a steady job. Gilbert was the only one who had been to a secondary school, called Mun. Sec. (Municipal Secondary), and he was one of the family readers. After he left home, he still let me read his library books, which he would bring in a little pile, on his way to or from the library. Once, I was grateful to him for loyally not telling my mother I'd read a very adult novel. It was called *They Wouldn't Be Chessmen*, set in ancient Crete, and retold the story of Pasiphae and the conception of the Minotaur. Its description of the woman, the bull and their sex-machine brought a new element into my Greek myths and my fantasies in the dark. Gilbert had left the book around, then after reading it must have realized with alarm that I might have read it too. He inquired discreetly: 'Haven't read that one, have you, Barbara?' When my mother pricked up her ears at the intonation and interrogated him, 'Why? What's it about?', he prudently said, 'Oh nothing... just... isn't she a quick reader?'

Uncle Gilbert's wife Iris wasn't a reader. She was smart and fashionable, the first woman in the family, and the first I knew, to wear trousers. Ron didn't like her and said it was to hide her skinny legs. I thought she was like a film star, with black permed hair, big brown eyes, loads of make up and glamorous clothes. She had a pony-skin fur coat, and Auntie Renee I think had a musquash. A fur was a woman's ambition. My mother used to say she'd like a Persian lamb, but by the time I thought of getting her one, she no longer fancied it. Auntie Iris was famous for her looks and clothes. There were rumours that she was fast, even that she'd had a baby before marrying Gil. There was a general family air of disapproval, an unacknowledged sense that Gil was too good for her. But she was kind and sweet, if a bit gushing, to us children, and once or twice gave us five shillings for Christmas, which was unimaginable wealth. She once gave me a pair of book-ends, saying, 'When you look at them you'll think of your poor little Auntie Iris.' One is missing, but the other is sitting on my desk, a little stylized bird on an oak base, yellow plastic with six cuts for a comb, a green pencil-shaped beak and a speckled oval body, Iris's bird from the thirties.

She had some right to self-pity. Her slimness became skinniness, and she got tuberculosis, then called consumption. Later, my brother got TB when he was a student, and my mother wondered if he'd caught it from Iris, though I think the gap of time was too large. Certainly no one ever stopped her hugging and kissing the kids. She went away to a well-known sanatorium called Craig-y̆-Nos, but couldn't stand it, came back, got better, and relapsed. She went to stay in Carew, the Pembrokeshire village where grandfather had been the baker, to be fed up by an old friend, Matt the Bridge. Iris came to be known, she told us, as the Little Maid from the Bridge. But country village life became unendurable, and she came home, to die.

Ron wasn't a great reader but he used to buy the yellow jacketed volumes of Gollancz's Left Book Club. He and my mother were very keen on A.J. Cronin, because he was in the fashion, because one of his novels, *The Stars Look Down,* was about South Wales and a Welsh miner who became a Labour MP, and because he was a socialist, writing about their class, their time, their ambitions and their losses. When *Hatter's Castle* was published my mother told me it wasn't a suitable book for me, and Ron hid it in a drawer. I borrowed it and read it on the sly. Ron had a tent in Brandycove, where he spent weekends with friends and girl-friends, swimming and canoeing and taking photographs. ('I don't know what Kitty's mother is thinking about, letting her stay in that tent with Ron,' Leah would say to

Gladys or Gladys to Leah.) I was allowed to sleep in his room when he was away, so had access to forbidden books and his diary. There was always a smell of sweaty socks around, but I would buy a bag of chocolate burnt almonds (half a pound for ninepence) and enjoy reading in a room I pretended was a room of my own. Sometimes it was *Little Women, Anne of Green Gables* and all the joys of their sequels. Of course I loved and enjoyed Jo – till she got married and became a Hausfrau – but *Hatter's Castle* gave me my first information about pregnancy outside marriage and its social consequences. It fed my deep private fear that I might end up with an illegitimate baby, a less unlikely possibility than going to prison. I enjoyed reading about sex but prayed I'd never be made pregnant before I got married. It was a doom lying just round the corner in wait for the growing girl.

Hatter's Castle wasn't the only banned book. I wasn't told not to read Oscar Wilde, but my mother said, emphatically, that 'Wilde was a rotter.' She had said it before about a character in one of my grandmother's romances, a vile seducer and womanizer, so I got the wrong idea about Wilde. I never heard of homosexuality until I was seventeen or even older. It was in the Upper Sixth, when we were allowed in the stock-room at the top of the building to read in spare periods, that some of us had had a puzzled discussion about the problem Queen Victoria had contemplated: 'What could they possibly do?' But we were baffled about men as well as women.

My grandfather sent off for a low-price offer of Odhams Press Classics for me and Bill. He once sent for a cheap *Century of Thrillers*, with a sealed section containing stories unsuitable for the weak and squeamish, which I tore open in longing. But this offer was for six Great Books. It was made in the *Daily Herald*, our daily paper. My grandparents were Liberals, but everyone else was Labour, though in our family the distinction was a matter of history not belief. Everyone was poor and insecure, and everyone was socialist. Only governments were Conservative. I never met a Conservative until I was grown up, and realized young people could be

Conservative only because of the Conservative Society, at college. Our newspapers, the *Herald* and the *Mirror,* had Labour headlines and editorials and letters. When the Prince of Wales spoke in sympathy for the miners I assumed he must be a socialist too. When I came to read Shaw and Marx I knew I'd been in the thick of the class war all my life. And we were Labour, they were Capital.

When the books arrived they were divided between us, except for a novel called *Tom Jones*. My mother was adamant. It was not suitable for a child. I was to wait till I grew up. My introduction to the eighteenth-century novel began. Nothing as thrilling as a banned book, but this one wasn't like Cronin's good read. Under the eiderdown, with a torch lighting my secret cave, I toiled through six hundred pages of long, elaborate sentences, discursive addresses to the reader, unintelligible classical jokes, baffling references to comedy – comedy! – and all in small print on cheap, crisp, brownish paper. I still have the book, in two volumes, with a hideous frontispiece of the novelist, and endpapers reminding the reader of Bacon's opinion, 'A good book is a true friend.' I was determined not to skip a line of this good book in case I missed something. When I came to the sexy bits they were so crude and boisterous that I didn't find them at all exciting. Nothing like Cronin's pregnant girl in fear of her tyrant father. How could you identify with anybody in *Tom Jones*? Its sex was boring, especially to someone who'd been swopping dirty words and verses and theories for years, since primary school. But I went on to the end. It took me years to get back to Fielding. When I began to lecture on the English novel I always managed to leave him out, or swop with someone who didn't like Richardson. (They never included *Pamela* or *Clarissa* in the cheap offers from the *Herald*.) I didn't teach Fielding until 1969, when I thought I'd give him another try, and put him into a course I taught at Northwestern University. I found him wonderful, though I still thought the sexy bits not sexy. But I had long ago stopped reading literature to learn those facts of life.

I borrowed books from Gilbert. My copy of *Gone with the*

Wind was a Christmas present from him and Iris in 1939. Another copperplate inscription, with love. He and Iris had ultra modern furniture in their flat round the corner in Carlton Terrace. I was particularly impressed by two thirties' armchairs that contained shelves in their wooden arms. We had one Dickens at home, my mother's copy of *Our Mutual Friend*. Like *Vanity Fair* and the works of Josephus, also my mother's, it was one of my unreadable books. Perhaps if I had been forbidden to read any of these it would have been different. I was delighted when I read Charles Lamb at school and found that Josephus was one of his unreadables too. From Gilbert I borrowed the children's Dickens, *The Old Curiosity Shop*, *Oliver Twist* and *David Copperfield*. I was irritated when David began to grow up and fall in love, being interested in sex but not in romantic love, especially the Dickensian sort. I preferred novels about children like Nell and Oliver, who never grew up. I borrowed *The Three Musketeers* and *The Mill on the Floss* from Olive, and devoured them both, at about nine. I remember going into my mother's bed, to wait for her warmth, after crying uncontrollably over the drowning of Maggie and Tom. I was Maggie. I was fair not dark but I had to have my hair curled, with curlers or tongs, I was told off for being a tomboy, I hated dolls, I told stories, and my brother, much nicer to me than Tom to Maggie, got a shilling from Uncle Ernie when I got sixpence. And I had all those uncles and aunts.

Gilbert was pitied for being childless, and always made a great fuss of us, so the family was delighted for him when, after Iris's death, he married another slim brunette, called Joyce, and had two children, Paul and Elizabeth. They were young enough to be my children, and I'd moved to London by then, so saw these additions to the company of cousins only once or twice. Gilbert was a very heavy smoker, like all the men in the family, and when I last saw him his thin, handsome, sensitive face was gaunt and yellow. He was dying from lung cancer, and I was calling on him, in his house in Fforestfach, to say goodbye.

Of all the uncles and the aunts, Ron loomed largest. He was only sixteen years older than I, and we lived in the same house, at close quarters, till at last I went away to university, then to work in London. My mother told me the flattering story of his first words when she showed him his new-born niece – 'She's got actress's lips.' My pride was quickly lowered when she looked hard at my not quite short enough upper lip and blamed Leah for letting the window fall on it – or had she dropped me on the brass fender?

Ron was not a frustrated intellectual or a reader. He was a mother's boy, like many Welshmen, spoilt and babied by his mother, whom he resembled and adored. He was extremely handsome as a young man, with a bull-neck and brawny shoulders, like Brando, and the dark good looks, though heavier and coarser, of Valentino. (Arnold had finer features.) Ron's hair was brilliant with Brylcreem, his ears stuck out, and his slightly-pop-eyes, rolling in excitement all the time, were like Eddie Cantor's. His girls came and went. They were introduced to the family, especially Nana, to join us at Christmas and trips to the bays. There was Rose the highly made-up Roman Catholic, 'Catholic' to us, a strong, brown, freckled girl called Bet, a marvellous swimmer who once defeated me at beach wrestling on the sands at Pwlldu, then a dark sincere beauty, Mary, my favourite, with whom Ron had seemed to have a long on-and-off relationship, and his last love, Kitty, whom he married, latish in life, after a protracted engagement over which there was much goggling and gossip. Once there was a bad quarrel and the engagement with Kitty was broken off. Ron had gone on a date with his old love Mary and stayed out very late, maybe all night. During the rift that followed I was told, impressively, that Kitty would walk past our house on her way to see Iris, friend and confidante, with her eyes shut tight so that she wouldn't see 22 Cradock Street or anybody who lived in it.

My knowledge of Ron's love-life was padded out by occasional furtive reads of his diary, though his entries were laconic. One said briefly that he'd lost all faith in Kitty, so I knew that he really loved her all the time, and it would be all right. It was, but we never went to his wedding, because he and my mother had a bad quarrel, scarcely speaking for months. After that he left home, so it may have precipitated the long-delayed marriage. He loved animals, like everybody in the family except my mother, who had to clean up after them, not only when they made a mess, but every day when they shed hairs on the floor and furniture, in those days cleaned with brush and pan. When one of his beloved dogs died, Gladys asked Ron, formally and in public, please not to have another dog because it was too much for her. He said nothing, frowned, went out, and in a day or two bought another dear little Sealyham, Dusty, to be house-trained and endured.

The quarrel was especially awful because Ron flung my parents' separation in my mother's face, and in front of me. It was from his cruel words that I learnt that it was a separation from choice, probably my father's choice. 'No wonder some men leave home,' he said, on two occasions. I never forgave him, though he and I hardly ever quarrelled. I remember not speaking to him for a day or two once when he took a cushion from my seat, for his own, when I was feeling tired, ill or just critical. Mother very occasionally said nasty things to him, too. She rebuked him for never fighting in the war. (He was an electrician at the docks, so in a reserved occupation.) 'My husband was man enough to be in two wars,' she said. And though he was flamboyantly generous as an uncle, she had to ask him to give her more for his housekeeping contribution, which she told me wasn't nearly enough. He acquiesced with a bad grace. I was nasty to him only inadvertently. Once he asked me, half-proud but perhaps half-jealous of my ambition and escape, if I'd come back to teach in Swansea, and I retorted contemptuously that I wouldn't dream of coming back home to live. Bill used to quarrel with him too, seeing more of him in the touchy adolescent time because he went to university in Swansea. But our animosities came late, after that long childhood when relations and relationships are taken for granted.

Ron was political, and sometimes instructive. I have a little leather address book with a gold crest, which he brought me back from Oxford, where he went to a school or conference organized by his trade union. He came dashing in, saying at his usual speed, in his usual excitement: 'I've got that scholarship to Oxford. In Ruskin College.' I thought he was going to be a real Oxford undergraduate, like characters in *Tom Brown at Oxford* and novels by Ethel Mannin, and was very disappointed, for him and the family prestige, when it was only a fortnight's summer school. Still, it was Oxford, and a bit of glory rubbed off. At some point Ron left the Labour Party and became a communist. Everyone seemed fascinated, even shocked. I was puzzled and asked him to explain the difference. He did, promptly and clearly: 'Socialists believe in nationalization with compensation, communists believe in confiscation.' I made a private decision to join the communists when I was old enough, and did, for a while. When I decided I was pacifist and told Ron I was going to Peace Pledge Union meetings, he was interested but disapproving, and warned me that I might get into trouble, as they tried to persuade soldiers to desert. Wrong about that, he had a realistic political sense, I think. He eventually left the CP, if he had ever formally joined, and moved Right, as he, like Arnold, became his own boss, a small capitalist.

My grandmother and mother vaguely disapproved of Ron's communism, but also thought it a bit of a joke. Ron was a snazzy dresser – he even had a pair of plus-fours – and one night when he was going out, hair shining, before he donned his trilby, wearing a heavy camel-hair overcoat which made his short-legged figure look squat, one of them pinned a newspaper photograph of Stalin on his back. The rest of the evening was a giggle and a speculation. When would someone tell him, where and how? We never knew. He had a double revenge. He never mentioned the practical joke. But a few days later my grandmother's treasured framed portrait of the Prince of Wales, in colour, with fair hair and bags under the bright-blue eyes, vanished for ever from the kitchen wall. A neat tit for tat.

When I last talked to him he even disapproved of trade unionism and voted Conservative. He was a great singer round the house, the song travelling with him, louder and softer. The earliest numbers come back, 'If you were the only girl in the world, / And I were the only boy', 'Oh Mona, you shall be mine,

/ When the good Lord sets you free', and 'Ramona, I'll meet you by the waterfall', which, even to my young ear, sounded old, their notes and words coming from an ancient time. My mother carolled old twenties' tunes. I remember her singing in the dicky-seat of a car just bought by my grandfather. We all piled in, and Ron and Gladys at the back sang 'Oh Dodeodo' and 'Bye-bye Blackbird' as we started off. Voices and faces had a happy shine on them as I looked round. As I grew older I'd join in Ron's songs. My top favourites were 'The Isle of Capri', my first encounter with the romance of adultery, and 'Oh Play to Me, Gypsy', a glimpse of brief encounters. 'Red Sails in the Sunset' was a love-story with a happier ending, but projected on to my father's distant voyages. 'September in the Rain', heart-broken and heart-breaking, sobbed out its pathetic fallacy. Long before I read Hopkins's great poem 'Spring and Fall', about the autumnal and winter grief men and women were born for in their spring, I'd met it, tears, seasons and all in Ron's pop songs: 'The leaves so brown, came tumbling down, remember?' Later our music fused, with 'Yours', 'I Don't Want to Set the World on Fire' and 'Smoke Gets in Your Eyes.' At some date, the Government discouraged soft love-songs as sentimentally morale-lowering for the troops, but I didn't notice much difference because I listened to Ron more than the radio.

When I was in the Lower and Upper Sixth, I used to go to the Swansea University hops in the Engineers Building, on Saturday afternoons, and started to catch up with Ron's dancing as well as his singing. I remember his going off to unimaginably glamorous dances at the Patti on Saturday nights, all dressed up and nowhere to go, my mother would say grimly. He always had somewhere to go, and his goings and comings were part of the jazz age. He played the piano by touch, and the ukulele. One of his and Arnold's friends, a round-faced, jolly man called Wally Cornelius, was an expert performer on the ukulele, and rendered 'And He Played His Ukulele as the Ship Went Down' with great power. Ron once demonstrated the Charleston to us, his big feet pointing quaintly in and out. About twenty-five years later, he had a go at the

Twist, laughing his head off, his short legs and strong arms zigzagging to 'Let's Twist Again' with abandon.

Lover, singer, dancer, Ron was most famous for his crazes. He was one of the few people I've ever known to have hobbies, though that word's too weak for his concentrated passions, discovered with the 'eureka' feeling, creatively developed, but never lasting more than about six months. He did electrical jobs in his spare time, mostly mending wireless sets – 'It's probably the valve,' they would say, as I took the set with a message for 'Mr Abraham the electrician'. He used the middle room as a workshop, though we also sometimes did our homework or played with our friends there. I much preferred doing mine in the kitchen, with a roaring fire, the wireless on full blast, everybody shouting, singing, laughing and quarrelling. 'How can you concentrate?' my mother would fuss. The uncles and aunts were always dropping in on their way somewhere, as we lived so centrally, and the inner glass door was always opening and shutting. Or being carelessly left open, to get my grandfather yelling: 'Shut that door! Were you born in a barn? *Cae y Drws!*' Ron had made one of the first crystal sets, my mother told me, but our wireless would often go wrong and he'd give it a bash, which would frequently make it work.

The middle room was where he made his huge, intricate Spanish galleon, during that craze. Then he darkened it to do printing and developing in a craze for photography, during which we were all photographed many times, and he kept changing one camera for another, going up the scale of expense and complexity. We would get his cast-offs as objects or hobbies were discarded, an old Brownie camera that never worked, a scratchy wind-up gramophone with some records, 'Wheezy Anna', and one I've still got, 'You call it madness, / Oh, but I call it love', sung in a thirties' heart-throb voice, husky, slightly fake American, with a sob or a break in it. Just like Ron. I also got his heavy Green Flash tennis-racket after the tennis craze, during which he'd play on the courts at Cwmdonkin Park, apparently rather well. I knew I was tremendously lucky to get it, as it cost a lot and was what the champions used at

Wimbledon, but it had been bought for his manual worker's muscles and destroyed whatever tennis talents I might have had. No wonder my backhand was useless.

Some crazes lingered on. He had a huge table-tennis table, at least six inches wider and a foot longer than the regulation length, and two good bats. It almost filled the attic in Cradock Street, and Bill and I spent many happy hours playing, though it ruined our game for ordinary-sized tables. To play with Ron was exciting, and he had more wit than to let us win, so the most we could hope for was to win one or two points. His service was thunder and lightning, but even more devastating were his occasional smash returns, at which you could only stand back and shut your eyes. He taught us to say table-tennis, not ping-pong, and score properly. We got our own bats from Father Christmas. He also taught us to put a spin on the ball, after which I developed a healthy sub-genre in day-dream, a serial story called 'Betty the Ballboy'. The heroine was a humble ballboy (I think a girl in disguise, but perhaps the cross dressing was a variable) who had to stand in for the champion at the last minute, and won a glorious victory. Ron left the craze behind, but the table remained, and friends and visitors used to play with us, at a disadvantage because they were used to smaller tables. Bill became a strong player, but I excelled only in my fantasy, the only one in which I developed an athletic theme.

Then there were goldfish. He started with goldfish in an ordinary round glass bowl, then graduated to a big rectangular one, with knobbly, fawn ceramic base and surround, and a figure of a boy fishing, a life-like statuette with a plaster shoe on the end of a real string. Then he had a tank in the back garden, with bigger fish, carp and shubunkin. 'That one looks as if he's wearing a plastic mack,' I said. 'Trust you to say something like that,' said Ron with a grin. When the aquarium iced over in winter I was sure they'd die, but they didn't. When he went off on holidays, to Devonshire (as we called it) and Pembrokeshire, we fed them for him. We played games too, in some of his crazes. The little hard-earth garden in Cradock Street had holes dug for miniature golf – very miniature, but the best backyard game was cricket. Grandpa, Ron, Bill and I used to play, in a very restricted space by the side of the house, with Nana's copper washing-board for the wicket, which gave a resonant twang when you hit it. Bowling had to be underarm, and confined to grounders, because a rising ball would hit a window. The game on the yard-wide ground was so confined that even a lazy girl like me could be proficient, developing an eye for the wicket, not having far to field, and allowed to bowl from nice nearby spots because of being so young.

Ron had a violent way of talking, his roughness seasoned with humour. On the other hand, a joking manner was a licence for rudeness. He would push in to a meal, shove the table to make room, spread elbows and shout, 'My stomach thinks my throat's cut.' If it was something he didn't like, or like the look of, it was: 'I'd sooner die some other way.' He swore a bit, 'Hell' and 'Bloody' and 'Christ', but not really much, and his strongest term of abuse, which I took to be a terribly bad word, was 'Lello' or 'Lel', which I've seen in a glossary of Gower dialect but heard, hurled in extreme scorn, only from Ron, and occasionally used more mildly by my grandfather or Leah. It may be a Pembrokeshire word. You use it like that other dialect work 'Gowk', not pointing out a fool, but uttering your own contemptuous low opinion. Ron used to tease us unmercifully. Eating too much, having your hair cut or curled, or showing fear, were held up to scorn. A timid boy was a pansy, I was a vulture or Greedy Greta or Bessie Bunter, and when I was a very small child he would deliberately frighten me with stories of the wolf and the bogy man. I didn't need Perrault or Angela Carter to tell me that acting out the *Red Riding Hood* story was part of the tradition, 'a rough kind of game'. Such games still go on. Angela Carter loved her grandmother pretending to be the wolf, and jumping on her, but she romanticized what I found far from funny. And Ron wasn't the only one who played rough. Teasing was a recognized way of playing with children. It was the other side of that caring and play. Even Arnold would jeer rather than praise, and throughout my early adult life I would expect the uncles' attacks on my hair, figure and clothes.

It was hard to know what to say in reply. Once, when I'd successfully slimmed after my first child, Ron had put on a lot of weight. He had teased me all my life about my being slightly overweight, but on this occasion he took me aside and asked me to advise him how he could eat less, or choose less fattening food. I was surprised, as I was once when Arnold said he liked my hair-style. We were much loved in childhood but it was a rough loving. Yet we were protected, held safe in the tide, wrapped in a blanket to watch Archie Jones's warehouse fire in the dark.

There was a brief period when I had a crush on Ron. In one photograph we have our arms round each other, like lovers. But mostly he was a glamorous film star come down to earth, rowdy, loud and fast-talking, apparently rich, a source of largesse. I still use the *Cassell's French Dictionary* he gave me, inscribed in his squarish flamboyant hand: *To Babs, with love from Ron, Xmas 1940.* I was overwhelmed with pride and a sense of maturity when he invited me to call him 'Ron', without the 'Uncle'. Once, he took me to the Albert Hall, our nearest cinema, and we sat in an expensive double seat, with a box of chocolates. That was real high life. Later on I must have seemed as unpleasant a snob to him as he seemed a crude, selfish and macho spoilt boy to me, but we stayed friendly, at a distance. After I got married, we visited him in his lovely house in Sketty, with a huge garden, his biggest and longest-lasting craze, and were shown his vast collection of toby jugs ranged all round the rooms on high shelves. My children remember the jugs, and his voice, the loudest and fastest voice they have ever heard.

My other important relation, who died eight years ago, and was a figure in my children's childhood as well as mine, was my mother's sister, Auntie Leah or Lea. She was married to her opposite, a dark, severe intellectual called Walter Incledon. He also brought a touch of male sternness to my childhood, sometimes telling me off (once for calling somebody 'You louse') and usually presiding in a fairly rebuking authority. He was a great reader, and had a collection of books in a glass-fronted case, kept locked. He sometimes lent me books, unlocking and locking carefully, but once refused the loan of *Condemned to Live*, one of the family-banned books I never got hold of. Walter used to buy second-hand books from Ralph's bookshop, subsequently Welshified to 'Ralph the Books', for the tourists and the Dylan Thomas fans. From him I got the habit of buying used books. 'Ralph's', as it was always called, became a source of excitement and education. I remember Ralph, a dark, dour, occasionally smiling, unforthcoming man, standing at the end of his very small shop just opposite the station. I bought slim volumes of poetry, a mixed bag – Douglas Goldring, Evan Walters, de la Mare and Anne Ridler. Walter was the first to introduce me to the poetry of Dylan Thomas. We were visiting the Incledons when they were camping on the top of a cliff, as I recall it, in Pwlldu. I can see him coming out of the tent into bright sun, showing me a magazine and asking in his uncompromisingly unenthusiastic tones, 'Have you read this new poet they're all making a fuss about?', and handing it over.

I remember bright, dislocated words and images. Dylan wasn't much talked about, never mentioned at school. My mother was very friendly with his friend Fred Janes's sister, Kitty Jones, who lived in Mirador Crescent, close to us in the Grove. She told Gladys various Dylan anecdotes, like the one about his eating chrysanthemums, which impressed me. But the tales weren't unearthed until he was famous. I must have often passed him in the street, and Bill and I would have been attempting cartwheels in Cwmdonkin as Thomas looked over at the star-gestured children. We walked the same streets and played in the same parks, but I saw only young men imitating Dylan, in appearance and in voice, usually in Aberystwyth pubs. Arnold had some Thomas stories too, but he was one of the Swansea people rather hostile to the man and the legend, partly envying the famous exile, partly on the good old principle that a poet, like a prophet, must be looked down on by the neighbours back home. For me, Dylan Thomas's absence is eloquent. Boys of my generation, or a little older, might have had him as role-model, or met him in the pub. Never girls. I met

Dylan Thomas only when he had turned into his poems. And, as I said, it was from Walter that I learnt of his existence, meeting modernism head-on.

I owe another first time to Walter. My first flight. The Nathans and the Incledons arrived for a day on the beach – probably the long, flat, firm stretch of Caswell Bay at low water – to find a plane on the sands. I'd never seen one on the ground, except in films. Planes were still fairly rare and if you caught sight or sound of one you'd call out to the family to come into the garden to see. It was a little biplane. A fifteen-minute hop cost half a crown. Walter was keen, and I begged hard. I suppose Bill and Betty were too small, because I was the only child to go. I was a girl pilot, astounded by my luck and courage, terrified and delighted by the swinging propeller, the heart-moving take-off, the far-away water and sand, the pin-people waving. Walter was a good photographer and leant over with his camera to catch views he'd never seen before. There's one in the family album, sky and window and struts and a section of wing. When we landed I knew life on land would never be the same again.

Leah was warm-hearted, talkative and loved to gossip. She didn't always think before she spoke, and was inclined to pass on opinion and narrative promiscuously, sometimes causing trouble. Her indiscretions were careless, not wilful, but they earned her the mythopoeic name 'Stirring-stick of the Devil', often condensed to 'Stirrer', and uttered with gestures and grimaces of family resignation. She was generous, affectionate, loved all of us children as much as her own, and became her sister's best friend after their husbands were dead and their children married. When my mother stopped going out, about fifteen years before she died, Leah would walk over or take the bus, depending on which house it was she came from, in Sketty or Brynmill or round the corner, in Richmond Road, parallel to Uplands Crescent, Dylan Thomas's street. They would sit by the fire, exchanging the stories of their children, in that rare reciprocity, without jealousy or emulation, which can be one of the boons of family feeling. Their children's health, schooling, adolescent ways and whims, love-lives, marriages, marriage problems, offspring, houses, illnesses, careers and finances made the drama of their talk. The family was their ruling passion. In my earlier years, Leah was important before I distinguished her individuality in the warm nest in which I started. She used to look after me when my mother was busy in the shop she and my father kept. (They tried two, both of which failed.) Leah would boast of the big breakfasts she fed me when I was two or three, making me eat two shredded wheats and a boiled egg with bread-fingers, in our family called 'dip-ins'. I would upbraid her for making me over-eat from the start and she would always say: 'Go on, girl. You're lovely.' And we were, always and anyhow, in her eyes. Women called each other 'girl' even in their fifties, and men were boys when they went to war, blameless and heroized in the eyes of politicians and women.

Grandpa called her 'Poor Leah', perhaps because she had been very hard up during the war, living so badly on a soldier's pay that she sometimes sold her rations to richer neighbours. She sold her engagement ring to a relative, who refused to sell it back in better days. Her name was often prefaced by 'Gawd 'elp', phrase of universal love and pity. Grandpa would press the penny or tup-penny bus-fare on her as she put on her hat to go back to Sketty. She was a golden figure. She loved clothes, especially smart hats. After Walter died she worked in a hat shop, where she was in her element. That hat shop was also a little hotbed of gossip. 'Take care what you say if you call in,' said my mother. Leah kept her blonde hair well into old age, though it was at its most glamorous for me when I was a child, and she wore it in great twisted or plaited knobs or 'earphones', like Yeats's 'great honey-coloured ramparts at the ear'. I loved the objects in the Incledon houses, in St George's Terrace, Trafalgar Terrace and Sketty Road, as sacred as our own. A black boy tobacco-jar, two vivid blue views of Italian seascapes, an elaborate bronze equestrian figure. Leah was famous for having a weak head for drink – not that a woman's drinking was put to much of a test in our family – and I remember her getting the giggles after one small port at Christmas. She had a wonderful innocence, summed up by her disclosure that she thought 'The Urinal', where Grandpa often bumped into friends and local notabilities, was a pub, like 'Number Ten'.

When the family grapevine breathed that she was pregnant with her second child (though her first, Betty, always described as 'the only child', was a teenager), I read the murmurs of disapproval – 'I blame Walter', 'Just like a man', 'What can he be thinking of', 'At her age' – as more ominous than in fact they were. Men were always after sex and women weren't keen. 'You know what men are,' my mother once said to me, assuming the common misandrist complicity. It was partly fear of conception, partly fatigue, partly ignorance all round. This was the women's talk against men. But not fully understanding I decided that Leah's health was bad and her life at risk from childbirth. For the next six months or so of her pregnancy I worried about the perils of labour, about which I knew nothing, except that she was over forty and I believed that to be dangerous. I knew my mother would be present, and that the birth would of course be at home. I imagined her death, and Betty the orphan, Walter the guilty widower. When the time came and my mother came back I heard the door open and shut, feeling sure there'd be bad news, and was amazed when she was all smiles at the birth. 'It's a little girl.' Perhaps it was my relief from fears nobody ever knew about that made me so fond of the baby, and prompted Leah, searching for a name, to say I could choose one. So I named her after a close friend, and a boyfriend's sister, Christine.

My children loved Leah, and one of their big treats was to go to her for tea. The Incledons made weak milky tea, compared with our strong stuff, but I never drank that anyway. Leah's teas were always just like our childhood Sunday teas, except that you didn't have to have bread and butter with the tinned fruit. She made delicious jam sponges, and tea always included sandwiches, ham or paste or salmon, with jelly, blancmange and trifle. The Incledons' trifle, unlike ours, was made with jelly, another distinction of the house. In childhood and later, I had the habit of picking up and reading any books lying round, and once when it was a *True Romance* or Mills and Boon, Leah laughed and said, 'I'll say this for Barbara, she'll read anything.' I would egg her on to gossip. She brought back tales of her brief brilliant career as part-time barmaid, when she was hard-up but liberated after Walter's death, tasting Babychams and remonstrating with hard-drinking customers, 'Not another one, Mr Jones. Go on – go home to your wife.' Sometimes she'd surprise me – like my mother – by permissiveness and a sense of history. Discussing one more family divorce she said, after the expected words of sorrowing disapproval at the commonness of break-up, 'Mind you, it isn't that marriage used to be any better. People were just as miserable but they never thought of leaving each other.' When she died, her death was mine. Her life contained so much of my life, in and after childhood. 'I won't be long after Leah,' my mother said, but she was, living for years with the big loss of someone to talk to. At Christmas I can't believe Leah's not on my present list any more.

I hated having to kiss all and sundry, as was expected of children. Especially obnoxious was Betty's Uncle Trevor, simply because he had big, black, beetling eyebrows. Of course we called every grown-up friend of the family 'Auntie' and 'Uncle' and compulsory kissing extended far and wide. 'Have you got a kiss for–!' ended many a merry meeting. One of my mother's friends, Uncle Sid, inspired me with a deep and inexplicable loathing. Sidney Noah Trot was a short, fat, bald, jolly man, a commercial traveller my mother had known for years. She and my father had a couple friendship with Sid and his wife Kitty, and felt great chagrin at my personal phobia for him. I couldn't bear to be in the same room with him, and at the dread sound of his laugh and greeting in the passage I would dash upstairs. They tried everything, from bribery ('He gave Billy a shilling') to moral persuasion ('He loves children and they haven't got any of their own', and 'He's so kind and fond of you both').

Poor man, he couldn't have been fond of me. After many years I was forced into his presence because he drove us to our holiday bungalow in Caswell, which we shared for two sunny summers with the Incledons, to sleep in heavenly bunks and feast on primus-stove-cooked picnics. I kept my eyes tight shut during the journey, but the reaction therapists are right, and his presence grew less dreadful. My mother would speculate on the cause ('I think he said he'd take your baby brother away'), but that was a common, rough joke and I knew it was a true, deep, instinctive, irrational repugnance.

Another friend of my mother's, from Pembrokeshire, I didn't like to kiss, though I liked her well enough, was Betty Sketty Hall, so called because she was housekeeper at the big house, Sketty Hall, now a function suite owned by Swansea College. My daughter Kate and I walked round it in April 1992 and picked king cups from its pond to take to my mother in Singleton Hospital. We once spent a weekend there when the family was away, and I have an old scar on my knee where I fell on one of the gravelled paths. I remember the long corridors and seeing my reflection in a distant mirror. I remember a Christmas party in the huge drawing-room, where kind Betty invited all our family and we played musical chairs, 'Man and His Object', and 'How Green You Are'. And I remember a cavernous kitchen, my mother showing Betty how to make pastry, and Bill asking innocently, 'Are you too old to make pastry?' It wasn't a happy question, because Betty Sketty Hall was engaged to Big Stiff, a sweet-smiling giant a year or two younger than she was. She was very kind to us and once rashly said we could choose any toy in Macowards, only to withdraw generosity when I chose a very expensive rubber raft that would anyway have been forbidden in our dangerous waters.

Another visiting character was Jack Harris, married to one of Mother's cousins. He was a scaffolder, and the only person I knew who'd been to prison. Mother said it was for not paying the rates, but we never really knew. He told us how in prison he'd learnt to split a match into twenty-four. I never liked him much, though he was an amiable man, but I regarded him with awe. And after all, I had that recurring premonition of going to prison myself. I certainly avoided kissing Jack.

I didn't much like kissing the real aunts and uncles. And family feeling could be aggressive. I used to resent being close-questioned and lamented 'Another bad report – your poor mother' or 'Your mother makes such sacrifices, I hope you realize it.' When I wrote to say I was getting married, but not in Swansea and not in church, I felt the pressure of choric disapproval in what my mother said and didn't say. But when I took Ernest home, they were warm and welcoming. When I did well, they congratulated me. When I had children, they took them to their hearts. When I went home, they were there. Ron once heard a broadcast I gave on Charles Lamb, and said, 'I'd never have recognized your voice, it's so changed, so English', but he was pleased as well. Arnold said a few years ago, 'Won't you need a car when you retire?' 'Why!' 'Well, you'll need it down here, not like London.' He took it for granted that I'd end up in Swansea. My swift, guilty, horrified rejection of the idea was half a century old.

Chapter 4
Blood Is Thicker than Water

I flounced out of the kitchen, shouting or muttering at my grandmother, who'd said something about my friends being a lot of old snobs, 'You can choose your friends but you can't choose your relations.' In a cooler, more ironic mode, I once asked my mother if she'd ever wanted to be an orphan. To my surprise she didn't take the question in the offensive spirit in which it was asked but laughed and said, 'Yes, I did. I always had four or five kids dragging after me.' I hated my relations. Not all at the same time, and not always the same ones. I used to assume that my brother and I hated each other because we fought and quarrelled all the time, but when I went away to university he wrote me affectionate, funny letters and I realized we were the best of friends, as we are still. I hated my grandmother on and off, but loved her in between. I hated my mother from the age of thirteen or so, pretty consistently, but only in her presence. The minute I left her I loved her dearly. I hated some of my cousins and uncles, and particularly disliked some of the relations on the fringe, like Uncle Ernie and his son John from Killay, who never took any notice of me, Maureen's Auntie Bessie, who had eyes in the back of her head and was very critical, Auntie Edie, a brown, skinny, smiling woman, and possessor of the rottenest set of teeth I've ever seen, and Betty's Uncle Trevor, because of his eyebrows. You had to kiss all the relations, near or distant, on arrival and departure. My main reason for wanting to leave Wales and Swansea wasn't ambition but distaste for the warm and swarming nest.

Two of my maternal grandparents' children, John and

Muriel, died in infancy. I just caught the tail of the Victorian assumption that one or two out of the litter might not survive. Nobody ever spoke sadly of the two babies, ghostly uncle and aunt. My grandmother never mentioned them but Grandpa said, 'Muriel was the most beautiful little girl you ever saw.' She'd died in infancy of diphtheria, and after that they started to use inoculation in the village. Leah, born after that death, was nearly called 'Muriel' but Nana went off the idea. I never knew anything about John, and there were so many Johns, like Williams, that he was invisible. I remember thinking they'd got plenty of children left. All the blood-uncles and the one blood-aunt had children except Ron. There were dozens of cousins, and the cousins were always there. We lived with my grandparents for about ten years, till my grandmother died, the balance of power and security shifted, and Grandpa (and Ron) lived with us. In both regimes the children and the grandchildren were always visiting, though you didn't think of it as visiting. There were formal invitations to tea, on Saturdays and Sundays, and occasionally to parties, but everyone dropped in every day and every night, without advance warning or a ring on the bell. If there was a knock or a ring you knew it was the coalman, a man with a wireless for Ron to mend, the Insurance, the Club or the gipsies. My mother once refused to buy pegs or have her fortune told, saying 'I know my fortune – work or starve', and the gipsy cursed her. She believed in that curse. After all, there was plenty of misfortune around. But our callers were mostly benign. The milkman poured milk out of a big churn into the jug, warm and foamy, and the baker handed in hot loaves which Bill and I would bite into, pulling off the crisp corners. Everybody else swarmed in and out. Nobody ever thanked anybody for having them.

The eldest cousins were Joyce, usually Joy, and John, often Jack. I was slightly jealous of Joyce because she was taller, slimmer, older, and had red-gold hair. I thought of it as ginger, but the grown-ups said 'auburn' or 'corn-coloured'. She sang in the choir, became a Sunday School teacher, had boy-friends and got engaged – all before any of the other girls I knew. She was always well dressed, and though I dressed up on Sundays, I was bored by clothes for the rest of the week, and got ink on my blouses and dirt on my frocks. John was about a year older than I and tried the Scholarship at the same time. He and I were the first cousins to go to a proper secondary school, and later on he took a Civil Service examination, Executive Division, like my husband. I was the first cousin to go to university. John was fair-haired and blue-eyed, like many of us, following the Abrahams. Elvert, Arthur and Leah were on the fair side, Gilbert in between, and the rest were dark, or got dark as they grew older. I always think of Tom Tulliver as looking a bit like my brother Bill and a bit like John, though they were more book-learned and academic than Tom. John eventually did very well in the Civil Service, travelling a lot, and living for a time in Holland. We never met after we left school, and not much after we went to secondary school. I liked John, though I was left out as he and Bill inevitably joined in a boys' camaraderie. Boys were supposed to be mischievous, so nobody made a fuss, except me, when John pushed a jellyfish down the back of my cotton dress, taking it out of the bucket of assorted salt-water life we carried back from the sands. I thought all jellyfish stung, and most were poisonous, but the awful thing was not fear but revulsion at the cold, slobby blob squishing down my back and not being there when I ran upstairs and tore off my clothes. There was only some indeterminate goo. I'd apparently assimilated the creature. When I came to read Sartre I appreciated his dread of viscosity. Another time John and Bill ganged up against me in an act of male destruction – less symbolic than it may seem, I'm sure. They vandalized my beloved dollshouse. I wasn't keen on dolls, especially big ones, but liked arranging and rearranging the bought and home-made chairs and table and beds and dreams in the dollshouse. It was a simple two-storey affair with a hinged front. I discovered the wrecked building as I went into the attic. The horrible boys had broken off the front and smashed everything inside. It was so simple and solid that they couldn't utterly destroy it and an uncle soon mended it, but I was outraged and startled to find my house in ruins. We hadn't even had a quarrel. Boys will be boys, they said. And I forgave John when I was in a play at school, and he lent me a tweed suit, with short trousers, to act a boy. He was about ten, so he hadn't gone into long trousers, then a great ritual change-point for boys. I walked about the school hall in his clothes, on the girls' side, in freedom and ecstasy. Trousers at last instead of skirts. I strode and swung my legs. It was forbidden and unknown territory, though I didn't feel that in the play itself, because I had to remember the well-rehearsed lines and movements, and speak Welsh. I remember my first line, spoken to two or three other children: *Peidiwch a siarad. Mae'r Sipsiwn yn cysgu.*

Joyce was the eldest cousin, so would have seemed bossy and superior and better informed whatever she'd been like. She kept dropping hints about the facts of life, in a garbled and alarming version. Men and women did Number One – or something like Number One – into a chamber-pot (known in our family as the po, though my grandfather called it the chamber). The mixture resulted in a baby, though how it got back into the mother I can't recall. We were too young to consider that problem. I had to be told about the stork and the gooseberry bush, and we actually had a gooseberry bush in the garden, as well as red currant under which a dead kitten had been buried, and I did not doubt the common myths of origin. But Joyce's story was so smelly. She also said that red-and-white stuff dripped out of women's bottoms from time to time, and she'd actually seen it. I was confused but she was confident.

Cousins could easily be offended. Once Joyce committed the sin of reading a *Girls' Annual* I'd been given for my birthday. We didn't have big parties with invitations, but a cousin or two and a friend or two would come, and we had a cake and candles. My June birthday usually meant that the kids could be turned out and left to their own devices. That day we were vaguely playing about in the scattered and disorganized way of childhood, in the garden. I came down the garden steps by the rambling rose to find Joyce leaning on the outside kitchen window-sill looking at my book, which I hadn't even opened, merely looked at the cover. There was a tear-storm, and the birthday girl was told off while Joyce looked innocently amazed, as well she might. When she rose to the height of singing solos in chapel, in her high soprano, acquiring Fred Nener, the handsomest boy in Mount Pleasant, and walking arm-in-arm with him in the street, it was more than cousinly flesh and blood could bear. I didn't want to sing, because I recited poetry, nor did I want to get engaged or married, but that didn't halt the advance of the green-eyed monster. Cousinage was a dangerous *voisinage* because it bred the melancholy of emulation.

My favourite boy cousin was a second cousin, Billie Molloy, son of my mother's youngest aunt, Emily or Em and Big Billie Molloy. I found Auntie Em remote. A small, bitter-looking woman with a mousy bun, she had once been very lovely, my mother said, with long golden hair down to her waist. She was a reader and a musician and had married Big Bill, a Glasgow engineer, after an unhappy love-affair, which explained her unhappy demeanour. Uncle Bill Molloy was huge, over six foot, which is even huger in Wales, especially pre-war South Wales. He was completely bald, with a big lump on top of his head, an impenetrable accent, the most astonishing glottal stop, and a sweet, beaming, big smile. Auntie Em used to joke wryly that she could never understand a word he said, but my mother would quote his adieu, 'Och, I'm awa' to my bed', usually short-ened to 'I'm awa'', to her dying day. There was a period when the Molloys suffered strangely from the generous attentions of a mad next-door neighbour who would leave boxes of food, tinned fruit, bread and cakes on their doorstep. I remember their anxiety and amusement, but not their solution to the Dickensian problem.

Young Billie Molloy came and played table-tennis, and because he was a boy, and older, and friendly, I liked his visits. We played, or vaguely walked round, perhaps playing ball, in the tiny backyard of their small house, 4 William Street, which I thought humble because it had no front garden, a door open-ing on to the street and a staircase leading upstairs from the kitchen. Emily adored her only child, and wanted him to be a reporter. He started at the *Evening Post*, in some kind of office job, but was asked to do evening classes in shorthand and typing, and I think left for another job. I had fancied journalism, about which I had the vaguest notions, so suffered with him when I learnt what you had to go through to write for the papers. He became a fitter, I think, like his father, and later on we lost touch, though for many years he used to keep up the Scottish connection by bringing my mother shortbread every Christmas. He was one of the few musical cousins, a fine pianist like his mother.

Em was the youngest child of my grandmother's generation, and my mother the eldest of hers, so they were close in age and had a lot in common. They sometimes exchanged confidences and gossip with me in earshot. Under cover of reading a book or one of the women's magazines found in every house, I learnt a lot in the kitchen in William Street, a street that no longer exists. A second cousin was unmarried and pregnant. You first knew about this because her name was always being mentioned then the subject dropped or changed when you looked as if you were listening. Gladys and Emily supposed their stage whispers and shorthand would mean nothing to me, but of course they demanded my attention and maddened my curiosity. Once, Em said, 'You can forgive an engaged couple, but the lodger!' I grasped the main theme, by some means, and wasn't surprised when the second cousin got married (to the lodger) and soon had a baby. But I had no idea what or why you could forgive an engaged couple. Engagement was more complicated than I'd thought. I was acquiring information, if patchily.

I was amused to read in Constantine Fitzgibbon's biography of Dylan Thomas that pre-war Welsh brides were expected to be virgins. His social history is fiction. Engaged couples were licensed, as Auntie Em said, and plenty of unbetrothed couples were yoked by pregnancies. It wasn't for nothing that wedding photographs were often greeted with ribald comment, 'A big bouquet for her big belly.' And many coupled couples didn't get pregnant. Of course sex was risky, furtive and uninformed but there was a lot of it about in Swansea.

Another second cousin, one of the tall, dark and handsome boys, was Kennie, son of Molly, famous for her fastidious pie-baking. She used to take off the pastry crust half-way through the cooking to add the sugar. I remembered Kennie when I walked down Bryn-y-mor Crescent one day years after I'd left Swansea, home for a holiday. There was a small man plastering a garden wall. He looked hard at me and his thin face and bright-blue eyes seemed familiar. He was very like Kennie and another cousin, Willie the Uplands. I remembered that the father of one of these boys was a plasterer, and looked questioningly at this possible relative as he sighed and put down his trowel. Our eyes met, and when he smiled I did too. 'I'm Barbara,' I said in a friendly way, remembering all those times I'd been called a snob. 'It's Will, isn't it?' He said 'Yes', and in a friendly, democratic family spirit I poured out all the recent family news, about the health of my brother, Grandpa's rheumatics, my flat in London, my mother's return to her work with the barristers. He looked gratified, interested and surprised, nodding and prompting with 'Well, well', until I dried up, hoping for news of Willie and Kennie. When he asked me if I would meet him that evening I said in an embarrassed way that I'd thought he was my Uncle Will, the plasterer. 'I am,' he said with a leer. I hurried away down towards the sea, blushing crimson and cursing family feeling.

There was a fringe of relations in the Hafod, an industrial quarter just beyond the station, where the copper works had been and which outgrew its beautiful Welsh name, which means Summer Home, the summer pasturing for the cattle. The small houses here abutted right on to the street. I recall visiting my great-uncle Mog, and his wife Mary, one of my grandmother's sisters. These were the Joneses, small and dark, like their houses. Mary had a big, friendly daughter named Enid, who called once in a while, and once or twice we went to see them. I thought Mog was a miner, because he was small and bent, but I believe he was in copper smelting. The Hafod, like Greenhill, which I never located, the Sandfields, Tontine Street, and St

Thomas, where Iris came from, and where the streets had the names of Crimean battles, Inkerman and Sebastopol, were the dark regions, dirty, poor, unimaginably common. I never heard anyone use the terms working-class and lower-middle class, but we were extremely class-conscious. 'Common' was the damning word, 'common as dirt'. There was a sense of class. Lower than us were the people from the valleys, who came into Swansea on Saturdays. They were Welshy, we said in the relativity of our racism, and very common. Greenhill and the Sandfields were less idyllic than they sound, and when you did something filthy or low, wiping your nose on your sleeve, or eating messily, or shoving past, you'd hear, 'Where do you come from? The Sandfields?', or 'Real Greenhill manners'. These place-names of mean streets beyond our pale had entered so deep into the family mythology that they were stripped of all pastoral associations. I was surprised when I found what Hafod meant, though not at all surprised when I was told that Grandpa, whose table manners were awful, and one of the reasons I couldn't invite certain friends home, had been dragged up in Greenhill. '*Shôn bach* from the Rhondda' was the lowest of the low. *Shôn bach*, used to describe anything from bad manners to upholstery, was Swansea for low class and kitsch.

My closest cousins were my Uncle Bill's daughter Maureen and Auntie Leah's daughter Betty. As we grew up, there were the younger cousins who turned up, new, amusing babies to be played with, taken for walks, taught to say 'Please' and 'Thank you' – Leah's two younger daughters, Christine and Margaret, born a long gap after Betty, Renee and Arnold's Norma, for years the cute baby whose clever sayings and funny ways were passed round the family, then her sister Jill, who became a teenager *terrible*, with green hair twenty-five years or more before punks. I wrote a star essay about Norma, the first writing in which I felt the pen take off in flights of wit and narrative, good enough to be shown to the teacher in the next class.

Maureen was one of my favourite cousins. I loved going to visit her. It was a great treat to stay the night. We had breakfast in bed, with shredded wheat on a tray. She had long ringlets down to her waist, and was always held up to me as a model little girl, perfectly behaved, helpful in the house and doing well at school. But I liked her all the same. She was younger, and couldn't or didn't boast and boss. I envied her the big house, long, rambling garden and expensive toys, including a rocking-horse, the only one I ever rode on, but my feelings held no rancour. The house was called The Croft. Having a house with a name was definitely upper class. Arnold and Renee had a house with a name too, Milton, after the village where Grandpa had worked as a baker. I think The Croft had been bought by Maureen's great-aunt, Auntie Bessie, a tall, smart, white-haired woman with curly hair and a dignified manner. She was lady-like and fastidious. We kept up the old tradition of having new clothes for Whitsun and doing the rounds of the relations to show them off. Auntie Bessie was generous and gave us three-pence or sixpence, but she was hard to please and would not exclaim with delight, like Leah or Renee or Iris or Marge, at the vision you presented in an organdie pink-and-white dress and a straw hat with cherries, but would turn you round slowly and find a tiny loose thread or an undone fastener. She was a mythological character, anticipating Mrs Ogmore-Pritchard. If ever I see a loose hem or a hair on someone's coat, I have the choice of being or not being Auntie Bessie.

Maureen had a playroom, something else I'd never met anywhere outside a book. She let me rummage in her big box of treasures and once gave me a little silver shoe which I kept on my mantelpiece for years. (She is still a generous giver.) She was a precocious organizing genius. I remember her raffles and her garden parties with bunches of lavender she'd tie and sell. 'She's got her head screwed on the right way,' my mother would say, or 'She'll be a good business woman.' She grew up to be very competent, certainly, and built her own house with her own hands, but did not turn into a business woman or – as I romantically expected – a lady of the manor. But she has taken to car-boot sales.

When Betty was old enough for school, four or five years after I started, I would take her up to Terrace Road, collecting her every morning near her house in St George's Terrace, returning her at midday and evening, grown-up and proud. I would stay and have dinner with them, in the underground kitchen, a large, dark, gloomy room where Leah cooked. The meals were eaten in their living-room, though, which was cheerful and light. It was one of the houses where I couldn't go wrong, because Leah was so easy-going and so fond of me, and those lunch-times were more peaceful than the noisy, teasing meals in Cradock Street. I was an honoured guest. If I didn't want to eat bread and butter or tomatoes or cucumber or bacon, that was all right with Leah and she'd find something else. Best of all, there were usually chips. Sometimes we bought fish and chips from a shop near their house, owned by a thin, dark, talkative Welsh woman who always called us 'Goo' girl' and gave us papers of 'crispies', bits off the batter, for nothing. Leah was a sweet lover and provider of sweets. And there was the glamour of Betty's books and toys, all different from mine. We used to walk up and down one of the steepest hills in Swansea, Constitution Hill. It was a terrible hill, nearly vertical, and exciting as Everest, if tamer. You'd look up at it and never believe it was scalable. A railway was once planned for it, but never came into being. I was sorry when Betty outgrew the need for my escort service and could go to school on her own. I reverted to the Steps and the Green, my old way to school. But we stayed close.

I liked having a cousin as close as a sister, without the disadvantages of sisterliness, as I saw them. Leah and Walter lived with Walter's mother and father, Grannie and Grandpa Incledon, a formidable couple, always sitting one each side of the fire, and dressed, at least by memory, in long, elaborate Victorian costumes. Grandpa Incledon, who outlived his wife by some years and married her spinster sister, had a white moustache and a venerable appearance. I found them forbidding and compared them disadvantageously with my playful, story-telling grandfather, but they were affectionate and gentle with Betty, and she loved them. After an obligatory polite visit to them, on the ground floor, we would descend to the basement. In the garden were loganberries and raspberries, as in no other garden. And there were Betty's dolls. I remember a soft doll with slanting eyes and a Dutch headdress, called Greta. I didn't care for my own dolls, but hers were different, partly because she hadn't broken them, so she had a large collection, partly because they were animated by her affection for them. We used to play a serial game of hospitals with dolls and animals, taking turns to be doctor, nurse and mother. The ailments were usually broken limbs, imagination not being clinically instructed, but even slight injuries would prove too morbid for tender-hearted Betty. On one occasion some grown-up conversation prompted me to diagnose one favourite – it may have been Greta – as suffering from heart disease. The game ended in heart-break, and we were told to play something nicer.

Betty was extraordinarily pretty, clever and artistic. She drew and painted and made things from papier mâché. She was famous, like Maureen, for being good, and I thought this unfair, since she had no sibling to quarrel with or be compared with, to tease or hurt or be teased and hurt by. I envied her for this, though not consistently. She was less free than we were, always going for walks between her father and mother, each holding a hand. It was better to have only one parent to reproach and advise, and to be one of two subject children. When my mother held my hand and Bill's, we could still skip about, free on one side.

For the first three and three-quarter years I was the only child. My parents loved me, played with me and told me stories. I had cats and dogs and two imaginary friends, Atalanta and Red Busby. Their names sprang from nowhere. When my mother discovered that Atalanta was a mythological character, she was impressed.

Imaginary friends are always there and do what you want, but when I was told I was going to have a brother, I looked forward to his arrival. He would be brought by a stork. Lying in the warm bed, close to the cool wall, I nursed my left arm in my right and sang him a lullaby, 'Bye little Douglas, Douglas, Douglas, / You shall have milk when the cows come home'. Or it might be my own particular pillow-song, with the name changed, 'Go to sleep, my Douglas, / Close your pretty eyes'. I was going to have a brother called Douglas, with red hair. When he turned up his name was William Howard Maurice, and he had fair hair. The William was after my grandfather, the Howard after the managing director in Father's firm, and Maurice, pronounced *Morereece* (French), not Morris (English), was after my father. I should have known he might not be Douglas, because my mother had told me I was nearly Pearl, my father's choice, or June, hers. My father had said 'Why not call her July?' so they compromised with Barbara. My mother said she got it off a tombstone in some village graveyard in Pembrokeshire, but I don't know why she needed such a remote source, since there were always at least three other Barbaras in every school class. I was sorry she hadn't chosen Tamsin, the other name she'd seen on a grave and fancied. Rupert and Sebastian are scribbled in my Baby Book, as possible names for my male might-have-been self.

The imaginary friends went away. I was glad I had a brother, not a sister. Even though we fought, first with clumsy punches and pinches, later with duelling expertise, I preferred him to a sister. My friends who had sisters were always quarrelling, first about their dolls, later on about clothes, looks and boys. I was protective and proud of Bill. Someone took me to play in the back garden when Dr Scurlock, our family doctor who resembled Father Christmas and always seemed very old, was circumcising the baby in our middle room. Suddenly there was a loud cry, and I felt frightened for him. No one would explain what circumcision was but I knew I hadn't had it. I'd had vaccination, but Billy was going to have that too. I was proud and astonished when he began to talk. I was in the presence of growing language. New words came from nowhere, every day. One morning we were in bed, and he looked towards the light and cleverly exclaimed, 'Window'. Two syllables, and no doubt about word fitting thing. He was a working human being. He was fond of me too. When I was five I was wrongly diagnosed as having diphtheria, and taken off to the Fever Hospital in the middle of the night, after they got the erroneous results of my throat swab. Billy asked for me next morning, looking everywhere for his sister, Diddy, and too young to understand about illness or hospitals, went on seeking until he thought of trying the real name the grown-ups used, and struggled to articulate Barbara. My mother often repeated this instructive tale of precocious sibling affection.

Meanwhile I was annoying the doctors, having been put to bed in a long ward, full of the diphtheria children, and later moved into a small isolation ward. When my mother rang up with anxious inquiry, the doctor was not sympathetic: 'Barbara Nathan, confound her. She's given the whole ward chickenpox.' This was much quoted, and I used to roll that new swear-word, 'Confound', over my tongue, in imitation of my mother's imitation of the cross, posh English voice. I remember that ward, because I was near the tall Christmas tree. I liked the little ward best, though I could see the children and the fairy lights of the tree only dimly, through a dividing glass wall. There were big dolls under the tree, coloured parcels and brilliant ornaments among its lights. I felt far away. I'd enjoyed the ambulance and I liked the food, especially the taste of the mince, different from ours at home where minced meat was made from the remains of the joint, while this was fresh. There were no toys in the little room, but someone brought me a cracker. I pulled it on my own and burnt my finger. 'So you won't be better in time for Christmas,' said the brisk nurse as she bandaged my hand. When my mother and Arnold came to visit me, they had to stay outside, smiling and talking through the window. We couldn't hear each other very well, but when they started to hold up parcels I gesticulated furiously, shook my head and waved them away. I knew that toys, once in, could never be let out of the germy Fever Hospital. They blew kisses and took everything away, much to my relief. My mother told me later: 'There were tears in Arnold's eyes.' She was a great conveyor of good feeling.

I was let out on Christmas Eve after all. I'd been rushed in after a hasty diagnosis because my cousin Betty had just been born in my grandmother's house. Auntie Leah returned to the nest to give birth. They were afraid the baby would get whatever I had. Now I was better, and the new baby had gone home. My mother helped me on with my beige leggings, lovely and soft, and we got on the bus from Sketty to Cradock Street. We were greeted by the best of smells, giblet soup, always made with goose giblets, and always eaten for dinner (lunch) on Christmas Eve. Probably one of the reasons neither Bill nor I have ended up vegetarians, despite occasional scruples. The presents next day were wonderful, including as a centre-piece the dollshouse, my first and only one, but best of all was the warm kitchen fire and the smell of that soup. A day or so later, when the Christmas thrills were wearing off, my mother broke the news that my two best toys had been casualties of the misdiagnosis. King of the Gollies and my teddy bear, Fairchild, had been burnt in the interest of hygiene. They are the soft toys I remember, with a Dalmatian called Dismal Desmond and a cat called Felix, after the song by Harold Lloyd, 'Felix Went On Walking'.

As we grew older, toys were divided according to gender, as they still are today. But I let Billy play with the dollshouse and he was amused when I put a little bit of shit-coloured Mansion polish in the toy lavatory. We also had our special games of make-believe. One of these I played before my brother was born. It was the game of weddings, in which I dressed up in old net curtains and paraded up and down with everyone singing 'Here Comes the Bride, / Big, Fat and Wide'. I'm sure that was somebody else's idea, but 'Meetings' was my invention. I'd drag, or entice, Billy, then a mere crawling infant, to come and sit under the table, which was covered in a brown, chenille-fringed cloth that came down to the ground and made a lovely private room. I suppose I must have heard my uncles talk about going to trade-union meetings. It was before any of them joined a political party, or my mother went on to the Executive Committee of the local British Legion branch, out of loyalty to my father. I know meetings seemed thrilling and grown-up. I've gone on enjoying meetings, a great advantage in academic life. Billy and I would sit under the table and talk, I don't know what about. My mother and grandmother regarded the call to meetings as a tyranny and threatened: 'Don't worry. When he's a bit older he'll have his own back.' I found that mystifying.

We slept in the same room as our parents, except when we lived for a brief period in London, where I suppose we had a room or rooms to ourselves. I don't remember. In the Cradock Street house we had stories, competitions and concerts every night after we went to bed. There was a serial story called 'Daredevil Dodo', about the adventures of an elf or gnome. He could fly and had interplanetary trips. He was Superman long before Superman. We had a game modelled on the radio programme *In Town Tonight*. It was called 'In Bed Tonight' and would contain, like the real programme, an overture of apt noises, then interviews with famous people. Sometimes they were characters from books, or Father Christmas, or invented people. We would hum tunes and try to guess the title, and played endless games of 'Truth'. We couldn't play the usual form of 'Truth or Dare' because we were strictly forbidden to get out of bed. One of us would say 'Let's talk about Christmas', so we would imagine it all from the moment of hanging up the stockings. And we'd discuss our presents. Compared with my children and grand-children we didn't have all that number of toys, but we never did badly, even when my mother was very broke. Bill's best present was his tricycle, gleaming at the bottom of the bed when he awoke, received with delight and some surprise – 'And I was good.' The period before Christmas was one of moral ordeal and blackmail. Uncle Ron once rigged up wires and a microphone through which he spoke in the voice of old Father Christmas, from the front room, to warn us about the relationship between good behaviour and rewards, never mentioned except in December.

When my grandchildren asked me to tell them the naughtiest

thing I ever did I decided it was frightening my little brother. I'd been frightened, so I passed it on. One of my favourite poems was Hilaire Belloc's *Cautionary Tale* about Augustus. I was always accused of being greedy, and he was my opposite, gobbling up his soup, then going off it, growing thinner and thinner to end 'like a little bit of thread' and of course thread rhymed with dead. I decided to make his ghost walk in the attic, right over our heads. There was a crack in the ceiling and I told Bill that if we looked hard enough at this crack we would see a little tremor. That was Augustus walking round the attic. I refined my narrative so that all I'd need would be to roll my eyes upwards and Bill would scream in terror. He tells me that he never believed in Augustus or the crack-moving ghost but used to pretend to be terrified. So perhaps I was the victim after all.

Betty was also one of my victims. She was soft-hearted and loved dolls. After 1929 my father, away at sea, was always sending us presents. One was an enormous pink plush doll, looking like a fat child in a baby-grow, all face and cloth body. Betty took one look and burst into tears of pure love and longing. I much preferred the African ship Bill had been sent, a wonderful long carved boat, made out of some creamy, crumbly wood, with detachable square-headed warrior boatmen. But Betty envied my doll. She wept easily. I didn't look down on her for this, far from it. I was always crying too, but my eyes went red and I looked ugly. Betty's tears would well up into her huge, round, pale-blue eyes – more astounding than any film star's then or now – and she would melt. She's the only person I've ever met who could cry and still look stunning. I was jealous of her for that advantage, and because she had curls all over her head, soft natural curls, much prettier and more natural than Shirley Temple's. And though Bill and I sometimes ganged up and teased her, she and Bill were close in age and would gang up against me. They were often posed for photographs, cutely arm in arm or holding a beach-tyre. So I rather liked making her tears flow.

One Christmas the grown-ups had retired to the kitchen to go on eating and talking and I went round the empty glasses in the front room and poured the dregs – almost non-existent – into my glass. I smuggled it into our bedroom, where Betty was staying the night, and began to show off gloriously, tottering and swaying round the room, jumping up on the beds and hiccuping loudly, in what I hoped was a realistic representation of drunkenness. I had only once seen a real drunk, an old man in the street, 'paralatic (not paralytic) drunk' as they said, but I'd seen drunks in the pictures. It worked. Betty didn't weep but yelled in terror, 'Auntie Glad, Auntie Glad. Come quick, Barbara's drunk.' Her screams brought the grown-ups to the scene and I was severely told off. On another occasion, when we were all on holiday in a chalet-bungalow in Caswell, I horridly pointed to a little pool of water some child's shrimp-filled bucket had spilled on the threshold, exclaiming meaningfully, 'Oh Betty, what have you done?', implying that she had accidentally peed on the porch. She took the implication at once, the blue eyes filled with tears, and I was ashamed. She was a real sensitive plant. But she toughened as she grew, and became daring and naughty in school. Bill and I once put in a day teaching her to smoke, but fortunately she never took to inhaling. We grew up to become the best of friends.

I went to elocution, Bill learnt the piano and the violin, but I can't say how far these variations were gender-determined. They were probably differences of interest. I liked reciting and acting, Bill was musical. My mother made up her mind that her children would have all the advantages she had lacked. I insisted that I was never going to get married, and she was pleased though she said she hoped I'd marry someone nice one day. In later life she often regretted that she hadn't known enough for us to apply to Oxford or Cambridge and, whenever she heard of some neighbour's child going to Oxbridge, there was a retrospective jealous self-reproach. Bill wanted to be an architect, but didn't like the maths involved, though Mother said he'd had to give up the idea because she couldn't afford to pay for him to be articled.

Both of us became teachers, like many Welsh children. We didn't have the know-how or the influence or the money or the role-models for creative high flights, but the strong work ethic, born of puritanism and poverty and class deprivation, made dropping out an unheard-of solution. Not for us a job on the local paper or running away to sea, and even those starts in life didn't guarantee a glamorous career in the end, like those outlined in the potted biographies on the back of old Penguin books. Class and nonconformist religion pushed us into conformity.

Bill was my closest ally, companion and enemy. Blood really is thicker than water. He was always Billy, as a child, Bill or sometimes William after he grew up, when diminutives were dropped. Like me he became a teacher and a writer, also a great fisherman and occasional journalist. He used to contribute a fishing column to the *Evening Post*, under the pseudonym Cambricus, and has written three excellent books about fishing. Both of us got into authorship by back ways. In many respects we were alike, fair, clever, bookish, nature-loving. If I suffered repressions and deprivations as a girl, he suffered the repressions and expectations of a boy in that lower-middle-class Welsh macho community, where men were proud of being 'tough guys', as Ron boasted. We fought like young cats or dogs learning to try our strengths and mark our territories, not easy in a house overflowing with family, where there was no privacy for boys or girls. And since the adults teased the children, so it was the accepted thing for boys to tease girls.

When I started to keep a diary of loves, ambitions, fantasies and facts, Bill would read it, as I read Uncle Ron's, and quote bits till I died of shame. During adolescence we went our separate ways, and when we were together his stronger sense of humour shrivelled my intensities. He once told me he couldn't understand the fuss I made about religion. He dealt with chapel, and ceasing to believe, with admirable quiet. Looking back, I think he probably matured more quickly than I did. But when I was fourteen or so and he was eleven, the gap was big. He would fool around, making marvellous monkey faces which I admired and disliked, joking and teasing until I would tell him, with superiority and dignity, not to be a fool.

I'd rather have a brother who was a thief or a murderer than a fool. When I had a letter from my mother telling me he had TB, in his last year at university, where he did well, making no fuss about his health, I felt guilty at my remoteness. I was in London working through problems of the early days of marriage, a thesis and part-time teaching. Before his illness he had come to spend a holiday with Ernest and me, in Capel Curig. We climbed our favourite hills and he fished, catching that most delectable of all fish, to my palate, brown trout. We stayed in a small, friendly hotel in Dolwyddelan, called Elen's Castle, where Ernest and I had spent part of our honeymoon, and in Capel Curig, with Mrs Hughes, who spoke broken English, always referring to her husband as 'she'. Ernest accidentally sat on Bill's fishing-rod, and his 'Christ' has stayed in Bill's memory. They always got on very well, then and later on when Bill stayed with us in London and came on holiday to Paris. We played Elizabethan songs (Dowland and Purcell sung by Alfred Deller) and Benjamin Britten, ate and drank, talked and went to the theatre. Once he sent us a huge pike, which we cooked with claret and oranges from a recipe in Izaak Walton, to whose pious and piscatorial pages Bill directed my attention. But as children and adolescents we came to occupy separate spaces. He had cultural clashes with Grandpa and Ron, both of whom thought it funny to turn off his classical music programmes, no doubt in a spirit of aggression. Once or twice he had long quarrels with them, refusing to speak for months. I envied his powers of silence. I often wanted to quarrel long and bitterly but I would threaten and forget. My hates and furies, like my early loves, were shallow.

Before those adolescent tempests and trials, Billy was the hero of boys' adventures. His Gower territory was wilder and wider than mine. Fishing took him where I never went, to remote trout streams and the rocks at the far end of that ancient tidal island, Burry Holms, where the little ruined chapel of St Keneth – my favourite saint, fed by the Titty Bell – stands. I would never have stood on the rocks of Tears Point or climbed down the slope of Kitchen Corner in Rhossilli, if it hadn't been for Bill. And he roamed further afield, to Llangorse Lake, when it was lonely, and to the salmon rivers of Carmarthenshire, like the lovely Cothi.

We both had a lot of freedom in those carefree days, even during the war. No doubt having an absent father helped. Billy would bring home carp and other coarse fish from Brynmill Park, where young fishermen learnt their craft on the big, sprawling ponds. Sometimes he would soak the fish overnight to get the mud out, and they were fairly edible. Once he arrived home calling through the long passage: 'Don't worry, Mum, but I've got a hook in my ear.' A friend's casting had gone a bit wild. Bill and my mother told the story slightly differently. She took him off on the bus to the doctor's surgery in Walter Road. According to Mother, the old doctor seemed to have been drinking. In Bill's version he was just inefficient. He chopped the end of the hook off, then drew it out, but when my mother demanded 'Where's the barb?' he didn't know what she was talking about. He had to be persuaded to extract the barb, being neither a fisherman nor a fisherman's relation. We knew about barbs, and about bait. Bill was always making bread paste for bait, not to mention keeping maggots in various kitchen containers, once found breeding smellily in the table drawer. 'I'll end up in Cefn Coed,' my tolerant mother would occasionally declare, rolling her eyes in the direction of 'the asylum' on the hill. She would direct the threat at both of us, but Bill's wrongdoings were more spectacular than mine.

He and one of his friends used to make gunpowder for harmless detonation in quiet spots, not for bombs. When a policeman called, he was Inspector Cornick, known to the family as a neighbour of the Sketty Abrahams. He got Bill to admit that he'd made gunpowder, then asked him how. He was answered by a boy who couldn't believe a grown man could be so ignorant: 'Don't you know how to make gunpowder?' The explosion had been achieved in a cave in Clyne Valley, a local beauty spot, and the police suspected sabotage or spies. My mother was relieved that Bill wasn't arrested for contempt of police. Earlier, in Cradock Street, Bill was given an air-gun by one of the uncles, and did his target practice from the attic window, within gunshot of Weaver's high warehouse tower, which came down in the blitz. Word got round that the police were making inquiries about broken windows, so my resourceful mother took the air-gun up to Gilbert and Iris in Carlton Terrace. When the constable called, she said truthfully, 'No, there's no gun in this house. Go and search.' I was on the fringe of these masculine excitements, but once I was let in on the mysteries. Bill and his friend John Waldron, who lived near us in the Uplands, liked playing with a short-wave radio, and I was once or twice allowed to send and receive signals, or at least be present at the transmissions. Once more the boys were warned by the vigilant police that such games were forbidden in wartime. They might be interfering with our radio communications. I boasted at school about being a radio pirate. No wonder my mild lying and stealing were never discovered. Boys had all the fun, danger, explosives, guns, radios, fishing-rods and visits from the police.

1. William John Abraham

2. Leah

3. William John and Florence Mary

4. Maurice and Barbara

5. Bill, Gladys and Barbara

6. (clockwise from top) Walter, Gladys, Bill, Betty, Leah (centre) Barbara

7. Betty, Barbara, Bill

8. Barbara, Girl Guide

9. Barbara at 16

10. Gladys and Arnold (Carlo)

Chapter 5
Daddy, Daddy, Can I Cross the Water?

What you forget seems stranger than what you remember. Leaving London and going to live with my grandparents is a blank. Perhaps it's blurred into the earlier years when we lived in Swansea, when my parents were trying to make a go of their general store, or their chip shop. All those terrible weeks when the firm crashed, Father lost the job, they sold the house and moved, are gone. We left just before I started school. The other day, as I was thinking about how I just missed being a little London kid in a London school, the dimmest of not-quite-jogged memories returned. I must have gone with my mother to see the headmaster of the school I would have gone to if there hadn't been the slump, Father's decision to go back to sea, and Mother's return to Swansea. Was or wasn't there a visit to a man in a room, staring children in a playground, and a little boy who said something to me in a Cockney accent? But we packed up and left, for a journey and a goodbye that have slipped through the sieve of memory.

Instead of going to school in Brockley, I went to Terrace Road School in Swansea. Just before you got there you passed the sweet shops, one on each corner, Mrs Davies for the boys, opposite the Boys School, and Mrs Lily for the girls, opposite the Infants and Girls School. You could see everything they sold spread out in a brilliant jumbled largesse. Prices started at a ha'penny, and there were some sizeable sweets, Trebor Treats for instance, which were two for a ha'penny. For a ha'penny, the standard price for our purchases, you could get a bag of soft, crunchy, brown, sweet coco-butternuts, not quite cocoa-y, not quite buttery, not quite nutty, but an exotic approach to all three, and four gob-stoppers, which might be the superior kind known as everlasting sweets. These pleased sight as well as taste because you took them out every minute or two to witness the regular changes of colour. My favourites were Sherbet Suckers, tubes of bright yellow paper filled with sherbet which you sucked through a liquorice tube. When my children bought them in their day, they had degenerated, and you ate the sherbet by dipping in a small sweet on a stick. There were lucky packets, which contained a sweet and a present. The little things you got in lucky packets or crackers were treasures, felt and gazed at and kept. I find it hard to throw away the plastic boats and whistles my grandchildren play with and discard after crackers are pulled. Having few things turned those few into fetishes and sacred objects. Once I got a love-charm, a silver heart.

We used to hang around those shop windows, before school if we were early, or on the way home. They were cram-full of hundreds of desirable goodies. If you had no money, you could just gaze. In the summer there would be an ice-cream cart outside the school. There was a bottle of optional raspberry vinegar to be poured over your cornet, another childhood lost flavour, like sherbet. When I read Eastern tales, and T.S. Eliot's 'The Journey of the Magi', I had no problem transferring our sherbet to those exotic settings. Once there was an old clothes man, offering goldfish in exchange for old clothes, but when my mother toiled all the way up from Cradock Street, a rough Welsh mile or two, with a bagful of cast-offs, he'd gone and I felt guilty. That became a bad time-spot.

Mrs Lily's shop was opposite the playground shared by the mixed infants and girls. The big girls and boys had different class-rooms, on either side of a common hall, but the boys had their own playground. The school colours, red and green, were mostly worn by the boys on caps and scarves. Terrace Road School was built on a steep hill, the two playgrounds steep asphalt slopes. We were always falling down and going home with cuts and bruises. A high flight of sharp-edged steps led you into the playground. It was a dangerous place used to measure your size and skill by the increasing number you could jump down. The steps were the site of the only violence I associate with school. A boy teased or hit my friend Valerie and I felt heroic and liberated as I gave him a quick punch, then ran off. The playground was the theatre of friendships, enmity, strength, fun and fantasy. We played singing games, girls only,

> Here we come loopy-loopy,
> Here we come loopy-li,
> Here we come loopy-loopy,
> All on a Saturday ni'.

One of the many local synonyms for mad or crazy was 'loopy', so the song may have been more abandoned than it knew. 'I Sent a Letter to My Love' was a thrill, whether you were the runner round the circle, choosing your love, or waiting and wondering if you were the chosen one. It wasn't all joy. For some games the big, bossy girls chose sides. The playground was full of cries, 'Whose game is it?' 'Can I be in your game?' Few fears are stronger than the fear of being the last chosen. When you were five even the top infants of eight seemed giants, and the oldest girls might be eleven. The catchment area of the school was mixed enough to include the children of professional men, in-betweens like us, and children we called rough, from poor and dirty homes. The rough girls were brilliant at skipping, which I loathed, especially when it was communal, with a long rope turned very fast by big girls. You had to jump in and try your luck as they chanted a skipping ditty, like 'Salt, mustard, vinegar, pepper'. Pepper was the signal for the rope to twirl like lightning, catching you in the legs, impossible to keep up with. My mother was a very good skipper, as she demonstrated, but I was not, and after several failures I stopped trying. As you grew older you could start games of your own, with the ritual 'Want to be in my game?' We had street games, too, in Cradock Street, round the left-hand corner, in Carlton Terrace, which led to school, and occasionally in Willows Place, a cul-de-sac round the other corner. Once I was asked to tea in Willows Place by a girl called Edith Jago. Her house was only about two minutes away from ours but the street seemed like a new territory partly because it was a dead end so you never had to go there, and partly because its houses and inhabitants were or seemed a bit poorer, rougher and commoner than us. It was the first time I'd been out to tea on my own, and when I was offered tea to drink, I felt very witty when I refused, saying I was a teetotaller. We played outside after tea, at sunset. The sky was rosy and I remember Edith's incantation, 'The sky is red, Mary's dead, fine day tomorrow.' The best street game was 'Daddy, Daddy, Can I Cross the Water?', a bit like Grandmother's Footsteps, but less subtle. Daddy stood in the middle of the road, usually Carlton Terrace, and we called out to be asked to cross the water, to be given permission or denied, challenged and chased. When you were caught, you were the next Daddy. When it started to get dark, and the street lights went on, Daddy became a threatening figure, larger than life. In the day we drew spirals or rectangles for hopscotch. Another of our street games I've forgotten all about, except its name, which was 'The Big Ship Sailed on the Ally-allay-Oh', with a corrupted trace of some real exotic ocean. Those games were played in the road, but I can't remember ever having to get out of the way of a car or a motor bike, though there were some about. I remember being taken round the block, through Cradock Street, Mansel Street, Verandah Street, then down Carlton Terrace home, clinging to Ron on the pillion of his first motor bike. My grand-father had a car when he was still fairly prosperous, but as his small yeast trade declined, he couldn't afford one. The uncles, Arnold, Gilbert and Elvert, would come and take us for a picnic or a run down the bays on summer evenings or at weekends. At the end of the street were the tramlines, where the rattling trams swayed past, lit up at night, and from the front room in our house you could see their reflections beamed on our ceilings as they turned into Mansel Street, a points boy adjusting the points. All over the house you could hear their clanking and clattering. One of the lost sounds, like the most nostalgic of all, still sometimes heard in reality, the night-boom of the fog-horn in the docks or the Mumbles.

All I remember of my first day at school is the long, white pointed Quaker collar on Glenys Dodson's cotton frock. Her big sister Muriel had an identical frock and they were the first sisters I knew to dress alike, like Nancy and Priscilla in *Silas Marner*. It was a fairly common thing up to the thirties. My mother tells me I came home saying I'd made two friends, Glenys and Valerie Williams. Valerie was very thin, and looked even thinner because she had short, neat, straight ginger hair, with a straight, neat fringe. She had a merry, freckled face, and like me loved books, day-dreams and acting out fantasies. Glenys was solider, with intelligent eyes and a sense of humour. Valerie's father was a commercial traveller, Glenys's a coal-merchant. I didn't find that out on the first day, I expect, though as small children we were all quick to ask about our father's professions. 'My father's a policeman', 'So's mine' was a common dialogue of fictions, perhaps as a social boast, certainly as a protection. I don't know if children still tell that story. Of course nobody ever asked what your mother did. They knew, though a few mothers, including mine eventually, went out to work because they had to. Gilbert's wife Iris worked in a dress shop, and was much criticized by the family for it.

After the first day or so I was taken to school by one of the Infants School teachers, who lived near us. Her name was Mrs Roderick. Though she was an ideal reception-class, motherly type, mild and smiling, I had been told she was a widow, the first I ever heard of, and I was daunted at the thought of talking to someone with a dead husband. So I was silent as we walked the uphill road to school. But soon I was allowed to walk with neighbouring children, to my great relief. We sat in school two by two at ink-stained desks, with seat and lid and foot-rest all in one piece. I remember the grain – was it oak or pine? – of the greyish wood. One of my few memories from the early days is being told 'Hands on heads!' and 'Heads on desks!', as the commands ran. In Sketty School, where my cousins Maureen and Norma went, the infants used to have a rest period in the afternoon, lying in the hall on straw mats, and that was thought highly progressive. For us the only respite was playtime, which was very active, and the only rest those brief times when we obediently laid our heads on our folded arms on the desk-lid.

I loved school, but there were black days. Once I was kept in, so that the Infants School head, Miss Jones, should attempt to show me how to knit. I'd made a mess of my first effort. She looked at the knitting in mild amazement, sorrow rather than anger. The keeping-in was less a punishment, I'm sure, than a kind of attempt at remedial work, but for me it was deep shame. I can see and feel that scrap of once-white, stringy-thread knitting, filthy-dirty, knotted, and holed with dropped stitches. I went home crying, because it was the first time I'd been punished, and I couldn't keep it secret because Miss Jones had made me late for dinner. I remember the weird language of school commands. We were told, in mysterious metaphor, to 'Pay attention' and 'Make haste'. I was puzzled by a lack of relation between the words and what they signified. How could you 'make' haste and 'pay' attention? Instructions were barked out by a teacher whose name may have been Miss Price, the first of the strict ones. I remember a boy called Billy Solomon, who drew amazing ships and horses. My own brother was good at drawing, but he was nearly four years younger, and it was Billy Solomon who first introduced me to the notion of great natural talent and art.

Infants and Juniors get a bit confused. I liked drawing, but we used what were called 'pastels', which disintegrated and messed up your clothes. The pastel-drawn work of art got easily smudged and spoilt. Ink was an enemy, and I always had inky hands. We learnt how to mix colours in paintboxes, and it was a revelation when blue and yellow made green, a terrible disappointment when five brilliant colours only made mud colour. One of the unimagined things I tried to imagine was a new colour. Why should there be only seven colours? But I never quite got there. The names of colours were lovely, especially in the big paintbox my mother bought me. Burnt sienna, cobalt blue, Prussian blue, indigo. Colour spread out over everything, one of the big joys and mysteries. Why did the bright electric light bulb's yellow turn into red globes and bars on the retina when you shut your eyes? Why were the numbers and the days of the week coloured? One was white, two and three blue, four brown, five red, six and seven bright yellow, eight blue, nine green, ten red. You could spend time translating all the things you couldn't see into colours you could see. But I came down to earth when I tried to draw and paint. I could only do trees and girls, girls in long dresses with their hands behind their backs because I couldn't do feet and hands. I preferred playing with colours. My coloured pencils were people. I made stories for them. A long blue pencil was the prince, and a rich yellow a princess. Happily ignorant of phallic symbols, having seen only a little boy's willie once or twice, I created girls and boys, men and women, beggars and lords and ladies.

I detested 'hand work', the elaborate making of useless little things. It involved putting numbers on a piece of cardboard, then cutting out and reconstructing it into little crooked, useless boxes. Lacking dexterity, I hated that almost as much as knitting. I hated science, later on in High School, because our first lesson, supposedly physics, consisted of weighing with fiddly weights that slipped through my fingers. And I had read H.G. Wells and Jules Verne, and looked forward to experiments.

I remember Miss Frood, dread headteacher of the Big Girls at Terrace Road. She lived in a glass room on the right of the platform in the hall, with the head of the Big Boys on the other side. I was once summoned to her presence, and left my classroom in terror, ascending to her room to be astonished when she smiled at me, with her creased cross face, and explained: 'I've sent for you to tell you your writing has improved. Good girl.' I loved reading and writing as intellectual exercises, but loathed the formation of letters, first print and then the nightmare of joined-up writing. The sentences in my exercise book were as filthy as my knitting, and produced with almost as much torment. I remember Miss Clements, young and pretty, and Miss Griffiths, a little older, who taught Welsh, wore her hair in a bun and was sometimes strict. She once sent me out for talking in the Welsh lesson, when I was about eight, as we were just starting to learn the language. I thought she was condemning me to permanent exile, and for several days did not go to Welsh but loitered out of sight, lost and guilty and vague, in a corner of the playground. I was eventually discovered by my class teacher, Miss Clements, who was very cross with me, for being rude and for staying away from Welsh, so I wasn't allowed to be a fairy in the Christmas play. But I was a boy in one Welsh play, and the King in our Jubilee celebrations. Auntie Renee made me a crimson velvet cloak, while my mother sent away for a gold crown. I remember one of the common people approaching with a basket of fruit, and saying: 'Have an apple, your Majesty.' Like Perdita in *The Winter's Tale*, I discovered the transformational power of costume. I felt powerful, dignified, superior, and male.

I liked learning Welsh and I still have some of that early vocabulary, though we learnt book Welsh, useless for conversation. I was delighted when I went home and Grandpa, who prided himself on his pub-and-street Welsh, started to greet me with '*Shwmâe*' and demanded, '*Cae y drws*'. He made the demotic greeting, '*Shwmâe*' go a long way. We weren't a Welsh-speaking family. I learnt to say 'Please' and 'Thank you', 'today' and 'yesterday', 'It's a fine day', 'It's a rainy day', 'I'm closing my eyes', 'I'm going to sleep', and 'I love you', all useful phrases, as well as words for parts of the house, days of the week and seasons of the year. For St David's Day we learnt to mouth the National Anthem and pretend we were singing all the words. I started to feel Welsh, and liked the Land of my Fathers, the legend of the good hound Gelert, and the story of the Prince of Wales, though that confusingly cut across nationalist sentiment. We sang 'Among our ancient mountains and in our lovely dales, / O let the prayer re-echo, God bless the Prince of Wales!' but it was years before I discovered that it wasn't a prairie echoing – I had thought it sounded oddly like the Wild West, but put it down to poetic licence. It was many more years, on a coach-trip in the

Rockies, before I realized that the Welsh mountains were called ancient for sound geological reasons.

Sometimes we had visiting students, and when I was about ten one of them asked some questions, wrote in an exercise book and said, 'You're intelligent, aren't you?' I didn't know, and it was the first time I'd heard the word. When I first went to school Grandpa used to ask 'Are you a good scholar?' and tell me how he'd had to stand in the corner wearing the dunce's cap – 'Mind you, I was always mitching.' I didn't know if I was a good scholar or not. My grandmother called teachers 'governesses', as they had been called in the National School when she was a girl. Like my mother, she had been a bright girl who had to leave school early.

One of the teachers, called Miss Couch, not Welsh, gave us stars for achievement, and asked general knowledge questions. I found I could answer the questions and felt competitive about winning stars. I began to feel clever, which made a change, since I'd been told off so much for bad writing, talking, being fussy, being rude, singing out of tune, and terrible sewing and knitting. We did mental arithmetic, which I quite liked, though I tended to be answering the first question when they got to the fourth, but long division and German method multiplication were nightmares and I sometimes thought I'd never pass the Scholarship.

We had a book called *Chips from a Book-Shelf*, but my copy had a brown-paper cover on which I'd started to write the title of 'Hiawatha'. The 'watha' showed through my correction so I always thought of it as *Chips from a Bookwatha*. I loved it when we were read 'Hiawatha', and asked my mother if she had a copy. She produced her Longfellow but I rejected it. 'That's poetry. Hiawatha's a story, and doesn't rhyme.' I'd been moved by the magical incantation,

> From the forests and the prairies,
> From the great lakes of the Northland,
> From the land of the Ojibways,
> From the land of the Dacotahs

and the unheard-of names, old Nokomis, Minnehaha, and Chibiabos the sweet singer, but I didn't know it was poetry. Poetry was 'Lord Ullin's Daughter', which I read dramatically, the tears coming to my eyes as I got to, 'I'll forgive your Heeland (Highland) chief, / My daughter, oh my daughter!' Poetry was my examination piece for elocution, 'The Lute Player' by Sir William Watson, 'She was a lady great and splendid, / I was a minstrel in her halls'. Poetry was rhyme.

I loathed covering books, but Grandpa did it beautifully, and showed me how to cut slits for the spine and corners. The books he covered were nice and neat, and I still fold parcels in the same way. I can't remember reading in school, but I remember the first story I read, about a kitten. I remember the pleasure of knowing I'd read a whole story on my own, and therefore hadn't just read a story but demonstrated to myself that I could read. I was a reader. I was in the back parlour, or middle room, alone, and the book was on a table by the window overlooking the garden, or rather the long, narrow, concrete path that became our cricket-pitch. I read the story again, savouring prowess. I know the story was illustrated by a picture, and I think it was coloured, and I believe the kitten had a red, spotted bow. A little later I read another story to my mother, about a goblin called Hoppikins. Hoppikins was an anti-model. His story began: 'You love your mother, but Hoppikins didn't. You go to school, but Hoppikins didn't. You do your lessons, but Hoppikins didn't.' That's all that comes back. He was a liberating character.

As we moved up the school, friendships grew too. Glenys Dodson and I used to have philosophical discussions, at a very early age. We were fascinated by the problem of immortality. It was impossible to believe in going out like a candle, but equally impossible to believe in eternal life. When you tried very hard to imagine, in either direction, you came to a vertiginous threshold thinking couldn't cross. As Stephen Dedalus says, it made your brain feel very big. Like Stephen we played the game of placing self in the street, then expanding outward to county, country, continent, globe, then universe. We too recited verses about existence. My version was

> Nathan is my name,
> Swansea is my station,
> Happy is the man
> Who makes the alteration.

I think Valerie Williams taught me that jingle, and wrote it in my autograph album. She and I used to play a serial game of being orphans ill-treated by a wicked guardian. It was mildly masochistic, but of course not as strong as my night fantasies. I never asked my friends if they had them, but when we played, I got the impression that for them as for me the dangerous games were daytime tamings of night-time indulgence. Looking back at the intensity with which I imagined victimization, and the way it developed into sexual fantasy, I wonder about its origin. I had a sheltered childhood, so from what in nature or nurture did these imaginings spring? I sometimes wonder if I was abused, before I could have known what it meant, and then forgotten about it. There is nobody in the remembered times and places who could have been guilty. But most of the shared play was innocent. And the greatest fear was one that flourished in broad daylight.

The Scholarship exam. Spoken of with bated breath as 'The Scholarship', it cast a big black shadow. If you failed you went to the National School, soon leaving for some dirty or dead-end job. If you were a girl you were doomed to work in Woolworths. Whenever I behaved badly in school, or got nasty comments under the heading 'Conduct', I was threatened with Woolworths, sometimes by my mother, sometimes by other, always female, relations. So the Scholarship was a terror twinned with the terror of Woolworths. The thought of an examination wasn't as bad for me as for other pupils who'd never taken an examination of any kind. I had the experience of the annual scripture exams and my elocution exams. When I did Grade One in elocution I remember telling friends at school, 'I've passed an examination', rolling the syllables out one by one. Still my heart thudded at the thought of the arithmetic exam. I'd be all right in English, and if I was lucky, and didn't get too many questions about sports and explorers, I'd pass in general knowledge. I had only learnt to do long division and German method multiplication after months of agony and help from patient Uncle Gilbert, who was good at figures but knew a different method of dividing and multiplying. This kind of computation still held traps for anybody as careless and as nervous about numbers as I was. In the end it was all right. I had only been able to remember Scott and Shackleton in the dreaded question about polar exploration – my cousin John had also known Amundsen, which I did not. The rest was easy, though first seeing the shiny clean question papers and being told when to start and stop was awful. I was one of the lucky ones.

School was the scene of crime and punishment. In the Infants and the Juniors I was aware of a tall, dark, handsome, spectacled, clever boy called Ellis Evans. I don't think I ever spoke to him, admiring from afar, but once when a teasing uncle or arch aunt asked me who my best boy was, his name slipped out, to be raised shamefully from time to time as a family joke. One day I committed one of the two standard sins, talking or being cheeky. As a punishment I was sent to sit on the Boys' side of the class. The Big School separated the once-mixed Infants but the first class was transitional, containing both sexes, though seating them on different sides of the room, divided by an aisle. Sulky, shamed and scarlet, I was shown an empty seat. I was sharing Ellis Evans's desk. I sat down and stared straight ahead. The morning dragged by and when I got home at dinner-time I told my mother I felt sick and thought I had a bilious attack coming on. What we would now call a bug or suspect to be food poisoning always came under the heading of bilious attack, or feeling a bit bilious. I spent the afternoon in bed, and though I felt guilt at telling a lie and pretending to be ill, that was nothing to the relief I felt at not having to pass an afternoon next to Ellis Evans on the Boys' side. Next morning I was back, feeling apprehensive as I proffered my excuse note, but it was accepted, and I was back with the girls.

I was never hit at school, but some teachers sometimes threatened to strike a pupil on the hand with a pointer, and I remember a naughty boy getting it. I think it was used by one of the strictest teachers, Miss Morgan, who had iron-grey hair screwed into a tight bun, and a cross, heavily lined face. She was unpopular because she was strict, and the rumour went round that she scratched behind her ears and made sores. I was frightened of her, though she was a good, old-fashioned teacher, another one whose bark was probably a lot worse that her bite. Once, she pounced on me for answering a general knowledge question before she'd finished asking it: 'What is the oldest building…?' I knew she must mean Swansea, so I shouted 'Swansea Castle'. It was barely visible then, just a stone or two showing beside or behind the old *Evening Post* building, to emerge in reconstructed grace and strength long after the blitz. My precipitancy incurred Miss Morgan's wrath, but she just frowned and growled. You had to be very careful. You must not be too quick or too slow, too clever by half or too much of a dunce – too dull, we'd say. You mustn't be too talkative or too silent. Between extremities we picked our way.

One teacher I liked was Mrs Davy. We gave her the nickname of Humphry Davy as soon as we were taught about mining and the Davy lamp. Her husband had been a customer of my grandfather's and I was afraid he'd tell her the nickname and get into trouble. He did, but told me she had been amused. Once I was ashamed because I pushed open the door of one of the children's lavatories to discover Mrs Davy crouched uncomfortably on the low seat. The doors had no locks, and you had to jam them with your feet, so it wasn't my fault, but I felt guilty of I didn't quite know what. Those lavatories were cold and smelly, and you tried not to go if you could possibly help it, which often meant you got slightly wet knickers. Often during our happy but insanitary childhood I'd have a sore bottom, like a baby. And you didn't often change your knickers. I'm sure our habits were clean and hygienic compared with those of the really poor, but we took for granted smells and dirt and discomfort that would be disgusting today. The bedrooms in houses like ours held full chamber-pots by the morning, and using them couldn't always be a private activity. The women of the family used to 'empt the slops' every morning.

One of my favourite teachers was Miss Rowe, who took us in the Scholarship class. She was an intelligent, plump, attractive woman with one blue eye and one brown. I believe she's still alive. On Friday afternoons we were allowed to do more or less as we liked for the last hour. We could bring sewing or some hobby from home or play a quiet game. Valerie Williams, Renee Davies and I used to organize raffles. They were confined to the neighbouring three or four desks, because we couldn't get too noisy or disruptive. Everyone brought some object, everyone got numbers written on bits of paper, and everyone got something they hadn't brought when the tickets were drawn out of a box. Precious objects and junk circulated merrily. Once Valerie cheated, placing a ticket where she could push it towards me, so I would get what she had brought, a Bible. It was the first one of my own I'd possessed, and very acceptable. Its old green cover appeared on my shelves, in various places, in various houses, for many years, but it seems to have gone for good, leaving its successor, a black imitation-leather Bible I got as a Sunday School prize for good attendance. It had a feature I'd longed for, bibliographically exotic, handy and beautiful, a gold-lined thumb index.

Names of boys and girls drift back. Ellis Evans I heard of as an academic, a lecturer, I think, in Singapore, and I always meant to read an article I'd seen by him in a bibliography of English studies. I supposed it was my Ellis Evans. I hope Billy Solomon became a painter. There was a small, dark boy, a friend of my brother's, called David Davis, whom I'd rather fancied, but since he was three or four years younger than me, he was another source of guilt. Some children had exotic names. There were Mimosa and Phineas Brayley, tiny, delicate-looking siblings with very dark hair and olive skin. When Mimosa said 'I've got a Japanese name so perhaps we're a bit

Japanese', that seemed quite likely. We had been asked to put our hands up if there was any foreign blood in the family. We all knew that foreign blood was prestigious so it was essential to claim some. I boasted that I had a Russian grandfather, Nathaniel Nathan, and an Irish grandmother, Rose something-or-other, and threw in for good measure that my other grandfather's ancestors came from North Devon and included Richard Blackmore, famous author of *Lorna Doone*. Our teacher was impressed and everyone in the class had heard of him.

Then there were Ninette and Warwick Furneaux, who lived a few doors down in Cradock Street. Ninette and I played hop-scotch. We chalked huge spirals on the pavement, like Matisse's *Escargots*. Warwick was a friend of Bill's. Bill came home one day to report that he'd seen Mrs Furneaux, an enormously fat woman, washing, 'And her titties came down to the floor.' 'Fancy washing in front of people like that,' observed my mother.

Another interesting name was Venus Bennett, borne by a fat little girl with an enormous fluff of light-brown hair, but in her childhood no beauty. I hope she grew up to carry off her parents' daring. Then there was the Charlccombe family, whose name I can't even spell confidently. Teddy and Lew were the boys, and lived two or three houses up from us, in the big house on the corner. Teddy used to come and play with us. Once, we all crawled into the forbidden space just beyond the attic, separated by a sliding panel, and consisting of a flimsy lath-and-plaster floor under the roof. Suddenly Teddy's leg went through. We were afraid he'd be hurt, but managed to drag him carefully through and back without injury. We left quickly and we didn't say anything about it. It never occurred to any of us to wonder where his leg had gone. When we went to bed that night we knew. There was a big jagged hole in the ceiling and on Mother's blue silk eiderdown, from which we used to pull out the feathers, was a big pile of dirt and plaster. I have forgotten the row, if one followed, though Mother may have had a good laugh, especially when we were so astonished at the loft floor having any connection with the bedroom ceiling.

One little girl at school smelt. She was the first person I'd met who did. We couldn't have smelt all that sweet ourselves, bathing once a week, washing in the wash-up in a cold back kitchen, with Puritan Maid clothes-washing soap, yellow and strong. No one had heard of deodorant. We didn't change our clothes very often, and never had coats and heavy garments dry-cleaned. I don't think there were dry-cleaners for years, and when one opened, Ron was the only person I knew who could afford to take clothes there. Joan no doubt stank of poverty. Two or three of us ganged up on her, like birds mobbing the sick or feeble. Somebody lost a penknife and we suspected her, because she was so poor. We laid our detective plans with care. I went to ask her, assuming a casual manner, if she could lend me something to sharpen my pencil, 'A pencil-sharpener, or something.' She did not produce the missing knife and I had a nasty feeling afterwards that I hadn't been as clever as I thought.

One of the best things about Terrace Road School was the journey there and back. Before long I didn't need an escort, and before my brother started, and later when he went his own way, I used the walk for games and reverie. Every day, going and returning, I made a compulsive count of the cracks, or spaces between the stones, on the tops of front-garden walls in Carlton Terrace. I awarded prizes to the wall with the most. I could have told you the number for nearly all the walls in the street. I always hoped they'd change, but they never did. It wasn't mere numbering, the walls had character, and the count was an act of judgement.

A little way along Carlton Terrace you passed the Dulinskys' house. Rita was a close friend, and I still have a copy of Hans Andersen she gave me for my eighth birthday. It has her inscription *To my dear friend Barbara*, and very good illustrations by Harry Clifford, Thumbelina pink and green in a walnut shell, and three Danish elf-princesses spread out like fans, hollow behind, the story said. The Dulinskys were Jewish, and though there was no overt anti-Semitism, some people tended to say 'They're Jews' with a deprecating inflection. Mr and Mrs Dulinsky, Rita and Sonny, were small, dark and exotic-looking. They were in the poultry trade and their house had a funny smell, emanating from all the piles of poultry waiting to be plucked, being plucked and having been plucked, on their big living-room table. They were always very amiable. Years after we'd grown up, my mother met Rita, who was working as a secretary, very attractive and smartly dressed, and she declared that she didn't want to get married.

A few doors up the Terrace lived the Jenkins family. He was an architect, not a commercial traveller, as I mis-remembered, a small man with a black moustache. I remember his first-footing on New Year's Day, after midnight, a lucky, dark man. My mother was very attached to Mrs Jenkins. The elder child, Joan, once went to a fancy-dress party as an eighteenth-century French aristocrat, a count or marquis, with a white powdered wig and a wonderful skirted silk embroidered coat. She came down to show us, and I remember Ron calling out to my mother, 'What's-her-name Jenkins is coming down the road, all dressed up.' Joan was too old to be of interest, apart from that glamorous appearance, but Billy Jenkins, her brother, was born on the same day as I was. Like my cousin Bob, he had a harelip. Bob was born about ten years later, when some surgical breakthrough must have happened, because Billy's lip was much more visible as a defect, until he grew up and had a moustache. My mother said she met him long afterwards, and he looked handsome. As a child he had problems with speech, of course. I don't remember anyone teasing Billy. Our mothers were close because of that birthday, and I felt lucky that it wasn't me.

A few doors further on lived another disadvantaged boy, Roy Gallie, who was 'spastic' (as we said then), again someone you felt sorry for, glad not to be him, meditating on luck and injustice.

By this time, on the way to school, you reached the Green, a big steep grass slope with a flight of steps in the middle, leading up the hill. The steps led up to the higher ground of Heathfield, in the middle of a long, rough grass slope known as the Green. The Green was good for rolling and climbing, and was surmounted by a high stone wall you could balance on if you were daring. Beside the steps grew barley, rural and beautiful, and a dark-green plant someone told me was wormwood, though I now think it was mugwort. I loved its pungent smell, and used to crush it in my fingers and stuff it up my nose. I did that with garden mint too, till a bit stuck high up my nose and I was told off for being silly. I couldn't get enough of those strong smells. I was addicted to my mother's smelling-salts. I could reach them from my bed, where the little green bottle sat on the mantelpiece, and took increasingly strong sniffs, till the ammonia smelt too strong. There was something delicious, sinful and dangerous in these lusts of the nose.

At the top of the steps was Heathfield. Valerie Williams lived in the big corner house with a father I thought must be immensely rich, a maid, a car, a bathroom, many rooms, and an impressive language barrier. 'It's me,' I once said, and he corrected me, saying kindly, 'No, it's I.' Valerie was the only one of my close friends to come from a Welsh-speaking family, but like many others, they didn't bring their children up bilingually, and indeed spoke fast Welsh to each other, as English families used French, to say something in front of the children they didn't want the children to understand. Valerie's house was lovely, but her front garden coming down beside the steps into Carlton Terrace was too steep to play in.

Round the corner, facing a cul-de-sac where we went roller-skating, was a disused quarry, Heathfield Quarry, where we explored and climbed. I loved the parks, especially Cwmdonkin, made famous by Dylan Thomas, but parks were tame compared with the sands and the sand-dunes in Swansea Bay, the old West Pier, really dangerous, rotten and full of gaps, with iron ladders you could climb. The quarry was as dangerous as the pier, wilder and more solitary. Ours were the playgrounds of the adventurous. Climbing was something physical that I loved, not being organized or competitive, enjoyable in solitude, a stimulant or accompaniment to fantasy. Once I was trying out a new descent and got stuck on a rock-face. I felt an odd, numb, jammed sensation in my chest as I foolishly tried to climb down with my back to the rock. I couldn't move, afraid both of falling and my pain. (I felt that same sensation many years later when I was hill-walking with my husband on the Snowdon range or on Tryfan. Again the click and numbness, and fear of moving.) As I hung in Heathfield a man on the road down below caught sight of me, and I recovered enough to shout that I was stuck. Like someone in a story shouting to someone in a story, he called out, 'Hang on, kiddie, I'm coming.' Immediately the numbness and panic unfroze. I climbed slowly down on my own, spoiling his rescue, but saying thank you. And feeling heroic.

Looking back, I'm amazed at the freedom we had to wander about on our own, often in dangerous places. Half the time the grown-ups didn't realize what we got up to. The roads were of course less dangerous, not yet crowded with cars, and we had the joys of playing outside in the long summer evenings, and in winter under the street lights. When I was a little older, but still only fifteen or sixteen, I went about on my own, in the blackout, sometimes on very lonely roads. In those days we had a freedom that's gone.

One of my Junior School friends was Peggy Petters. She sat in the desk in front of mine. I know the year because when Peggy asked me how old my mother was, I had no idea, not because she made a secret of it but because I was vague about ages, so I added on my age and said she must be at least thirty. Twenty-one seemed a reasonable age to start child-bearing, but actually my mother was thirty-one when I was born. Peggy boasted that her mother was only nineteen. I argued that you couldn't have children when you were only nine, but she persisted. Her interest in parenthood wasn't purely fantastic. In some ways she was my superior in knowledge. She had a brother called Johnny, and one day when we were chasing each other on the way to school, I tried out an interesting new word, a bit of schoolboy slang, from *Chums*, one of my uncles' old annuals. 'You are a funk!' I shouted. They stopped in their tracks.

'Barbara,' Peggy said.

'You mustn't say that word.'

'What word?'

'What did you just say?'

'Funk.'

'What does it mean?'

'Coward.'

'Well, it's like another word, an awful word, and you'd better not say it, especially in front of grown-ups.'

'What word?'

They refused to enlighten me, sharing shocked and knowing leers and nudges. I pleaded till we had to run the rest of the way to school, and at last Peggy promised to tell me, if I could walk back with her some afternoon, and be a bit late home.

A day or two later, sitting behind the bushes on the Green, I was told the Petterses' version of the facts of life, and the new word. It was all accurate, but I refused to believe it. Nobody could possibly ever do anything so disgusting. Peggy was an unreliable narrator, with a mother of nineteen and an incredible theory of procreation.

Accompanying the new knowledge, which I came slowly to accept, with the help and hindrance of other bits of legend and theory, like those of my cousin Joyce, came a new genre of literature. It took the form of rhyme, anecdote and riddle, and it was the Dirty Joke. The chief source was a little girl called Lydia Thomas, who lived in Cromwell Street, at the top of Primrose Hill. At the bottom was a huge Spanish chestnut tree, and in autumn we would eat the delicious nuts, peeling off the bristly cases. At the bottom of Primrose Hill were some iron railings, I suppose to support the feeble, but not going far up the hill, and used by us for acrobatics. Bill once broke a new front tooth on those railings. They led to Lydia's house, and if we met her on the way I would ask, 'Any more DJs?' There often were, though I never knew what her source was. She added her fiction to Peggy Petters's facts. Her jokes played with metaphors of flag-poles and brushes, and her rhymes flaunted the new word. It confirmed what Peggy had told me. Primrose Hill gathered unpastoral associations. I never breathed a word of any of this at home.

One night we had a boy visitor, perhaps one of the second cousins, or son of a family friend. Perhaps it was John Killay, son of Uncle Ernie Killay, Grandpa's brother. Mother went out or upstairs for a while and he told me a long dirty joke, featuring the appearance of bagpipes during a fire at night. I found it incomprehensible. As I was trying to make it out, he asked me scornfully if I had heard this sort of story before, and as I said eagerly 'Oh yes, I know lots of jokes like that', my mother came in. As I feared, she had heard. When I was in bed, she came and asked me what I'd meant. Knowing it was no good trying to pretend I was asleep, or telling a complete lie, I cast about for a joke that was harmless but not so pure as to arouse suspicion. Lydia Thomas's repertoire was out of the question. Desperately, I quoted the feeble riddle, 'What goes down white and comes up yellow? A baby's nappy.' To my surprised relief, my mother accepted it. But then she asked if he'd been telling me dirty stories, and if so, what. Reluctantly I retold the obscure bagpipe story as best I could. After all, I didn't know what it meant. Gladys did, kindly explained to me the meaning of the bagpipes, and said if I wanted to know anything I was to ask her. I'd have died first. I was covered with shame at having to be told by my mother that grown men's private parts resembled bagpipes. I'd glimpsed those little boys' penises, and had never heard of testicles, so I was still puzzled about those bagpipes.

Chapter 6
Happy as a Sandboy

If somebody did something stupid, going out after washing their hair, casting a clout before May (was it the month or the flower?) was out, or choosing an unsuitable best boy or fancy woman, you said 'Why are you so dull?' or 'What a lello!' or 'She wants to have her head read' or 'They're loopy' or 'He's not right' or 'You're not all there'. Abuse was often affectionate, like 'Good as gold but dull as hell'. If you were vivid in a new dress or suit, it would be 'You think you're it!' or 'There's a man for you, a dab by here and a dab by there!', which Grandma, my grandfather's mother, was supposed to have said when Evie, her pet grandchild, went out with a corporal flaunting his two stripes. If you were rejoicing in a new doll or train or book, love, or a sunny day, you 'were landed' or 'as happy as a sandboy'.

I never thought of sandboys as boys. They were creatures made out of sun and sand and salt. Once I turned round on Swansea sands and saw my elder daughter Julia running along the beach as fast as she could, laughing as she ran. That was it. She was happy as a sandboy. And so were we, though we didn't know we were lucky children, with Swansea Bay and the Mumbles and Gower as our playground. We were a quarter of an hour's walk from the sands and a short ride from the south Gower beaches, rocky Bracelet, sandy Langland and Caswell, and the big dramatic limestone headlands of Three Cliffs, Tor Bay and the Worm's Head. I'm one of those Swansea and Gower inhabitants who regret the invasion of touristic pseudo-Welsh 'The Gower', formed on the analogy of 'The Mumbles'.

Gower was always 'Gower', without the definite article, and I wish it could go on being so. I can't recall when I first saw or felt the sea. When I was small I paddled with my dress tucked into my knickers, like grown-up women. South was where the sea was. When you could see the North Devonshire coast and the houses over in Ilfracombe it was going to rain. Every hill led to a sea view. From Townhill, Mayhill, Terrace Road, Mount Pleasant and the back of our Uplands garden, you looked down on the bay. The sea stretched from east to west. Ships sailed straight along the horizon or into the docks or the Mumbles. When I first left Swansea to go to University College, London, evacuated to Aberystwyth, I was surprised to find shingle instead of golden sands, but the sea was even nearer, its rhythm and crash sending me to sleep, in Seaholme, the house in Portland Street where we lodged. Next I moved north to Llandudno, with more sea, and the magnificent bulge of the Great Orme, on whose slopes I decided to get married. I moved to London, where I can scarcely believe the river is tidal, though one of my daughters, Kate, is a mudlark who brings back treasure trove of old pots and clay pipe-stems. There I started to miss the sea, like a person. Every time I went back to Swansea, the return meant an immediate climb to see the sea, and breathe.

The first wild place you could go to without grown-ups, first with big children, then your peers, then on your own, was Swansea sands. To go down the sands was to go anywhere between the old West Pier, by the docks, and Blackpill. The sands were lovely to look at, dark brown from the tide or yellow in the sun, but littered and polluted with trippers' rubbish, mud dredged up from the Channel, and sewage. The bay curved from the derelict West Pier to the three points of Mumbles Head, and the Mumbles train's twin carriages moved all day between the two points. The first boats you knew by sight were the dredgers, the tugboat and the pleasure-steamers that crossed to Ilfracombe or round the Gower coast for evening cruises. I remember going once with my mother and brother, leaning over the side, seeing a fish, and being proud of not being sick. It was calm as a millpond, my mother said, but I knew I wouldn't have been sick even if the waves had been mountainous, as they were in Mother's stories about Father's storms. I boasted of being a good sailor, savouring the phrase. Though the sea wrecked my parents' marriage, my mother would say, 'The sea's in your blood.' This was confirmed when I recited Masefield's 'Sea-Fever', beginning, like everyone I've ever known who has quoted from the poem, 'I must go down to the sea again', certainly not the archaic and affected, 'I must down to the seas'. Having a father who was a sailor was romantic, though I wished he was a captain not a chief steward. And after a while, when I got used to missing him, I wanted to be like my friends and have a father at home. I didn't want to be different. I wished my mother was happy.

The big sewage pipes ran at intervals into the sea, emptying their contents at high water, concluding in brown but sea-smelling pools when the tide was out. We were told not to paddle in those pools, but the pipes were lovely for playing. You could run along the sand and spring up on to their high sides, to balance, jump and fool around, then jump off the end. The beach was threaded with little streams, clean and running, nameless except for Vivian Stream and the river that ran down Clyne Valley to become Blackpill. We played round the old pier, but paddled and tried to swim in the more salubrious regions near the Slip and Brynmill. Swansea Bay was really no good for bathing. At high water you could get deep enough quite quickly, and there were no dangerous gullies or pools or undertow or currents, but the water was never clear. All kinds of bits and pieces floated round you. And at low tide you walked for miles to get even thigh-deep, plodding patiently, lifting your legs high in and out of the squish, feeling soft, nameless ooze between your toes or hurting the soles of your feet on the ripple of hard banks. Sometimes you gave up and went back, relieved if a friend suggested it first. Though we lived by the sea and played in it, we weren't taught to swim. My uncles could swim, but only Renee out of the aunts. I doubt if my grandparents ever went in except to paddle, and my mother always regretted that she'd never learnt. I used to go to the old Swansea Baths, by Victoria Park, until they were closed some time in the war because of a polio epidemic. Once, I cut my lip on the rough bottom, trying to dive at the shallow end, and that put me off for years. You didn't learn to swim at school, but with the help of a few lessons from Ron and Walter, and a rubber ring, I learnt to float, do an erratic dog-paddle, and eventually a side-stroke which I still resort to when tired or lazy.

The beach had many pleasures. There were old lumps of peat which were the remains of ancient forests. Wood became peat and peat became coal. You could pop bladder-wort and skip with long strands of some other seaweed. You could look for shells. The best ones, always rare and now gone for good, were the exquisite ancient oyster-shells worn into transparent mother-of-pearl slivers. Mother-of-pearl was on my list of beautiful words, which I added to from time to time. It was a word that meant more than pearl, a poetry half understood. And the shells were silvery, gold, copper, rainbow, in frail saucers and half-moons. We were told how real pearls were made and searched amongst the big, thick, newer oyster-shells, still pretty ancient, because it's more than a century since the rich oyster-beds flourished which gave their name to Oystermouth, the village at the west point of Swansea Bay. You found shells of mussels and cockles and whelks too, and some-times after the weekend you could pick up ha'pennies and pennies left in the sand by the careless, happy trippers who came down from the Rhondda in charabancs.

We looked down on those valley trippers, 'common as dirt', my grandmother would say, and hardly ever went to Studts fun-fair, patronized by the noisy crowds talking Welsh or Welshy. I went once or twice, and dreamt of winning a goldfish in a bowl, a huge teddy bear or big soft doll. We were never allowed to go on the chairoplanes, the height of fairground pleasure as they whirled round high over your head, at a dizzy pace. Everyone said they were dangerous, and no doubt they were. Ron's Kitty had a brother who had broken his collar-bone when one of the rotating cables gave way, someone said. But they were never short of yelling whirling riders, and we looked up in longing. *Shôn bach* could go, but not us. When I was twenty-two I went to the August Bank Holiday Fair on Hampstead Heath, and there were the chairoplanes, and nobody to stop me. My companion was a young German POW, spending a weekend with some friends of ours who lived in West Hampstead. The flight was as blissful and terrifying as I had always imagined.

We were allowed to go on the big dipper, the cakewalk, the dodgems and the swing boats. I was afraid of them all. The swing-boats were fun if your companion was as cowardly as you, swinging low in a gentle, cradling rhythm. Uncle Ron once took me, and though it was a great treat, the pride and pleasure came and went with the dread that clutched my stomach as we rose and fell, the horizon falling with us. I loved climbing but dreaded swinging.

When I was a little older I went down to the old West Pier, with a friend or my brother, who would fish from the end. This was one of our very best places. It wasn't visited by any grown-ups in our family, except perhaps by uncles who fished, and they didn't know we went there. I don't think my grandparents and my mother knew how derelict it was. If they had, it would have been a forbidden playground. Like the Heathfield Quarry, it is a visible absence from Dylan Thomas's protected parkland, for old Swansea boys and girls. Even a walk along the old pier wasn't child's play. The pier was falling to bits. The wooden planking had huge gaps where it had rotted and fallen, and you had to step, stride and even jump over the spaces, looking far down at the iron supports and struts, and the quiet or crashing waves. The planks still in place were soft, crumbly and rotten. You could work bits off with your foot, if you dared. It was a place where you could imagine danger, and the danger was real.

Less risky but more frightening to me was an old iron ladder fixed to the side of the pier. It was vertical, splendid to climb up but sickening to climb down, especially if you broke the unspoken rule and looked down as you climbed. When you'd reached the half-way point you wanted to go back up or down, but it was too late. The ladder must have been about forty feet high, a tremendous height to a child. When the war started, the old pier and the docks were out of bounds for security reasons. After the war I went back, with Bill, and found childhood memory hadn't exaggerated those thrills and risks. Recently I went to see the new Swansea barrage with my cousin Betty and her husband, Harold Smith, and suddenly realized I was back in our old haunts. We were walking along the rebuilt pier, solid stone steady beneath our feet, no crazy planks and rusting iron but the water down there below, and at the edge some of the old timbers, massive and red-brown. The smell of salt and rotting seaweed is still there too. The new marina has red-brick apartments, tarted-up old ships, bars, restaurants and shops, but on the sands just west of the pier there are still one or two paddling children, sand-castles, buckets and spades, and dogs.

We knew the whole curve of the bay. Every summer my mother bought season tickets, one and two halves, for the Mumbles train. It ran along the bay, separating the beach from the promenade. We'd walk down from Cradock Street to the terminus, where there was a shelter to wait if there wasn't a train in. The train was bright red, with two coaches and a wonderful hoot. It looked a bit like a tram, though there were no overhead lines. When I introduced my husband to Swansea he teased my family by calling our famous train the Mumbles Tram, arousing local patriotism I thought I had outgrown. Destroyed by short-sighted planners, it was a unique means of transport. For us it was the vehicle of summer journeys to the first Gower seaside, Bracelet Bay.

The journey round the bay was a series of pleasures, punctuated by the familiar stops. First there was the grim fastness of Swansea gaol, with high, stony walls. Mean streets were succeeded by a terrace of smart boarding-houses, still there with old ads for bed and breakfast and new ones offering television and *en suite* luxury rooms. They still have the old white-painted verandas and names like 'Seahaven' and 'Bayview'. Then you came to the Slip, with one of the several arches which led across the railway line from road to sea, and the Vetch or Vetchfield, where my uncles watched the Swans win or lose on Saturday afternoons. When they first talked about them, I didn't know the Swans were human animals. I saw my first and last football match there, taken by my grandfather to see Swansea Boys playing. There was the smallest and most boring of the Swansea parks, Victoria Park, whose attractions were the Patti Pavilion and a floral clock, brilliant before the war but ugly when it was restored. Next you came to the Rec, a recreation ground enlivened by circus tents or the fun-fairs, or a waste of dry and battered grass where boys and men in shirt-sleeves idly kicked balls about. Then came Brynmill Lane, leading to two parks. At the entrance to Singleton Park is a fake-medieval lodge built over the archway, one of my enchanted dwellings, admired for its supposedly ancient pointed arches, windows and turrets, and for its small compactness. Just right for my romantic community of children without adults, constructed out of imagination and eccentric architecture. My castles in Spain were mostly built out of Swansea pseudo-Gothic and mock-Tudor. After the park you came to the university buildings, tiny compared with their later spread, opposite the small golf-course, which seemed vast and wild. Then past Ashley Road stop, undistinguished except for a couple of dolls-house villas, to Blackpill. Here Gower and the country began, at the old Roman bridge, where the river ran down from Clyne Valley. This was the half-way point, the turn in the bay where you looked straight ahead to the Mumbles with the lighthouse and the three pointed rocks. The lighthouse might be a misty shape, or invisible in sea-fog, or a clear and shapely telos. It flashed its warning by night, and marked the destination of every August day. After Blackpill you came to West Cross, an expensive sub-urb before the housing estate lowered values and caused a class exodus, Norton Road, then Oystermouth, with its ancient castle and rows of swaying coloured boats and buoys, and last of all Mumbles Pier. The train stopped, we got out, the driver changed places, and the second coach became the first. There might be blasting there for the new sewage works, the first explosions we ever heard. We might go on the pier, which had slot-machines where you could get a penny fortune or pull a lever, threepence a go, and stamp a silvery slip of metal with your name in print for the first time, or see the famous Mumbles lifeboat, saver of lives, braver of storms. We'd walk up the short, deep, tunnelled road round to the cliffs, where there were harebells and thrift in the soft, sweet, cropped grass. A short scramble took us to the rocks and caves and beach, a wide strip of shingle, then golden sands.

My mother would find a sheltered spot on the rocks, or a small sandy inlet, and we would undress, pull on our cover-all bathing-suits, and make for the sea or the rock-pools. Memory sets a small white cotton hat on Bill's head, and gives him a shrimping-net and pail, and a fisherman's smile. I go off to find a pool big enough to lie in, with rocks to sun myself on, red anemones to poke and shrink, and long tails of seaweed for a mermaid. You could look out at the ocean, see if it would stay fine or rain, and pretend you could swim as you held on to a rock with one arm or found a stony corner to prop your head. The pools were dark and deep, with crabs and pink, crimped sea-plants, but they held you safe and warm and floating in a secret embrace.

Using an inflatable tyre, exercising great caution, and with occasional grown-up help, I moved from pretence to reality and learnt to swim. I always loved floating and I remember that first feeling of lying back in the water, looking up at deep sky from the sea's softness and comfort. And coolness, in those summers when it was always warm. The sky might look doubtful before we set off. Weather prophets in those days didn't have to compete with radio forecasts, and though we took the *Evening Post*, which had a weather entry, I don't remember anyone quoting it. It would be my grandfather, standing by the back door, looking at the sky, saying, 'Yes, now look. If you can see enough blue to make a Dutchman a pair of trousers, then it'll be fine.' I still stand by my door in Llanmadoc, or on the balcony of my flat in Earls Court, hoping Grandpa's weather-sign will work.

We used to have hard-boiled eggs, bananas, plums and

Welshcakes, with fizzy pop in one of Manny Thomas's bottles. Sitting on the rocks after bathing and climbing, damp and sandy, barefoot or wearing short-lived rubber bathing-shoes, we eat lunch, wave off the wasps, then go our separate ways again. My mother calls out, 'Don't go round the end, out of sight' or 'Don't go out far' or 'Hometime, now'. We peel off our wet things, or they may have dried in the sun. My mother carries everything except the shrimping-net, and we catch the next Mumbles train home.

When I went to High School I made friends with rich girls who went away for holidays, Margaret Hartshorne to France, Christine Palmer to Switzerland. Christine brought me back a blue gentian brooch and I invented family holidays in Tenby and Saundersfoot, where I had been for a day trip. I was ashamed of never going away in the summer.

The parks were beloved playgrounds too, if tamer and more crowded than the bays. We took our dog for walks in Cwmdonkin and Brynmill. We had the same dog for much of my childhood, the fat and loving Sealyham from Uncle Bill's kennels, called Nippy. She was famous for her habit of scrambling up on the chair beside you and gazing with a sloppy look in her big brown eyes, sympathetic if you were sad, eager for a walk if you were willing. We had cats too, but they came and went, leading their secret catty lives. One cat without a name worried my mother by becoming too attached to me. I was convalescing after having my tonsils and adenoids out. A quick operation was performed in the central clinic, after which you were laid on the floor with other children, in rows, to get over the chloroform, then taken home by your mother. For several days after my operation I had nothing to eat but ice-cream in milk, and this diet, together with the experience of being chloroformed, which gave you a whirling-in-outer-space sensation, made the event a great treat. While I stayed in bed and read, our cat used to stay with me, lovingly swishing her tail in my face and turning over my pages until my mother began to think it was a sign I wasn't long for this world. Long after, I realized that cats are fascinated by paper. Our famous cat was Charlie

Cousins, named after a local architect. He had a second home, if not a third, being one of those cats that vanish for months on end. He wasn't a loving cat, nor did anyone want him to be, because he had a twisted mouth and a nasty dribble out of one side. Our last Swansea pet was a ginger cat of small brain called Ginger Rogers, who lived to be eighteen and never minded letting children play with him. My elder daughter Julia used to dress him in a ballet dress or baby clothes, making him dance or trundling him in a pram. He never scratched a child – scrammed, we would say – but never learnt to sheathe his claws, so he was not everyone's favourite.

I am not a dog lover or a believer in pets, but as an unprincipled child taking the environment as it came I felt proud and grown-up and sporty when taking Nippy on her lead, and letting her off in suitable spaces. The first time I took Nippy to Brynmill, also known as the Swan Park, it turned out to be less than suitable as a playground. I let her off the lead on the green near the bandstand, but in Brynmill you're never far from the winding chain of lakes, and she made a dash for the water. When my friend Sheila Norman and I caught up a bit, she was swimming strongly towards a couple of swans. I'd never seen swans do anything except idly and elegantly paddle, sometimes with one foot nonchalantly shipped over the tail, but as Nippy came closer these swans took off, rising and spreading their great wings, flying low just above the dog, flapping in anger and menace. I heard for the first time that strong beat Yeats evokes in his great swan-counting poem, 'The Wild Swans at Coole'. These were the tame swans of the park, but they rose up into savage power, and I thought Nippy's end had come. All we could do was stand at the edge and shout her name, hoping she would hear us and return, without the swans. We screamed in urgent summons and fear, and much to my surprise she turned and swam to us, dripping and terrified as we lifted her out of the water. My fearful respect for wildlife dates from that morning. I always give swans, geese, horses and alligators – encountered once too close on the Okefonokee swamps, far from Gower – a wide berth. But even alligators weren't as frightening as the Brynmill swans.

It was our favourite park, far superior to Cwmdonkin, which I conclude was Dylan Thomas's favourite because it was only a stone's throw from his house in Uplands Crescent. Bill used to fish in Brynmill, but even girls, who never fished, could walk dangerously over the linked lakes, on wet, slippy, five-inch dividing-stones, too small to be called bridges. There was the children's playground, with two metal roundabouts, one like a Christmas tree, which tilted sickeningly, one a horizontal disc. We were forbidden to go on these, which suited me as I didn't like them. There were the ordinary swings, on which big boys and girls stood up and said they'd swing right over the top, but on which I preferred to sway gently. There was a tennis-court for the young grown-ups, and a bowling-green for the ancient. There were a number of fascinating, smelly cages for wildlife, a provincial ill-kept zoo. We knew no better than to love it. The golden pheasant and speckled poultry of unknown kinds were dull, but there were peacocks that would occasionally oblige by opening up their great fans of feather. I learnt with surprise that they were the males and the dowdy, though quite pretty, littler ones were females. You had to think about why humans were different. But it was their beauty, not gender, that was important. We'd stand still for ages, knowing there was nothing you could do except wait and hope and hope. Sometimes the tails would open, sometimes they wouldn't.

Best of all were the monkeys, who would make faces back at you if provoked by a grimace, or chatter crossly at their bars. My father once brought me home in shame, though he was laughing, because I'd loudly drawn attention to the swollen, scarlet, private parts of a monkey. That was my one memory of going anywhere in Swansea with my father, and it may be displaced from a memory of London Zoo. I have one childhood memory of London sightseeing, feeding the pigeons with my parents on the steps of St Paul's. We must have gone in but what I remember is the birds on the steps, and they flew straight from the past when I went to St Paul's fifteen years later, coming to London to finish my degree. The height and shape and site of those steps were right, exact match for memory.

In a remote corner of Brynmill Park, by the exit nearest the sea in Brynmill Lane, amongst bushes and trees, lived a fox, who passed his obscure life enclosed in a hutch. We would go and visit him. You couldn't see much, as he mostly kept out of sight, but you could smell him yards off. That impressive BO was unforgettable, and whenever I scent a fox on the wind, most often on the sea-paths or in the dunes in Whitford, I owe the identification to that sad stink in the park.

Cwmdonkin lacked wildness, and it was part of our Uplands backyard, enjoyed and taken for granted. The biggest Swansea park was Singleton. It had wild woodlands, a stream, fields and shrubberies. It also had a group of Druid stones, a kind of imitation Stonehenge used for the eisteddfod, or so we were told. They were excellent for hide-and-seek when you were very small. And in the formal botanical section, known as the Educational Gardens, there was a small, dry wishing-well. You could climb in, and, with a little help, out again. And of course you could have a wish. You didn't throw money in, presumably because it was too easy to take it out, so we would throw one leaf for one wish. Last year I went back to find it was just the same, the bottom full of the previous autumn's leaves. As I bent over, a passing man called out, 'It's not really a wishing well', and I said: 'Yes it is, we used to wish here when I was a child.' I went there with my first boy-friend and wished love would last for ever.

Trips down the bays were family occasions. During the war many beaches were mined or staked, but before 1939 we occasionally went on big family parties with the aunts and uncles and cousins. 'Muldoons Picnic', my mother would say, obscurely, on these and other family occasions. I can't remember my grand-parents on the beach. We would go to Oxwich or Horton or Crawley Woods where Bill and I always hoped to see a snake. There were plenty of grass snakes but I didn't see an adder until I was showing Bishopston Valley to my husband, and a small bright shape slid by our feet. As a child I recall only the odd cast skin. Bishopston Valley was a place of danger and delight, because of those invisible snakes, and because the river went underground. Its shifting bed was muddy, and you often went home with filthy shoes. I went here with the Guides, to which I graduated after becoming a Sixer of the Elves, in the Brownies. We used to sing cheerfully, 'This is what we do as elves, / Think of others not ourselves', which I found more acceptable than the patriotic Girl Guide promise to honour the King, which I began to have doubts about early on. But the knots were more interesting in Guides. The war stopped camping, but the next best thing was going on all-day hikes. My mother brought us up to be great walkers, and the Guides continued the training. We learnt to cook in the open, on camp-fires. First you marked out four triangles of turf, with pointed knife, then folded them back neatly, feeling, cutting and gently tearing the fibrous roots. You edged the square with a rim of flat stones, which contained the fire and was the hob. You collected twigs for kindling and bigger bits of wood for fuel. Then you lit the fire, never using more than one match. My mother had to be frugal, but she had never been a Guide and I would wince at her prodigal way with matches, as she struck one after the other, lighting the kitchen fire here, there and everywhere. My fires must never be lit with more than one match. Lighting the fire was a primitive joy and it still is, first in the making, then when the crackling says the fire's going, and at last when it glows red at the heart. In my Llanmadoc cottage we have an old Victorian grate, falling apart, and lighting the fire there is part of holiday and home-coming. Someone in London once asked me what I did down there, and I said: 'Put wood on the fire and look at the flames.'

We cooked potatoes in their jackets, in the white ash, dampers made with flour and water and filled with jam, sausages on sticks, and eggs in bags. You buttered the inside of a brown-paper bag, dipped it in water, put the egg in, and suspended it over a red-burning glow. And at the end we toasted marshmallows on bits of twig. When I introduced my children to camp-fire cooking, using my old billy-can for frying the sausages, they objected to the dressing of ash and twig, and really only enjoyed the marshmallows. Julia asked where she should wash her hands before eating. For us as children the spitting wood and smoking capricious fire and gritty food were all part of the pleasure. And the walk and fire-making and open air put the finest edge on appetite. When I was a student at farm-camps, one in Gloucestershire and another in Herefordshire, we didn't cook on the fire, but sat around it in the dark, singing some of the old Guide songs, 'There Is a Tavern', 'O Jemima', 'John Brown's Baby Has a Cold upon Its Chest'. There were new ones, 'Wrap Me Up in My Tarpaulin Jacket', one of the most melancholy marching songs, songs from the First World War, 'Tipperary' and 'There's a Long Long Trail a-Winding', which my mother said my father loved so I never liked parodying as 'There's a Long Long Worm', and funny ones like 'A Woman Stood at the Churchyard Door'. I remember one plaintive song from the camp near Leominster, where at Enfield Farm we worked for Farmer Paske, who let me drive his tractor and harrow and plough, 'Man's life's a vapour full of woes, / He cuts a caper down he goes, / Down-adown-adown-adown-adown-he goes'. It still brings back the smoke and sparks of the fire. This was singing in the real dark, but even those camp-fires at high noon, their flames paled by the sun, had a sacred wildness.

When I was nine I went away from home for the first time, though not far. Gilbert and Iris invited me to spend a few days with them, camping in Pwlldu. It was also the first time I'd slept in a tent. Iris and I had a double bed in one tent, Gilbert slept in another. I was told not to touch the canvas when it rained, and put out a finger to test the warning's truth. I woke on the first night to feel a centipede crawling over my chest, bravely picked it off, and went back to sleep. Pwlldu is a romantic place, with a storm beach of pebbles and a dangerous line of rocks, the Needles, at the point. But I remember the civilized pleasures too, eating Smith's Crisps as we walked on the cliffs, and savouring Iris's camp cuisine, out of tins and packets. We never had tinned soups at home and for the first time I tasted Heinz cream of tomato soup, oxtail, Irish stew, Lancashire hot-pot. I loved the exotic names and strange pungent taste, of strong seasoning, sweet sourness and the canning process. That was the second adventure for the palate, after the funny taste of hospital mince. Those novelties were not outdone by the first olive or the first caviare. There were biscuits too, not the Marie and Betta we had at home but Garibaldis and jam waffles. But despite the wonderful tastes, and the fearful delight of sleeping under canvas, I got homesick. When my mother came down on the bus I clung to her and begged to come home. Parting was too hard.

Later on we would hike to Gower, toiling through the town, emerging from the long, steep Gower Road to reach the common and the real country. We often walked eight or ten miles, each way. I remember when they brought out Snowfrutes and Snowcreems, and we stopped a Wall's cart on the way to the sea and argued over the tastes. Sometimes we were turned back or stopped by rain. My mother was a less scientific weather prophet than my grandfather, her predictions rooted in loving optimism not folk-science. She couldn't bear to think that her children and grandchildren and great-grandchildren could get rain not sun. She would smile hopefully up at an implacable black sky, as we looked doubtfully at our sandwiches and bathing things: 'I've got a feeling it's going to be fine.' We would walk on the sculptured limestone cliffs, from Bracelet to Pwlldu, from Porteynon to Rhossilli, over the high ground of Cefn Bryn from whose sweet, marshy top you see the sea glitter all round and know you inhabit a peninsula. And there were larks and wild ponies. I remember walking in Caswell or Bishopston with my friend Christine Palmer, seeing the deep-green grass shine and knowing what Wordsworth meant by its glory.

We were brought up in wildness, to be prudent. We might climb in the quarry and on the crumbling old pier, but we learnt never to take risks with the sea. We knew better than to be vague about the tides. We weren't allowed big rubber mattresses and boats and animals, pretty and amusing in the shop and on the shore, in case they took us out to sea. We didn't go out of our depth but swam waist or shoulder deep, parallel with the shoreline. After a meal we had to wait at least an hour, perhaps two, before going in the tide, if only for a paddle. We were warned about cramp. We weren't allowed to stay in more than ten minutes for the first swim of the season. We saw the warning flags put up in Caswell, so it was more than family superstition. People really got drowned.

We knew some of the North Gower bays were dangerous, with the cross-estuarine currents and deep gullies and inlets where you can get cut off without a cliff path for your back door. We were told about the tides, their hours, days and months. We were shown the coves and caves where you might stray at low water and forget time and tide that wait for no man or woman. I remember Arnold or Ron or Gilbert holding me in a strong hand, telling me to feel the undertow dragging against my small legs and pulling me off my feet. One of them took me to the rocks on the dangerous side of Caswell or Pwlldu, and pointed to the light, clear shape of the current. The natural world was small and tamed and comforting in parks and gardens but we also played on the edge of wildness, free but fearful.

Chapter 7
Madame Parsley, Kate Kolinsky and the Yellow God

Everyone had a party piece, a song or recitation, to be performed sometimes at parties and always at Christmas. Christmas Day began with the lumpy stocking in the cold dark and ended with a family concert in the front room, which smelt deliciously of cigar-smoke. My grandfather or Gilbert would recite 'The Newsboy's Debt', a poem about an honest newspaper boy, selling papers on a street corner, who dashed across the road to pay a customer a penny he owed him, because he'd made a mistake or hadn't got the change, to be run over, I forget by what kind of vehicle – a horse-driven cab, I suppose. Leah had a narrative poem in which the moral was clearer, about a poor widow with a crippled son living in a remote village where the boy was the only one not to have work. Every other stanza ended with his anxious, 'God has a plan for every man, / But where is his for me?', while every other stanza reassured him and the reader that 'God has a plan for every man, / And he has one for you'. And so it turned out in the end. The crippled boy slowly and painfully crawled up a hill to light a beacon fire and save his native land. When I try to place the story historically, I run into difficulty. Perhaps it was set in France. It couldn't have been the Napoleonic danger to England because the lighting of the fire was crucial. The plan for every man was consoling, and I applied it to girls too, especially when prison or an illegitimate child loomed large.

The best poem of all was my mother's favourite, though I

heard Ron say it too: 'The Green Eye of the Little Yellow God'. When I first heard it I was so young that I thought the hero's name was Madkaroo, and didn't have the faintest idea what it meant to be worshipped in the ranks, nor why the god should have vengeance. After a while I did spot the colonel's twenty-one-year-old daughter in the broken-hearted, grave-tending woman, but certainly not at first. The story grew more lucid with the years, until I read Wilkie Collins's *The Moonstone* and recognized in his long, complex narrative the story so succinctly telescoped in the poem. Mother recited it whenever asked, until her ninety-eighth birthday in January 1992, her voice firm and solemn, trembling and low when she got to the bit about the moonbeams in the room, the slippery floor, and the discovery of the knife sticking in Mad Carew's heart.

Ron used to make me cry and feel guilty about my presents with 'The Little Boy That Santa Claus Forgot'. I believed in Father Christmas so long that sometimes I still do, but that heart-rending ditty dimmed the magic of a Christmas stocking, 'I've heard the Christmas Carol, and I've seen the Christmas Tree, / But I must have been a very very naughty little boy, / 'Cos he never brings nuffin to me'. How did we know, as we did, despite those mid-December threats, that naughtiness had nothing to do with it? That poverty could keep even Santa Claus away? Grandpa's vein was more jovial, though his rendering of 'The Boy Stood on the Burning Deck' was always cut short because it was going to get rude after 'The skipper had brought his little daughter'. Nor was Grandpa often allowed to finish his version (I believe a radical parody, though this is only a guess) of a poem beginning 'It was Christmas day in the workhouse, / And the paupers were…' I forget what the paupers were doing but the climax was: 'You can take your Christmas pudding and stick it on the wall.' I suspect that end too is a family bowdlerism. I used to have to recite my favourite, Robert Louis Stevenson's 'The Lamplighter', and my mother's favourite, Masefield's 'Sea-Fever'. The repeated, 'I must go down to the sea again', made me feel sad about my father. I had to be persuaded many times before I'd perform, and doing so was agony until I was half-way through the first verse. From then to the end it was fine.

When I became an intellectual snob, especially about literature, indeed not knowing anything else to be snobbish about, I was divided from my mother by poetry. She was very keen on the work of Ella Wheeler Wilcox, possibly by now a poet retrieved for the woman's canon, but to my fifteen-year-old taste a dreadful poet whose name, a lyric in itself, was the only good thing about her. For some years I had admired her verses, especially a long narrative love-poem called 'Maureen', a poor woman's *Aurora Leigh*, which has merged with *The Rosary*, one of my favourite novels from about eight to fourteen. I began to go off Ella Wheeler Wilcox, and once when my mother gave her frequent recital of the sad poem about having once 'Lived in the shade of a dark brown eye' I pronounced it trash. I'm sorry to say that at some point my mother chucked out the *Complete Poems*, because I went to have another look at 'Maureen' about ten years ago, and all that remained of Ella Wheeler Wilcox were two miniature suede-covered booklets, two inches square, one called *Poems of Passion* and the other *Poems of Tenderness*, or something on those lines. My mother liked higher things too, and recited that excellent poem 'The May Queen' about which James Joyce was so rude, and 'Break, Break, Break', surely the best short elegy ever written. I remember my mother's voice saying 'O for the touch of a vanish'd hand, / And the sound of a voice that is still!', and I knew she was thinking about her mother, and that sometime I'd be thinking about somebody dead I'd loved and lost. When my mother was in her last illness, I was working on a lecture for the Tennyson Society, and used her old Everyman Tennyson, with her strong signature on the flyleaf. And she introduced me to Victorian novels, *The Lamplighter*, *A Peep behind the Scenes*, Dickens and George Eliot. She was a fast, opinionated, demanding reader. When she had white nights in extreme old age, she passed the wakeful hours reciting the poems she had learnt by heart in childhood.

My mother hadn't been much to the theatre in her youth, and couldn't afford to while we were growing up. As I said earlier, she didn't even come to our school plays, because her clothes were too shabby. But she would tell me over and over again about the 'guisers' who used to go round the villages in Pembrokeshire doing the old mummers play of St George and the Dragon when she was a girl. She was terrified when they came into the house, in mask and costume, to perform in the kitchen, chanting and fighting, and have Grandpa's elderberry or cowslip wine afterwards. She liked to quote the doctor's list of the illnesses he could cure: 'The itch, the pitch, the palsy and the quitch.' I was surprised when I found nearly the same words in the play of the High School anthologies, *The Daffodil Poetry Book*, though its 'the phthisic, the palsy and the gout' are not as powerful. Gladys's version also included 'The plague within and the plague without.' She had seen melodramas played in the villages, like *Murder in the Red Barn*. Once in a Swansea theatre she had seen *The Silver King*. She used to tell me the story, and I loved the bit about the father, cut off from wife and children, lingering outside his child's school to catch a glimpse of son or daughter, I've forgotten which. Of course I thought of my own father. It must have been in the very late forties, when I was living in Bloomsbury, that I saw a production of the play at the old Bedford Theatre in Camden Town. I recognized each character, scene and speech as if I'd seen them before. But tears came to our eyes only because we were laughing so much. An old man next to me in the intimate wooden seating of the gods, wiped his eyes and said: 'I'm laughing now but when I first saw it I was really crying. Isn't that a funny thing?'

We listened to the wireless all the time. I remember stories read by A.J. Alan, that great ghost-story writer and reader, and *Mary Rose* and *Dear Brutus*, with Nova Pilbeam playing the unborn child allowed a brief haunted reappearance and the unforgettable line, 'Daddy, I don't want to be a might-have-been'. Second-rate drama can be as potent as cheap music, and Barrie's plays were sentimental and overwritten but grasped the deep myths. Later on we used to go to plays at the Grand Theatre, in the gods, for sixpence. I remember Emlyn Williams's *The Corn Is Green* and *Night Must Fall*, with a wonderful local repertory actor playing Danny the murderer. I can still hear him singing 'Mighty Like a Rose', which identified him and made your flesh creep. For years I could hear his voice saying something sinister and smarmy to the heroine, but only the inflection of two words remained, the thin ghost of a rhythm. Then I suddenly retrieved them: 'Any objection?' We didn't have teenage crushes on actors but I recall that dark boy, so good at being sly and creepy. I saw Emlyn Williams once or twice, more of a local hero to us than Dylan Thomas, and had his photograph pinned up in my bedroom when we first heard of pin-ups. They must have been just coming in. We saw the classics too. The Swansea Little Theatre had left its Mumbles home, where Dylan Thomas acted for it, and used a building near the Guildhall, then always called the Civic. There I saw the great plays, and knew they were great. I was spellbound by *The Cherry Orchard, The Three Sisters* and *The Wild Duck,* but the play that really knocked me out, and forced its modernism into my mind, was Karel Capek's *The Insect Play.* That was the first work of art I knew which was politically thrilling as well as breathtakingly theatrical. It made you feel pity. It made you laugh and cry at money and property.

Of course there were the pictures, at least once a week. We went to a children's Saturday morning cinema show, held in the YMCA, unjustly called by us 'the flea-pit'. The boys would stamp and whistle, and it was strange having no grown-ups. There was lots of Charlie Chaplin, Laurel and Hardy, and a serial horror movie that always started with an animated image of a house whose lit door and windows made a grotesque face. But I liked the real pictures best. There was such a choice – the Albert Hall, the Castle, the Elysium, and later on the Plaza, with a man who played in the interval on an organ that rose and fell amid rainbow shifts of light. There were two high boxes, decorated with statuary and huge bases of flowers, and I knew the King and Queen would sit in these when they visited, aloft and lit by colour and beauty. There was a little hole in the elaborately carved circle in the ceiling, which would open and shut. The Plaza was the most glamorous building I'd ever been in, and must have helped to form my taste. While the organist played, the words would come on the screen, with appropriate images, and 'Tiptoe through the Tulips' and 'Tea for Two' still return, clear to eye and ear. The first cinema I went to was the Albert Hall, a stone's throw from our house in Cradock Street, with my grandfather. He took me, at the age of three, to see *Old Bill in the Trenches*, which sounds unsuitable, and proved so. I had a terror of loud noises and once the soldiers started shooting I began to yell, and had to be taken out. Grandpa told me he stopped on the way out to tell the usherette that he'd be back to see the rest of the film when he'd taken his granddaughter home, and so he was.

I don't think Grandpa went to the pictures much, perhaps because of the rheumatism which kept him at home. Much later, I went with him to see *Gone with the Wind*. My grandmother and I saw one Mary Pickford film, *Secrets*, but Pickford, deeply admired by Nana, was a bit *passée* then, and my favourite stars were a romantic pair, Janet Gaynor and Charles Farrell, who appeared together, reassuringly, over and over. My grandmother and I sat back in those soft seats and shared the dream. Perhaps my first Swansea young lovers, all beautiful, were modelled on those film heroes. But not all our films were soppy. I remember Claude Rains in *The Invisible Man*, absolutely terrifying as he slowly unpeeled the bandages to show – nothing. I remember the thrill of future fantasy in the film of H.G. Wells's *The Shape of Things to Come*. I remember a scene with a video-phone. My mother once said she thought her mother's visits to the cinema to see those films were some of her rare happy times. Certainly they were almost the only times I saw her enjoying herself. I revelled in the after-effect of going to the pictures, coming out in a drugged but self-indulgent state, into the daylight. You felt you were still acting, still with them, for five minutes. Hypnosis, I suppose, from being in the dark looking at the light. I've never felt it with a stage play or television. My grandmother read women's magazines, like *Peg's Paper*, and one or two romantic novelists. She liked Ruby M. Ayres, of whose work only one book comes back, *Man*,

Woman, and Sin, which must have been made into a film because the cheap little red-and-black reprint contained cinema stills of people looking desperate and wearing evening dress, one in particular of a woman descending a staircase and a man gazing at her from below.

My noise phobia was a nuisance when my parents took me to my first pantomime in some big West End theatre during those months in London. It might have been the Palladium, but it was certainly *Puss in Boots.* When the principal boy came on, singing 'I'm Gonna Getta Girl' while doing a loud tap-dance, I couldn't stand it, and had to be taken out of our expensive seats in the stalls. I remember the nearness of the voice and the dance, and the great height of the performer, a yard or two away. And I was frightened by the loud banging of the drum in the annual Hospital Carnival, a big event in Swansea culture. I wasn't frightened but impressed by one of the fancydress entries, a man walking in a vertical coffin, in chalk-and-death's-head make-up, singing, 'I'm Dead but I Won't Lie Down'. Funny at the time, he returned after many years to haunt me after I'd gone to see my father laid out in his coffin, to be polite to the undertakers, and against my mother's advice. At night I dreamt of Father singing the carnival song, smiling with his real dead shrunken yellow face.

Another terrifying character was a man juggling plates in the annual Travellers Party, for children and friends of commercial travellers, posh and select. The juggler made no sound, but I was afraid he'd drop the plates with a crash, so once more had to quit the scene. This phobia passed away, like other day and night fears, but one fear that pursued me well into adult life was the common dread of moths. It started with butterflies, cabbage whites in the Cradock Street garden, from whose lovely fluttering I would run, screaming 'Buck-eyes'. It was a flapping-wing phobia, which hit me badly one day when I was alone in the attic, having a doll's tea-party with real cake crumbs, and a sparrow flew in to join us. My mother thought the skylight had fallen in when she heard the yells. I got used to living with my children's budgerigar, Wee Hughie, who spoke a fine mixture of Scots and Danish, but to this day I'm not keen on winged creatures flying indoors.

Most little girls, and many little boys, used to go to dancing class. This is a feature of provincial, and some local London culture and education, that is still going strong in some parts. I went to a Saturday morning dancing class patronized by my cousin Maureen. It was conducted by Madame Parsley, of whom I keep only a vague memory of middle-aged benevolence. I fancy she had a younger assistant who helped with the more ambitious stunts, like the splits, at which I was not successful. I liked watching the girls who could do it, lying comfortably on the crotch, legs stretched flat along the shiny wooden floor. They were members of another species. I learnt to do the polka, the slow foxtrot, the quickstep, the waltz, the veleta and the military two-step. When you'd been going for a year or two you graduated to dancing on your points, or toe-dancing, which Maureen did beautifully. A ballet dancer, Belinda Quirey, once told me it was disastrous for girls whose legs were still growing, but no one knew that in Swansea then. I loved the ordinary ballet-pumps. I was once in the big event, Madame Parsley's Dancing Display, held in some local hall or theatre. I was a teddy bear, enjoying the picnic, and wore a Union Jack apron in the chorus of a number called 'Little Miss Empire'. It was wonderful being dressed in a proper dressing-room, under bare lights, being made up, holding your upper lip stiff for the lipstick, and having your hair waved and curled up at the ends and back, at a proper hairdressers, a far cry from the curling-tongs on Sundays, which left you with a row of crimped hair and a strong smell of scorched paper from the testing of the tongs. Sometimes your hair smelt a bit burnt too. A surviving photograph of our little painted faces surrounded by Marcel waves, makes plain the film-star model. I wasn't keen enough to stay on with Madame Parsley, though I left with a faint hankering after the blocked wooden toes of the 'toe-shoes'. I preferred elocution classes. Perhaps elocution was the tail-end of the tradition of female accomplishments. I remember just one boy in the communal class I attended, and my brother never went, or wanted to, so has the advantage of keeping something of his Welsh accent. Mine seems to have been elocuted away, to return if I'm talking to someone with a strong accent and remain in a few pronunciations which probably only linguists can spot.

My first teacher was a dark, voluptuous woman called Kate Kolinsky, a small-town Jewish Elizabeth Taylor, with a shadowy husband in the background and a black velvet voice. Auntie Em or Auntie Leah asked my mother, 'Why are you sending Barbara to her?', to which Gladys replied: 'I'm interested in her voice and her teaching.' Someone had heard a story about her answering the door to the milkman or the baker or the window-cleaner in her under-wear. Swansea was easily shocked, and Kate was a flamboyant flower. She taught chiefly by example, and we all learnt to imitate her buoyant modulations in our thin, young voices. We learnt some pretty awful poems, like 'Where did you come from, baby dear? / Out of the everywhere into here', and some good ones, like 'Tiger! Tiger!' We spent a lot of time rehearsing for plays and shows. One piece she taught me to recite was a famous American tear-jerker, 'Little Boy Blue', which begins 'The little toy dog is covered in dust, / But sturdy and staunch he stands'. The toys are left in their places and told not to move by Little Boy Blue, who never comes back to play with them again. (I once recited it in a Chinese restaurant, as a duet with Marjorie Kaufman, an American colleague from Mount Holyoke who had also learnt it in childhood, after feasting on ginger-fish.) Another poem I loved was 'The Minuet': 'Grandma told me all about it, / Told me so I could not doubt it / How she danced the minuet, long ago'. I associate it with a short play we did, learning our parts from one of those greyish books published by French, the first acting text I'd ever had, very glamorous. We dressed as crinoline ladies, and all I remember about the play is the book and my dress, the most beautiful dress I've ever possessed. It was made by Renee from yards of pale, apple-green satin with little pink rosebuds, its huge skirt stretched over a big starched petticoat with hoops. There was also a poke bonnet, made from a bought frame, covered by Renee with bottle-green silk, its poke filled with rosebuds. I kept the bonnet till the silk frayed and faded in the attic with old clothes and tea-chests, where we dressed up. There was a crepe-de-Chine Chinese kimono, lime-green with storks, a present from my father to my mother. 'I must have been daft to let you play with it,' she said years later. We used to pull out the silver paper from the chests smelling of ancient tea, regarding it as treasure trove.

I wore the crinoline for the play, and experienced my first stage fright. I'd heard the word, and as my heart began to beat and my mind to empty, I knew I was feeling it. The curtain rose, everything was a blank, but the words came to the cue, and panic ebbed away. I wore the dress for years, sometimes at the big Hospital Ball, held every year, a fancy-dress affair. I remember my partners' admiration and amusement as we danced off and the crinoline tipped up at the back. At these parties pleasure was divided evenly between seeing how many boys asked you to dance and how many ices you could eat. I remember eating fifteen, queuing up, then going with the ice to the back of the queue again. My children say there's something peculiar about eating fifteen ices and fifteen of Grandpa's doughnuts, but I think it was a greedy coincidence. The ball was thrilling. I don't think we got asked to dance much, because the males were mostly older than we were – we were fourteen or so – but the girls danced with each other a lot and there was always the expectancy of the Paul Jones, hoping the music would stop when you found yourself opposite a handsome boy. There was a real orchestra, in evening dress. And the gorgeous riot of bloom and fruit and figure, gold and orange and purple and lime-green, in Frank Brangwyn's panels, my first big encounter with paint.

At one party a friend of mine had a fit. She lay twitching on the floor and had to be carried into another room, where I waited with her beside the couch till her father came and took us home. When he got out to let me off at my house, he came to the door with me and whispered that she wasn't to know it had been a fit. We were to say it was a faint, in case knowing about it brought another spell on. I felt responsible but precarious, tempted to say 'I know a secret about you' and then have to tell. I'm thankful to say I resisted the temptation. I don't think she had another fit.

I remember the tunes we danced to, 'The Merry Widow' and 'The Blue Danube' for the last waltz, and one Paul Jones, 'It's a Sin to Tell a Lie', which I found poignant because a past love came circling in front of me, and the music stopped at the very words, 'So be sure it's true, / When you say I love you'. I'm not sure exactly how they fitted, but I sensed bitter-sweetness as we danced but didn't speak. All this with the brilliance of the great Brangwyn Hall. We knew it was important because when the Civic Centre was finished in 1933, all the schoolchildren were taken on a conducted tour, made notes and wrote essays with detailed descriptions of the materials and design and furniture of every room, from council chamber to Brangwyn Hall. I seem to remember one room had panels or seats of Australian walnut.

Kate Kolinsky's pupils went round reciting at various concerts, chapels and eisteddfodau. We were entered for competitions, and sometimes got small cash prizes. We'd say the same poem over and over again. I remember saying 'Abou Ben Adhem', which I still admire. Best of all was the school eisteddfod on St David's Day. March the First had a special atmosphere like Christmas, only quite distinct. The girls from Welsh families wore their costumes, with flannel shawls and tall black hats. There were no lessons, only the day-long eisteddfod, at which we recited and sang and played, and prizes were announced for the competitions in writing. In my first year I won one of my only two first prizes. It was for recitation, and the poem was by Walter de la Mare, about a girl who told stories.

> 'Once... once upon a time...
> Over and over again,
> Martha would tell us her stories,
> In the hazel glen.

I loved Martha because I loved stories and she had grey

eyes, like me, and got me the prize. And it is a good poem. As I said it I felt for the first time, as I feel now, the delight of voicing your feeling with that of a poem, feeling for the poem's feelings.

In my last year I won a prize for translating a poem by Catullus, which didn't please me because I'd dashed it off, but had worked fervently on the poem I hoped might win the Bardic Throne. That was my never-to-be realized ambition. You could compete for Bard in the sixth forms. I hadn't succeeded the year before, but in the Upper Sixth I expended all my craft and lyric impulse on the subject 'Salute to Adventure'. The other subject was 'The Fair', and I hadn't liked either, but interpreted adventure as a response to the natural world. It wasn't a bad poem, though it had some rather obvious allusions to not sailing with Ulysses and not hearing the sirens, and was very intense about nature. I cribbed black ash-buds from Tennyson, via Miss Matty's lover in *Cranford*. I've always admired understatement, but it is not my native element. What made defeat worse was that possible winners had to be told in advance, because they couldn't prepare for the chorus of Druids who would write a poem in praise of the Bard and respond to the Chief Druid (Miss Stewart, senior history mistress) when she asked for their assent to the enthronement. So we were told it was between me and Sylvia Jones, who had won the year before. She was heading for Oxford, having stayed an extra year, as our school insisted, to take the entrance exams. She was said to be rich, wore expensive clothes and wrote rather good facetious essays in the school magazine. I remember an amusing paragraph about the current Persil advertisement, which showed a grubby little ghost envying another with a Persil-washed shroud. In short, she was my rival. And she won. Her poem was set in a bustling Welsh fair, praising the beloved, '…it was Sian I really looked at'. As the Druid sword was drawn from its sheath, imitating the National Eisteddfod, and '*A oes heddwch*' was answered '*Oes*', in one heart there was not peace but green-eyed envy.

When I was about sixteen, and had taken a couple of elocu-

tion exams with Madame Kate, my mother decided to switch
my teacher. The new one was Mabel Tait, and Mother went to
ask her if she could give me lessons at a reduced rate, because
we weren't well off. Miss Tait agreed, and I never thought anything of the effort on my mother's part. A year or two later we
were asked for the usual fee, but I can't remember if we paid it
or not. Madame Kate was a prima donna role-model, Miss Tait
an excellent and well-qualified teacher. From her I learnt about
enunciation, modulation, inflections, the physiology of breathing and speaking, diaphragmatic breathing and the chink in the
glottis. We had done tongue-twisters with Madame Kate, fun
for the tongue and a kind of weird poetry, 'The Leith police
dismisseth us, / And the sea ceaseth and sufficeth us' and one I
still can't say quickly, 'Are you copper-bottoming 'em, Mum? /
No, I'm aluminiuming 'em, Mum'. With Miss Tait there were
exercises in breathing and articulation. I practised vowels and
consonants, did scales, and learnt to throw my voice and vary
its pitch. I also enjoyed my teacher's conversation. I thought of
her as a woman of the world, the first I'd known. Unmarried,
she had nothing spinsterish about her but was at ease with herself and the world. She talked to me as an equal, as our
schoolteachers often tried to do but were somehow blocked
from doing by the old-style school environment. Miss Tait
would talk about being a student in RADA, and when I told her
I hoped to go to University College, London, said, 'You never
get to know London the way you do when you're a student',
which made my horizons shrink and stretch. I liked her flat, a
light ground-floor one in a modern block, Belgrave Court. She
died years ago, and I didn't keep up with her – you never do.
Sometimes I see the paler brickwork where her brass plate used
to be, with name and letters after it, A.L.A.M. and L.R.A.M.
She taught in a pleasant, uncluttered room, with grey or green
walls and carpet, and plates on the wall as well as pictures.
There was a ceramic bas-relief of a female head, and a reproduction of one of Vermeer's portraits of a woman.

Mabel Tait's own voice was a fine one, but she projected her
example with restraint. I couldn't imagine her acting in the the-

atre, while Madame Kate was always centre-stage, vibrant and magnetic. Miss Tait knew a lot about poetry and liked Shakespeare. We usually had a piece from Shakespeare for the higher grade elocution examinations, and every now and then one of the old extracts rises out of context – in the lecture-room, theatre, or study – to sound voices from the past, mine and my teacher's. There's Juliet: 'The clock struck nine when I did send the nurse'; Oberon: 'Ill met by moonlight, proud Titania'; Katharine of Aragon dying, and Katharina the Shrew put down by her husband's servant, 'Why then, the mustard without the beef'. I stopped being declamatory and trying to sound thrilling, and applied my voice to meanings and words. I took the examinations up to the silver medal then stopped because I was going to university. I also stopped learning poetry and drama by heart, until I did some acting, first in the Civil Service and many years later with the Birkbeck Players. I used to miss the week's piece I had to learn for Miss Tait, sometimes scrambling through it late the night before. I still have my old elocution exercise-books. Even if you had the text, you had to write it out for the teacher's marginal notes. She usually let me choose my own poems, and I liked fairly long ones, 'The Lady of Shalott', 'Lepanto' and 'The Highwayman'. I loved G.K. Chesterton's 'Ballad of Saint Barbara', though as a pacifist I regretted that my namesake was the patron saint of artillery, battle and sudden death. I preferred Alexander Smith's spas-modic lyric 'Barbara', which has splendidly sexist metaphors: 'Thy love the trembling rainbow, / Mine the roaring cataract, Barbara'. No doubt about the three syllables there: I hated my name to be contracted to two. I liked reciting Alfred Noyes's 'The Highwayman', and Miss Tait told me to click my tongue against the palate at 'Tlot, tlot', which impressed some of the girls at school when we all read poems in English, though my friend Dulcie Morris thought it was showing off. Nansi Evans informed me, gently but influentially, that I'd probably go on admiring Chesterton but would almost certainly grow out of Noyes. Not quite true. I've grown out of both, yet out of nei-ther. 'White founts falling in the courts of the sun, / And the

Soldan of Byzantium is smiling as they run' and 'The landlord's black-eyed daughter, / Bess, the landlord's daughter, / Plaiting a dark red love-knot into her long black hair' are memorable lines addressed to the eye, the ear, and the love of story. When I discovered that a friend and fellow-scholar could also recite 'The Highwayman', it was a special affinity. Tastes change but nothing you've really loved can completely fade, poems or people. Nansi was a great teacher, but made me self-conscious about aesthetic judgement. I started to discard things prematurely, to look beyond what I was enjoying.

My big gap was music. I was self-conscious about this too, but I couldn't do much about it. My mother had played the piano and in later life enjoyed classical music on the radio and television, but nobody in her world went to classical concerts. Our musical education in school was non-existent. We were taught theory by a nice woman who couldn't imagine what it was like not to transfer notes from sight to ear. I could read music a little, but when we were told to compose tunes I would make pretty visual patterns, which got reasonable marks. We never had good music played to us, except on one occasion, when someone played a record of Sibelius's 'Valse Triste' and 'The Swan of Tuonela', and told us about programme music. That was interesting, in idea and illustration, but it never happened again. When I got to the Sixth I realized that some of the girls loved music as much as I loved literature, and would talk in a fond, familiar way about Mozart and Beethoven. As I read modern poetry, they listened to modern composers, Debussy and Shostakovich. I actually acquired an extract from Shostakovich's *Age of Gold* ballet, which I played over and over on Ron's old wind-up gramophone. My first record, enjoyed for itself and because I was pleased that I could like real music. I can't remember who gave it to me, perhaps a friend of Bill's. I loved jazz and swing, but that was different music, for dancing and dreaming. When I discovered jazz interested intellectuals I was surprised, especially as jazz turned out to include things I'd heard and liked. But I knew I didn't know anything about music, and was impressed by those who did.

Aylwin Pearce, a large, clever girl with a sharp nose, whom I knew in the Guides, told me that she used to whistle symphonies to pass the time, and obliged with a bit of Beethoven. I was even more impressed when Sheila Norman, another friend in Aylwin's class, a year ahead of mine, whom I had thought of as interested only in books and boys, like me, turned out to be at ease with music too. She said one day, 'Oh, Aylwin loves Mozart – you know, boring old tumti- ti… tumtiti… tumtiti, on and on and on.' Sheila introduced me to opera, and she and Aylwin and I used to queue for the gods when the Carl Rosa came to the Swansea Empire.

All the cousins learnt the piano from Uncle Walter, but we were a disappointing bunch of pupils. Only Bill, who preferred the violin, and Walter's own middle daughter, Christine, had some touch and ability. The rest of us tried for a while and gave up. I used to rub out some of the ticks he'd put against the pieces I was to learn, and though he must have noticed, he was kind or resigned enough to say nothing. It was embarrassing to have to get out of it, when he was an uncle and the lessons were free, but I expect my mother made some excuse about my having to work for the Scholarship, and I'm sure he wasn't sorry to get rid of me. I can still play one short piece called 'Playtime', with Uncle Walter's ghost looking over my shoulder.

Every Christmas my mother used to say, 'Go on Walter, play Handel's "Largo"', and he would. I was impressed that my mother knew about Handel, who remained for many years the only composer I'd heard of, and the composer only of 'Largo' and *The Messiah*, hard to escape in Wales. I liked it, especially singing the Hallelujah chorus, but it didn't seem all that different from hymns and voluntaries in chapel. Once, we were all picnicking in Oxwich, less noisy and crowded with boats than it is now, when a summer storm burst over our heads. We took shelter with other people in Oxwich Church, one of the beautiful, tiny Gower churches, the only one right on a headland overlooking the sea. The church was dark, the sea roared, lightning flashed, thunder crashed, and my mother said: 'Go on Walter, play Handel's "Largo"'. To my surprise he did, cool as a cucumber. I felt proud when everyone listened, and clapped at the end, even though we were in church. Playing the organ in a storm was heroic and romantic. Music needed such seasoning to appeal to me. I was too ignorant to take it neat. In our house the women were busy, and didn't listen much to the wireless, and Grandpa and Uncle Ron would switch off or change wavelengths when that old classical row came on. As he grew more seriously interested, that was a source of irritation to Bill, who had quarrels with them over music. That was his culture crisis, I suppose, like mine when I turned up my nose at Mother's Ella Wheeler Wilcox.

Bill and his friends used to discuss music, and listen to records and broadcasts. I remember their talking about orchestration, and realizing I didn't have the faintest idea what it was. And how could one performance differ from another when the notes and keys and time were all marked? (I'd learnt enough from Uncle Walter to know that.) I did not go to a concert until I left school. But one summer night when my mother was out visiting, and my grand-father had gone to bed early, I turned the wireless on, hoping there'd be a play. There was a concert, so I listened, conscientiously, to two items, one which I've forgotten, and the other 'On Hearing the First Cuckoo in Spring', which I liked because you could hear the cuckoo. It was easy, image-making music. Next day I cautiously told one of the musical girls – a big, jolly, red-cheeked girl called Gloria – I'd liked the Delius, and she said: 'Well, that's a taste for pure music.' Once more I didn't – and in this case, still don't – know what was being said. But I felt flattered – on the move, culturally speaking. When I went to London and my English friends said 'Of course you are musical, being Welsh', or 'The Welsh have a gift for music', I told them they were wrong. Music for most of us, our time and our class, was dance-music, lowbrow music, and of course hymns.

We sang hymns all the time in chapel, at Sunday School and at school. Even at school I was fated, as my grandmother would say. I was singing, with the rest of the class, when the teacher passed my desk, in the front row, and said with a frown,

'Barbara, you're out of tune. Please stop singing.' I did, for about two years. One day another teacher happened to pass my desk when everyone else was singing, and said with a frown, 'Barbara, why aren't you singing? Is it because you're Jewish and don't sing hymns?' I often got asked if I was Jewish, because of being called Nathan, but since I hadn't been told that my paternal grandfather was Jewish, I said 'No.' I was pressed, so explained that Miss Clements, kind but musical, had issued a veto. Miss Rowe, amused, told me I could and should sing again. I did, and it wasn't too bad. It takes time for me to learn a tune but I know when I'm out of tune, and when anyone else is too. I was liberated, after all the embarrassing silences in school, though I hadn't stopped singing up and down the house, like my uncles.

When I went to University College, London, evacuated to Aberystwyth, I started to go to the weekly concerts given by their excellent music department – alas, just closed down. They were always called 'music concerts' and took place in a big sunny room, a trio or quartet, playing Mozart and Haydn and Schubert. At first the music was a strong stimulus to reverie, but then it began to take over my attention, and wholly absorb the mind and feelings. Music was like and unlike literature. The emotion it expressed, or aroused (Which was it? What did I know?) might be melancholy and joyful at the same time. There were extremities and unities and collisions. Was Mozart radiantly exhilarated or heart-breaking, or both? And how?

I was briefly in love with a violinist, who played rather well, and the combination of love and music was heady stuff. This helped my involvement in music. Something had started. Uncle Walter was unlucky enough not be over-age or in a reserved occupation (like my uncles who went to work in the docks), and was called up. He had some safe but dreary clerical job in the Army, and Auntie Leah and my mother begged me to write to him. I wrote about going to a concert, and he wrote back, sternly music-loving as ever: 'Are you getting to like music or are you being "arty"?' For him, auto-didact, musician and reader, the affectations of the arty must have been unpleasant. I was being arty, but on the way to being hooked on the arts. There was no real painting, till the Brangwyn panels. I loved the reproductions of paintings on the walls in school, and they were good, Marc's *Red and Blue Horses*, outside Miss Cameron's room, so associated with guilt and fear, a Monet bridge over water, and Van Gogh's *Portrait of the Artist as a Young Man*, which I loved enough to hang up in a cheap reproduction. Ron used to tease me about it. My father, on his return, copied the copy and gave it to me. It hangs in my bedroom.

Art wasn't ever talked about because it wasn't known. When I was about eighteen I went to the Swansea art gallery, the Glynn Vivian, and the first painting I ever looked at (after the Brangwyn panels) was a still life of fruit by Alfred Janes. I met him years later, and was able to say sincerely for once: 'I've always liked your work.' His fruit included bananas and a pineapple, and was bold and grotesque, a bit cubist, with a hard black edge drawn round each object. As I stepped back to have a look from a distance I nearly crashed into an arty-looking young man who said: 'Are you a painter?' 'No,' I said, stunned by the compliment. 'Why?' 'You're looking at that picture as if you know about painting,' he went on. Stepping backwards or forwards in galleries, I sometimes think of the young man in the Glynn Vivian. I suppose there were other good pictures, but I was taken only with Fred Janes. My friend Glenys James, who knew less about painting than literature, but always had something to say on cultural subjects, told me she rather liked Orpen, so I went and looked but was not excited. The Glynn Vivian also had lots of gorgeous Swansea china but I didn't know enough to look at that.

Despite reading Tennyson and Ella Wheeler Wilcox and reciting Chesterton and Noyes, I found poetry was a third best. Give me a novel, a play and a poem, and the poem would not get a look in. I decided that there was something wrong about this, especially as I liked writing and reciting poetry. So I willed pleasure for the first time, vowing to concentrate on poetry and see if I couldn't intensify and inform my response. I read everything in the *Golden Treasury*, and started to choose volumes of poetry for Sunday School prizes. I chose the works of poets I'd heard were good, or had liked in single poems – Robert Bridges, Francis Thompson, Alice Meynell, Rupert Brooke. I read them cover to cover, silently and aloud. Francis Thompson I particularly admired, having a fellow-feeling for the victim of 'The Hound of Heaven'. I too was perpetually pursued by God, always hot on the scent. I stopped buying novels at Ralph's and chose some of the slim volumes on his poetry shelves. I was in unknown territory, but the books were dirt cheap, only a few pence. A little volume of Anne Ridler remains a gem amongst the forgotten others.

My favourite anthology was the one we used at school, *The Daffodil Poetry Book*. I bought an old copy a few years ago, and back came the schoolgirls' clear young voices. We had to choose poems to learn and recite, and the repertoire of our choices was small. I was not the only one to pick Brooke's 'The Soldier', though by the time I left school I was beginning to worry about his patriotism. Moira Davies, good at games and to become a physical education teacher, said in her deep Welsh voice some lines I liked from a poem about crocuses, 'Hymen's Torch, their beautiful and half-forgotten name'. Our teacher told us Hymen was a god. Christine Palmer liked a poem from some other collection, a parody of Hiawatha which I didn't find funny. That was about the time some of my friends were discovering comic poetry, which I didn't like, my lack of response making me wonder if perhaps I didn't have that sense of humour on which we all prided ourselves. It was nearly as important as sex appeal, and easier to spot. Dilys Peregrine had a cool and deliberate voice, trickling like water-drops, and I can hear her reciting a poem I didn't get to like for years, Harold Monro's odd little dialogue between a nymph, who had some beads, and a faun, who wanted them: 'Nymph, nymph, what are your beads?' he asks, several times, and she repeats several times, 'Green glass, goblin'. 'Give them me, give them me,' he entreats, but she is adamant, repeating, to the end, 'No'. I liked more Alfred Noyes, 'Come Down to Kew in Lilac-time', another poem popular with everyone, and Bridges's 'Snow', which I

could repeat in my sixteen-year-old voice, 'A pure white man-
tle blotted out the world I used to know'. Christine Palmer and
I thought Bridges's 'Nightingales' one of the best poems ever
written, and I can still read it with pleasure, though not most of
his other verse. My introduction to Thomas Love Peacock was
his strange poem, 'The War-Song of Dinas Vawr', with its
swinging rhythm and tricky, neat diction:

> The mountain sheep are sweeter,
> But the valley sheep are fatter;
> We therefore deemed it meeter
> To carry off the latter.

My family was always extolling the virtues of Welsh lamb, so
it was good to have their opinion confirmed, though I didn't
know then that Peacock was a gourmet as well as a poet and
novelist.

My best and longest-lasting discovery was Yeats. His
'Daffodil' poem was, of course, 'The Lake Isle of Innisfree'. I
liked it enough to ask for more, inquiring of Miss Harris, the
school librarian, if we had anything by Yeats. She gently corrected my pronunciation, and I was surprised to find he didn't
rhyme with Keats. I bought his *Last Poems*, soon after it came
out in 1939, to find that it was not only brilliantly unlike anything I'd ever read – including, of course, 'The Lake Isle of
Innisfree' – but was sexually disturbing and elating. I hadn't
known that classy literature, and modern poetry, could be sex-
ier than dirty jokes. Here was a wonderful dramatic poem, 'The
Three Bushes', musical, plain and clear, mentioning the male
genital organ, which I thought of by our family name, 'Jimmie'.
I knew the words 'phallus' and 'penis', but they were Greek and
Latin. Here it was a rod, and became limp, though what that
meant I didn't know for years, long after I'd met the organ in
question, one way and another. The lines throbbed, 'Or should
hand explore a thigh, / Must the whole creation cry?' I knew
exactly what that meant, action and question. Everyone said
Yeats was a fine and important modern poet. And here he was
writing poetry which spoke to the body, as well as to the mind,

and whatever they meant by the heart.

The public world scarcely entered into that provincial culture. I didn't recognize Yeats as a political poet for several years. De Valera, and the Germans in Ireland, are memories of headlines. The thirties' poets weren't known, though I bought the first skimpy number of Roger Roughton's *Contemporary Poetry and Prose* in Swansea market. It had surrealist poems, including one by Dylan Thomas, which opened up cracks in everyday life, but weren't anything to do with the world of headlines, Samuel Hoare, Russian bombs on Spanish cities, Neville Chamberlain and Anthony Eden. My mother brought me the news of that shameful treaty in 1938, though we were innocently glad of 'Peace in Our Time'. Mussolini was wicked to invade Abyssinia, but came into our lives chiefly though a playground chant:

> Will you come to Abyssinia, will you come?
> Bring your own ammunition and a gun.
> Mussolini will be there
> Shooting peanuts in the air,
> Will you come to Abyssinia, will you come!

Chapter 8
High School Snobs

I was eleven when I left Terrace Road Juniors for Swansea High School. There were three secondary schools for girls in Swansea, Delabeche Dustbins, Glanmor Cowsheds and the High-School Snobs. The Dustbins were mere alliterative insults, and the Cowsheds got their name because they were wooden huts put up for the Army, I think, in the First World War. There was lots of light and air and Glanmor was supposed to be a healthy place to go. Delabeche was a stone's throw from our house in Cradock Street, and the High School (later rechristened Llwyn-y-Bryn) was about twenty minutes' walk up Mansel Street and Walter Road, just before the Uplands. You turned down a drive and there was a collection of old and new buildings which were the school. The girls who went there were the High-School Snobs for various reasons. The school was reputedly the best for academic results, though by no means everyone chose to go there. It had been a Girls Public Day School Trust foundation, and had a smack of the strict, old, lady-like tradition. The buildings consisted of a Victorian house, joined to some First World War temporary wooden structures with verandas and a big red-and-white modern block put up in the early thirties, with balconies, a modern gymnasium and modern laboratories. There were Edwardian bits in between. It was rumoured that whatever you put your name down for, as you did at the Scholarship exam, only those at the top of the list got in to the High School, but I've no idea if this was true. I was separated from Valerie, who went to Delabeche, and Glenys, who went to Glanmor.

One friend who moved up with me was Dilys Peregrine, who recited the Nymph poem. Dilys was a thin, brainy girl whose intelligence showed on her face. She also learnt elocution with Mabel Tait, my second teacher, and eventually taught with her. She liked poetry and had an individual voice. When we were about eight, Dilys and I went on a picnic. We walked from George Street, where Dilys lived, down the Mumbles Road to Blackpill, then up to Clyne Valley, feeling grown-up and proud that we were allowed to go on our own. It was a good walk, of several miles. We wandered up the valley and round the woods, felt hungry, ate our sandwiches, were frightened to meet a man we thought looked like a gamekeeper, who stared at us and said 'Good morning', then decided it was nearly evening, time to go home. Neither of us had watches and when we arrived back it was only about two o'clock. Our long day had been three or four hours. The high tower of the Civic (now called the Guildhall) with its far, visible, big clock-face didn't exist then, or we'd have seen the time as we turned by the old Roman bridge to walk back along the Mumbles Road. I was pleased to have Dilys changing schools with me. I walked to school from Cradock Street along Walter Road, past one or two shops, including Belmont, one of the smartest dress shops in Swansea, then along the dull, house-bordered way to school. This was no enchanted way with aromatic green plants, high steps, and Primrose Hill's sweet chestnuts, but there was the thrill of passing boys on their way down the road to Dynevor, the boys' equivalent of Delabeche, and the Grammar School, the boys' equivalent of our High School. So it was still a primrose path.

My mother bought my uniform from the clothing club, run by the expensive shop, Sidney Heath. We could never afford to pay cash. The most glamorous garment was a dark-green blazer with a shield on the pocket bearing the school motto, *The Journey of High Honour Lies Not in Smooth Ways*. You could choose between silk and poplin, for the shirts. I was surprised when I got to school that the well-off girls wore poplin, but the poorer ones like me wore silk. Like all schoolgirls at the time, we wore hats, dark felt in winter, panama in summer, with the green-and-silver school colours on the ribbon. The head-mistress, Hannah Mackay Cameron, had advanced views on uniform for girls and we wore navy-blue tunics, in a straight piece, split to the waist, with an overlap. Under these swinging panels, good for walking but unbecoming to growing girls, especially those with big hips, you were supposed to wear long, woollen, navy-blue knickers and white cotton linings. Miss Cameron investigated some things, even using a personal tape-measure to check the length of sleeves and skirts on tunics and the blue or green or beige summer dresses, but underwear wasn't scrutinized, so most of us wore dark cotton or winceyette pants with no linings. You had to wear gloves, stock-ings, and have house shoes to change into at school. My mother scraped the money together for the deposit, and I wore my blazer all the summer in anticipation of September.

At the new school I made new friends. There was Hilary Sumner, daughter of a Swansea auctioneer, surveyor and estate agent, Margaret Hartshorne, daughter of a chemistry lecturer, Christine Palmer, lover of poetry, and Dora Roberts. I don't remember what Dora's father did, but she was the envy of the class because her family had one house in Knoll Avenue and another in Rhossilli, most spectacular of the Gower bays. Dora was always the first to go swimming every spring, and the first to get a tan. I still saw some of my old friends from Terrace Road, but we gradually drifted apart. My new friends were middle-class. I became a High School snob. It no longer seemed easy to ask my friends home to play. Many of them lived far away, like Margaret in Caswell, and Hilary in West Cross, then a well-to-do residential area. There wasn't a chance of dropping in during the evening. I was friendly with one or two girls from school who went to Mount Pleasant Girl Guides, like Sheila Norman, who lived in a small house not far from mine, and in the same social bracket. Friendship with her was no problem.

My mother found it hard to buy my uniform and other clothes, even on the club's instalment system, so she econo-mized on her own wardrobe. She stopped buying clothes for herself, so she would make excuses about not coming to school plays and the annual hobbies exhibitions. She kept at a distance from the High School. Once at a medical examination, to which mothers had to come, she was touchy and critical about a well-dressed woman with a posh English accent who'd breezed in saying, 'Where's my child?' 'Her child,' said my mother nastily. 'The old snob.' Even in her last years she would quickly brand people as snobs. Sometimes they were, but sometimes they just happened to speak in middle-class accents. It was her strong inverted snobbery that I picked up and augmented. I struck out new lines in snobbishness for myself. How could I ask my middle-class friends to tea when they probably had gleaming bathrooms and indoor lavatories? When they invited me, I found my suspicions confirmed, so I didn't ask them back.

Social life became problematic, but work was fun. We went on with Welsh and started French, later Latin. We were the *crème de la crème* all right, those of us who had not only got to the High School but were in the A stream. In the so-called good old Grammar School days there were whole lost sections of children in the B and C streams, who would leave early, and never do School or Higher School Certificate. In our school, the A stream regarded the B stream as dumb, and hardly any of them crossed over to the As, after the streaming in the first year. Your destination was settled early. Nor did the streams mix socially, even in the playground.

I was lazy, absent-minded and dreamy. The teaching was good only if you were attentive, already interested and proficient. The teachers were well qualified, and even the worst were excellent as purveyors of learning to those who needed no help, or who could get it from professional parents at home. I coasted on my English and history, was mediocre in most other subjects, hopeless at maths. I once made the great effort of going to the maths teacher and asking her if she would explain quadratic equations. As always with algebra, I was floundering, but I disliked passive stupidity. You got an hour or so of elucidation, then you were put on to exercises, and if you hadn't understood the explanation you were doomed for ever. I had

159

just realized that I was lost in the system, so I made a desperate bid for recapitulation and retrieval. That wasn't in the tradition. Miss Rhys looked at me with her pleasant horse face, half-smiling, half-frowning, and said with great goodwill, 'Well, Barbara, it's strange that such an intelligent girl shouldn't be able to do algebra. Perhaps the weakness runs in the family?' Nobody in our family had ever done algebra, I wanted to say, except second-cousin Leslie, whom I had never met. I didn't ponder the question of nurture or nature but knew it was no good doing anything except go back to my seat. So I failed every algebra exam I ever took, except for one, after I had by some chance grasped the principle of arithmetical and geometrical progression. Arithmetic I struggled with, now and then getting my head above water, and geometry I quite liked. There was some sense in Pythagoras, something to be proved and demonstrated. I got by, which meant that I averaged a scrape credit in School Certificate maths, without which I wouldn't have gone to an English university. I would have done as well in a Welsh one, to be sure, but I wanted to leave Wales.

The girls who went to university tended to be the ones from well-to-do families. Most girls from families like mine left early or went to training college, to do the course leading to a primary teacher's post. I still have my school reports, which are pretty nasty. You would conclude from them that I was a delinquent, instead of a bright girl from a poor family, maintaining a big burden of guilt, sustained by domestic sacrifice and ambition, and travelling nervously up a social escalator. Year after year, it was a harsh verdict. I was talkative, fussy, fidgety, inattentive, self-engrossed and lazy. I got abysmal marks for algebra and needlework (my lowest was 7 per cent but I was often in the teens and twenties), which dragged my average down and down. Every time the report landed with a little thud on the mat (it was sent by post, I suppose because they didn't trust us), my heart thudded too. Woolworths still loomed as a possible fate. I once passed in needlework, the time we had to do a diagram of a hideous pattern, called a 'Magyar', from which we made shapeless bed-jackets. Showing you knew the pattern didn't need a needle, so I got by. Sewing was awful. We learnt to do French seams and run and fell, and my grandmother helped me. We made unwearable things. My hemming was once passed round the class, from girl to girl, as a prime instance of how not to do it. My friends passed the little disfigured scrap on quickly with averted eyes. Cooking was much better, because you didn't use needles. Actually we did for one of our great family dishes, a baked stuffed hake which was boned and sewn up, but that was the kind of functional crude stitching that was no trouble.

We made lentil soup, pouring the individual efforts into one boiler. The result was rather good but when I brought it home Uncle Ron took one look: 'I'd rather die some other way.' Nobody really liked it because it didn't have meat in it. As my mother said, our family pea soup, made with dried peas, ham or Welsh salt bacon and cabbage, knocked spots off school soup. Our long-suffering domestic science teacher, Evelyn Morgan, whom I saw last in 1990, once lowered my marks in the cookery exam, much to my fury. She'd happened to pass by as I was putting in the baking powder at an unconventionally late stage, after the liquid. The result, no doubt to her surprise as well as mine, was perfectly good. The golden mixture rose as if the raising agent had gone in correctly, but the proof of that cake was in the book of rules. However, I still do one or two things according to the Morgan method. I wait for a very faint blue haze to rise from the oil or butter for pancakes. I use a quarter of a teaspoonful, not a pinch, of salt, and I usually make cakes with plain flour, and raising agent. When I brought rules and tips home from school, my grandmother would scoff. What was wrong with a pinch of salt and self-raising flour?

We were taught French and Welsh by a small, fiery-tempered, attractive woman called Dilys Philips. She liked to point out connections between Welsh and French lexis, like the words for church, *eglwys* and *église*, and for sin, *pêchod* and *péché*. *Pêchod* is one of those Welsh words in no danger of being under-used. When I was working on the land, at a students' agricultural camp in Herefordshire, I went hitch-hiking to

North Wales with a new friend, who was doing English at Oxford. We narrowly escaped rape on several occasions as we travelled by night in long-distance lorries, and when we found ourselves in a little whitewashed chapel in Anglesey, sank thankfully into a back pew. The minister spotted us at once and after a welcome in English proceeded with the service. When he came to the sermon he took no chances but said the word *pêchod* many times, each time looking hard at us and translating for our benefit. No matter if we didn't understand another word, as long as we got the sense of sin. '*Pêchod!*' he bellowed, time and time again, '*Pêchod!* Sin!'

Dilys Philips told us the French picked up chops and poultry in their hands, which I found liberating, having always been too greedy to like eating with knife and fork and leaving so much meat on the bone. She drilled us in irregular French verbs. When I first went to France and the Parisian hotel-keeper addressed me in French, I was tongue-tied, and it took ages for me to pluck up courage and speak a little halting French in a Welsh accent, but I could have reeled off the forms of any irregular verb you might mention, including the useless subjunctive. Of course we were hampered by not being able to go to France, some of us because we were hard up, eventually all of us because of the war. We did German too, but by that time I'd begun to live up to my reputation for naughtiness and used to fool around instead of listening. Discipline is a funny thing. There were some teachers who simply got attention, without shouting or threatening, by presence and personality, others who did it with the aid of powerful nastiness, and a third lot who were just hopeless, and we knew it, they knew it, and we knew we could just do anything we liked short of, or not always short of, actual insubordination. So several subjects taught by pleasant, feeble teachers, like German and music, passed me by, even though I was in theory interested in learning them. Miss Cameron refused to let me learn Greek, because my report was patchy, and I saw her point.

A real old-style disciplinarian, the headmistress took the occasional maths lesson, during which we were all frozen with terror, even Fay Timpson, our eccentric maths genius. Miss Cameron told us that Greek kappa was hard so we should say we were going to the kinema, not the cinema. Since we never said the cinema, but the pictures, the information fell flat. She was very musical and drilled us in carol singing, making us sing 'In the Bleak Midwinter' over and over again because there was one note we kept getting wrong. She had a tight, smooth head of hair, grey and in a bun. I think of her as always wearing grey. She never smiled. Once I fainted because we'd been standing up for a long time in assembly. I suppose she felt guilty because when I came round I was helped to her room, gently told to lie on the sofa, and given sal volatile, which I'd met only in novels and never heard pronounced. I listened in astonishment to the almost tender tones: 'This isn't like you, Barbara.' Actually it was, though I didn't know it then, but I have fainted at least half a dozen times in my life, always from some obvious stress or strain.

Miss Cameron was severe and cold, but after she retired she took her little dog for walks in the Grove, past our house, and she and my mother often used to chat. My mother, who had never once been to see her while I was at school, told me she was a really nice, sweet woman. To us she was never nice or sweet. She had a beautiful speaking voice. I had never heard of the Book of Common Prayer, because we were Baptists, and our prayers and sermons were at best spontaneous, at worst made up in advance by the minister for the occasion. I assumed that the prayers Miss Cameron recited were her own composition, and quite admired them. Slowly it dawned on me that she tended to repeat herself. I checked after some words and cadences sounded familiar, and sure enough, days or weeks later, they came round again: 'Whatsoever things are good, whatsoever things are lovely, whatsoever things are of good report' and 'We have done those things we ought not to have done and left undone those things we ought to have done'. I'd found that last bit rather well turned, a neat reversal and balance. So she used her prayers over and over again. It seemed not unreasonable. It took me years to realize that she was reading somebody else's prayers, even longer before I knew they were nearly as famous as the Bible. I didn't see the Book of Common Prayer till I was seventeen. The hymns in school were different from the ones we sang in chapel, though there was some overlap. Common to both was 'O God Our Help in Ages Past' which we always sang at the end of term. When we sang it at our very last school assembly I had the poignant sense of an ending you anticipate will return as an ending, compounded by memory. Tears were in my eyes though I couldn't wait to leave school and Swansea. 'They [Time's sons] fly forgotten, as a dream / Dies at the opening day'. That singing was a farewell to school, to girlhood and to all hymn singing, because I'd left Mount Pleasant two years before. I don't count the church weddings and the occasional Christmas service with my children or grandchildren in Llanmadoc Church at the bottom of my garden.

We occasionally had schoolgirl crushes on each other, more often on the teachers. I held hands with one of my friends, and felt a physical closeness, affection rather than attraction, though I remember her brown skin, and even her individual smell. My crush on Nansi Evans, the second English teacher, was asexual. Proximity was important though I never dreamt of touching her, or even getting physically close. But I was drawn by her image. I persuaded my friend Sheila Norman, easy-going, amused and tolerant, to come and walk outside Nansi's house at night. Once we caught a glimpse of her going in, but since there was a blackout, you couldn't hope for a shadow on the blind. But waiting outside was a thrill. It gratified that romantic need to be near the beloved's house. I used to pass a big red fake Tudor house on my way to St George's Terrace, where the Incledons lived, from Cradock Street, and for a long time this house was a theatre for the common childhood fantasy of living in a community of children. When I was in Terrace Road, and for some years after, I varied the dramatis personae, always excluding grown-ups. But when I had a boy-friend and a best

friend and a crush on Nansi I revised the child's ideal community. We should all four live together on a desert island. We
would talk and walk and sunbathe and cook – there was no sex
in this technicolour dream. The characters were not connected
except by my fondness for them all. I knew I couldn't have a
lover while the other two were around, so I dematerialized my
feelings for Rob. At another stage I enjoyed fantasy with Dora
Roberts and Margaret Kydd. We would live in a wonderful
house by the sea, with a high tower from which we would look
at the waves. We called ourselves kindred spirits, after the *Anne
of Green Gables* books, and for a term or two we were insepara-
ble, in school and day-dreams.

In school Nansi was less romantic. She had a deep, slightly
anglicized Welsh voice, very good for Wordsworth. She told us
you had to be mature to like Wordsworth. It was much easier to
like Keats and Shelley. So we tried hard to like Wordsworth, and
it wasn't difficult when Nansi read extracts from 'The Prelude'
and the 'Ode on the Intimations of Immortality in Childhood'.
Her voice went on and on, up and down, as I looked out of the
Lower Sixth window, at a green pointillist garden, through a
blurred rainy pane. When she rendered 'Tintern Abbey', I was
so profoundly moved I couldn't possibly have looked at her as
she said 'Haunted me like a passion' in her beautiful, earnest
tones. She suddenly stopped reading, broke my passion, and
abused me for being inattentive. I was too weakened by
Wordsworth, her contralto voice and my injured innocence to
do more than mutter that I had been listening. But she knew I
liked poetry, and wasn't often touchy. She once asked me to
stay after lessons and gave me a lecture about behaving in a
superior way to someone or other. I was astounded by the accu-
sation. I never felt superior. School was very like Homer. The
mood-swinging gods were always descending to make mysterious and inexplicable demands and rebukes. They were in
charge of our destinies, and unpredictable, but we went on wor-
shipping them, with only the odd spurt of protest.

Nansi started a form magazine for the Lower Fourth. She
cyclo-styled it and asked for contributions. I contributed two of

the only three short stories I have ever written, one about a woman who went to heaven and hated it, the other called after a song of the day, 'Little Old Lady', about a little old lady who was always passing by with stolen goods from the shops. And a poem about Flanders poppies which began 'There were many little poppies out in Flanders', and told about white poppies turning blood-red. Years later Nansi was head of an Army school in Hamm and invited me to come and give the prizes. It was the first year of the miniskirt, and I had a very short dress and a very short Mia Farrow hair-style. It seemed a long way from the High School and Miss Cameron's ban on short skirts, daring hair and make-up. But Nansi said she remembered my Flanders poem and I was back there with a crush on the English teacher.

She was my role-model. She was unmarried but we were sure she had a love-life. We thought her beloved might be in the forces, and were delighted when she was seen with a naval officer. But he turned out to be her brother and we were disappointed. I tried to deepen my voice, and didn't have to try very hard to like Wordsworth. Nansi was a bit snooty about elocution classes but liked my reading. I didn't act much, though I wanted to. I overheard one teacher saying to another that I was stiff and self-conscious so wasn't to be given a big part. So of course I became a million times worse. The school productions were very good. When we were in the first or second year Miss Mountford, the senior English mistress, produced an enchanting *Bluebird*, by Maeterlinck, one of those productions that make a shape and colour in your mind for ever. In *Wild Decembers*, a play about the Brontës, I got a minute part, playing a penitent confessing just before Charlotte comes to make her visit to the priest. My days of stardom were behind me, in Terrace Road. The real show-stealer was Dulcie Morris, an original character with a very strong voice who played Emily Brontë. After the first night she was told off by Miss Cameron for her realistically hacking cough, which had upset some of the mothers, and had to be toned down for the last two performances.

At first I didn't like Dulcie, chiefly because she had read and mocked an intense iambic love-poem I'd written during a crush on our Youth Club leader. Long afterwards, when we were students, she explained that she hadn't understood then that people wrote poetry out of their feelings. Knowing Dulcie shaped my life. I didn't know what university to apply to, and Dulcie was applying to University College, London, because her brother, Glen, had done chemistry there. She was following or imitating Glen and I followed or imitated her. We sent away for the application form and hoped to get State scholarships to do English. UCL was a second best. I wanted to go to Oxbridge – anywhere there would do. But I didn't know how, and when I went, in fear and trembling, to ask Miss Cameron, she gave me prospectuses and forms, but told me it would mean staying on an extra year and taking the entrance exams. I couldn't ask my mother to let me do this. For political reasons I'm glad I went to London, but I sometimes feel angry that the school was so inflexible and out of touch. It would have been perfectly easy to do the Oxbridge entrance exams as well as the Higher, for good readers and quick workers. What was deplorable was the total ignorance of the school about our personal circumstances. The head and teachers must have known which pupils were fee-paying, as some were, and which weren't, but they knew nothing about our home backgrounds and needs. There were no parent evenings, no consultations about progress or ambitions or means. Miss Cameron announced one day at assembly that she had the Oxbridge forms, and asked from the platform if I was still interested. (I had tentatively asked her how you applied.) I said no, feeling like Jude the Obscure. So I went to UCL, which was evacuated to Aberystwyth, with Dulcie, also doing English, and Pat Jenkins, who had passed the Scholarship at nine, and was one of those gifted children who are good at everything. The science and arts Sixth Form teachers vied with each other for Pat's favours. She did German at UCL, and on graduation at twenty or twenty-one got a lectureship at Royal Holloway College (where I taught later) and wrote a brilliant thesis on Goethe's *Iphigenia*. I didn't get to know Pat at school, where she was of course the object of envy and admiration, but she is one of two High School girls of my generation with whom I am still in touch.

Dulcie and I began to be friendly in the Sixth, as we did the same subjects. Hilary Sumner, my best friend for much of my school years, had left early to take an agricultural degree in Aberystwyth. Hilary had polio and was away from school for a long period, and when she came back her ambitions had shifted. She once said something which startled me, and has often come back to me. We are in the Lower Sixth classroom. I am confiding my great ambition, stimulated by Nansi, to get away from Swansea but to come back and teach English in the High School. I feel daring even to dream of it but Hilary looks at me and asks, amazingly, 'How can you be so unambitious?' I didn't know what she meant for many years, but of course she was right. I did not go back to the High School, but even taking English at university was a conventional move, though understandable for a Swansea girl of my time and class. Ambition is relative. It was impossible to say 'I want to write' or 'I want to act' or 'I want to stand for Parliament'.

Dulcie and I were summoned by our form mistress, Miss Leask, in the Lower Sixth, to be told that we could be influences for good but had elected to take on the role of the school buffoons. We were flattered but tried not to show it. We liked Miss Leask. She was a character. About four foot ten, square, with short, straight hair, she came from the Shetlands and had the driest sense of humour I've met. She taught us Catullus, Virgil, Tacitus and Horace. Livy was the only Roman she failed to make exciting. I think Tacitus was the first prose writer who struck me, even with my feeble Latin, as having a style, and a style of his own. Of all my fantasies about doing something new when I retired, going back to study Latin is the least unreal, because of Miss Leask. She had a feeling for languages and poetry, and I still remember '*Passer mortuus est meae puellae*' and '*O fons Bandusiae splendidior vitro*'. Miss Leask was one of the teachers whose first name you never knew. Some were always cheekily called by their first name, though only behind their backs.

I was lucky in my English teachers. In the junior forms we were usually taught by Myfanway Jones, a large woman with a fine figure, in her fifties but seeming ancient, with a white bun and a slightly jutting bottom which earned her the nickname of the Lady with the Shelf. She was supposed to be able to carry books on it. She taught grammar and it was as exciting as computer games are to little boys today. Clause analysis became as interesting as finding rhymes for sonnets or writing blank verse, which we later did with Nansi, who asked us to write a sequel to Arnold's 'Sohrab and Rustum'. Mine began: 'In Ader-baijan, 'neath her father's roof, / Tamineh dwelt and dreamt of days gone by'. Margaret Kydd gave Tamineh a big hound to keep her company, a touch that was much admired. We never dreamt that Ader-baijan would crash back into our lives in the 1990s. Myfanway Jones was called 'Miff'. In relaxed mood she organized word association games, and I was rebuked for showing off when I said the word 'shop' made me think of 'butcher'. She was right too. I'd suppressed sweets as too obvious, but couldn't think how she knew. A bit like Miss Morgan in Terrace Road, she could look and sound terribly cross, and made us shake. But she would twinkle over her spectacles, and she gave me such high marks for English in one end-of-term examination that I forgave her everything. Even though I was pulled down as usual by maths and needlework, nobody said 'Woolworths' that term. Two high 90 per cent marks glittered in red ink. Miff was a great poetry reader, with a rich, posh Welsh voice. Once she gave me full marks for reciting Rupert Brooke's 'The Soldier', but for some reason the test had to be repeated and second time round I fluffed. To my surprise she said she'd count the first try. The Olympians could beam as well as thunder.

The senior English mistress was Mounty or Monty, Winifred Mountford. She too made grammar a superior game, but English literature was her subject, Shakespeare her peak. All through the school, literature was taught animatedly, by people who loved reading and who loved acting. When we did *Cranford* we acted it, and Dora Roberts, like many close friends given to telling home truths, said I overacted as Miss Pole. I remember doing Mole in *The Wind in the Willows* too, in the great scene where he gets a whiff of home and takes Ratty there in time for the Christmas waits, but perhaps that was in Terrace Road, where we also acted our stories. Doing Shakespeare was never disappointing. Whatever I have against the High School, it was not a place where Shakespeare was ruined. On the contrary, he was very much alive. Nobody forgot theatre. I remember acting Oberon for Miff. It was reading, not acting, but the readings were drama. Monty was a scholar as well as a director. As we ended one lesson, about to start *Macbeth* in the next, she told us to go home and read the play. She said we must think about the characters who are there at the beginning, the three witches. 'Think about the witches,' she said, 'and remember they are "weird sisters". Look up "weird". I know you think you know what it means but look it up all the same, in the big dictionary in the library.' Then she asks slowly and intently, here in my mind's ear, 'Are they just witches?' A shiver runs down my spine, ice-cold. When I read that 'weird' had to do with destiny, the shiver trickled again.

I was given the part of Macbeth for our readings. For me the Scottish play was good luck, and I thought of Monty about six years ago when I gave a public lecture on it. Someone had once said she had done a London degree and when I was writing my thesis I looked her up in the thesis catalogue and found she'd done a Ph.D. on the supernatural in Elizabethan drama. Never had scholarship been worn so modestly. She never called herself Dr, but Dr Mountford was part of my destiny. Schoolgirls are beastly. Miff's bum was a joke and Monty's rather large red nose was another. The legend of the nose was romantic, worthy of Rostand. They said Monty and her betrothed were in a car smash, he was killed and she had damaged her nose. When we were in the lower classes we used to twitch our noses in her lessons, but of course she never noticed. I didn't know if some truth lay behind the grotesque story, but she was a figure of restraint and sober dignity.

We used to wonder why so many of our teachers weren't married. Only one was in my time at school – Mrs Camps, a tall, very attractive and graceful French teacher, who used to speak tactful, slow French to us, and seemed to like Dulcie and me, even though we weren't great proficients in the language, because we liked the literature. And I suddenly found that French was literature as well as language. We doted on Lamartine, and I can still recite reams of 'Le Lac', but there were wonders ahead, Verlaine, Rimbaud and Baudelaire. Wordsworth began to look a bit dowdy, losing his sheen for a year or two. Mrs Camps was easy with us too. Glancing at the books on the mantelpiece she asked who was reading *Crime et Châtiment,* and I realized I could understand French, and reply, if briefly. Her interests were larger than French, too. She was one of several new-style teachers. Some of the older women had lost their lovers in the First World War, and others had been constricted into schoolmarmishness. Of course they all had more interesting lives than we suspected, conventional as we were, sorry for the unmarried, and expecting to be married, however far we might long to wander.

There was another young teacher, straight out of college: Elyned Lewis. Every teacher had to have a defect. Hers was a very slightly dark upper lip, a feature admired by Tolstoy. She used to bleach it and it was sometimes yellowish. Though a little less than wholly perfect to the distorting schoolgirl's eye, she was a wonderful teacher. She too talked to us as equals. She was only three or four years our senior, so that shouldn't have been remarkable, but it was. Her subject was history. She would talk about socialism, taking it for granted that intelligent people like us, being who we were, where we were, and when we were, would be on the Left. She or some other history teacher set us a debate subject, 'The Case for and against Nationalization'. Much to my displeasure, I was told to make the case against, in the old tradition of impersonal academic disputation. I was sure this would be impossible. I was a fervent and fairly well-read socialist, though I hadn't got to Marx and Engels yet. I got my socialism from the world around, with much help from Shaw. (Arnold lent me two volumes, *The Complete Plays* and *The Complete Prefaces*.) For the debate, I went to the library and

read the conservative arguments I'd ignored. To my consterna-
tion there were things to be said against the principle I held
dear. I put a case together, almost accepting it. It wasn't a proper debate with a vote, so nobody lost or won, nor did it convert
me from socialism, but it was an excellent exercise in trying to
negate your hypothesis. Though I may be the very last sup-
porter of Clause Four, that project did make a little dent in my
inflexible politics. For a while. I was really strengthening my
beliefs by thinking through the arguments against them. And
we were thinking about socialist values, a subject too hastily
glossed over by the Labour Shadow Cabinet today.

I was torn between doing history and English, but in the end
English won, chiefly because of the sensuous appeal in the subject. Elyned Lewis electrified me one day by saying casually,
'You'll be sure to get your studentship. Distinctions in history
and English at least.' I started to blush and protest, still a
schoolgirl, but then stopped and said I certainly hoped so. Had
I done history, perhaps I'd have been active in politics, as from
time to time I longed to be. I was a pacifist before I was a socialist. For many years I tried to be both, and still do. The most
congenial teacher, politically speaking, was Miss Bevan (called
Beaky because of her flaw, a very slightly beaked nose), who
taught us biology. She was another young teacher who treated
us as if we belonged to the same species, another non-
Olympian. Biology was the only science subject I liked, because
it was well taught, because it didn't involve mathematics or
manual dexterity, and partly because my interest was already
awake, in my body. I'd explored my eyes, my skin, my hands,
my feet and my vagina, learnt a bit about breath and voice, and
pored over the accuracies and inaccuracies in my mother's ten-
volume medical encyclopedia. Its vivid red illustrations of the
reproductive and digestive organs, skin diseases, and the devel-
opment of the foetus, supplemented the lore and literature of the
playground. There was no rote-learning and no meaningless
abstraction in biology. Miss Bevan was always telling us practical
things too, for instance, that it was better not to blow your nose
when you had a bad cold. We didn't do any dissection – I'm not

sure why not. But the Sixth Form biologists did, and there were always some of their specimens floating in dishes of evil-smelling formaldehyde on the side benches. We used microscopes, but I only remember being taught how to look at the slides, not what we saw. I liked doing the eye, but we were so lazy and selective that we tended to gamble on certain organs coming up in examinations, and not covering the whole body. So I left out the ear, amongst other organs. I've always had to think hard about the distinction between Eustachian and Fallopian tubes, and I'm much sounder on the aqueous and vitreous humour.

Miss Bevan also talked about politics, though very prudently. It wasn't safe and easy to be a pacifist, even if you were a woman. I was already one before I discovered Miss Bevan's allegiances. I read all the books on pacifism in the public library, I think because I came across them when reading about socialism. There were Beverley Nichols and Norman Angell, and many forgotten others. I read books about progressive education at the same time, probably because the education section was next to politics. I read about A.S. Neill's experiments at Summerhill, which seemed a great idea, though I disapproved of private education. This early reading gave me just a little sympathy for the argument that an exclusion of all private education might inhibit experiment, though I'm bound to say that the three people I met from Summerhill, in later life, were original and creative but handicapped – above all – not so much by learning to read and write very late, but by being used to answer only their own questions, not other people's. I'm in favour of an open and pupil-centred education, but with some experience of response to other people's minds and emotions. Not that three students make a Summerhill.

Dilys Peregrine was also interested in arguments for pacifism, and we decided to go to Peace Pledge Union meetings, held in a building somewhere near the GWR station. It may have been the Friends Meeting House. There were usually about twenty-five people at a meeting, and after the first embarrassment at being the only obvious school pupils there, we found it enlightening. It was politics in action, not mere talk.

On one occasion questioners tried to get speakers and members on the platform to discuss propaganda. I remember someone being asked if she or he would try to persuade soldiers to become pacifists. Without ever using the word 'desert' they were trying to trap PPU members into an admission that they would urge desertion. Such an admission would lay themselves open to a charge of sedition. We didn't quite understand this, but obviously something nasty was going on. Politics was coming close. At school next day Miss Bevan took Dilys and me aside and asked if we were really interested or just coming for fun, and accepted our assurance that we were genuinely concerned. She told us about the *agents provocateurs,* and the real dangers. The PPU meetings were open, and the members were vulnerable.

A little later all the employees of the local authority, which included schoolteachers, were required to take a loyalty oath. Those who refused were suspended, and Miss Bevan was amongst them. But some teachers who had no difficulty in supporting the letter of the declaration, like Nansi, who had brothers in the forces and was militant in patriotism and support of the war, disapproved of the oath, and its consequences, and also refused to sign. They were also suspended. Everyone in school was excited and took sides – mostly the side of free speech and thought – and after some time the suspended teachers were allowed to come back. Politics came into the classroom.

That was one of two occasions when the school was in the news. The other was domestic, in every way. Miss Cameron announced in assembly, always called 'Prayers', that some girls were using make-up blatantly, wearing their hair long, loose and curly, displaying jewellery, and sometimes tinting or dyeing their hair. The edict went out: school regulations about skirt and sleeve length must be strictly kept, no jewellery was to be worn, long hair must be neatly tied back, not be artificially coloured, and no cosmetics were to be used at school. I think she banned them out of school too, but that was stretching restrictions impossibly far. She was behaving exactly like Mr

Brocklehurst in *Jane Eyre*, forbidding curls, one hundred years later. We murmured, but conformed. Most of us tried a little discreet powder and lipstick at weekends, and I'd been biting my lips to make them crimson for Sunday School as long as I could remember, but we didn't dare appear fast and common by wearing make-up in school. Most of the teachers exercised restraint too, though Miss Stewart, senior history mistress and deputy head, had raven-black hair with suspiciously purple glints, and Dilys Philips, the French mistress, wore make-up, which seemed justified by her subject. She dressed well too, and cared about her appearance, sometimes spinning round when writing French verbs on the blackboard to demand excitedly if her slip was showing.

I tried to discuss politics with adults, like Uncle Ron and Hilary Sumner's father. Uncle Ron because he was a communist, Bob Sumner because he tended to ask 'And what do you girls think about the world?' in a way that was disconcerting but likeable, to be respected and answered. One man a conservative, the other a communist, they both showed antagonism to pacifism. I was staying with my friend's family after the Swansea blitz and I think the Sumners thought their evacuee was a dangerous import, though Hilary's pacifism was all her own. But nobody in the outside world sympathized with Miss Cameron and her strict notions. 'Like a nunnery,' somebody said. 'What a way to educate girls.' A history of social and personal repression had formed Hannah and her values.

To be or not to be in favour of the war effort was in a way the only political issue of our teens. This was no doubt because there was a strong local pacifist movement in Swansea, but also because all the other issues were remote. We talked about socialism, but since there was a national government and no elections, it was indeed all theory. Though it was theory with a time-fuse. No wonder the 1945 election created such tension and such power, fooling conservative expectation. Everything had gone underground. Politics had turned abstract, for the young, then released into action. And for men and women in the Army, not abstract, but waiting for power, for election. I was born in the year of the first Labour government, two years before the General Strike, three before women over twenty-one got the vote. My childhood and school time made me a socialist. But politics was an intermittent concern.

It was in High School that I began to think of houses being beautiful. We had a glossy and shapely oak staircase in the old part of the school, and the architectural diversity of the buildings made the eye grow and speculate. The gardens, too, were landscaped. The aesthetic sense was growing. Outside Miss Cameron's room was a lawn with a large and magnificent cedar. Glenys James wrote an essay about this in the school magazine in which she praised its spread, not with the apt Tennyson quotation, 'The cedar with its many-layered shade', which impressed a character in *Cranford*, but more tritely, from 'The Brook', 'For men may come and men may go, / But I go on for ever'. Unfortunately it didn't. They found that the roots or trunk were rotting and it had to be cut down, leaving an ugly scar on that velvet green. In the garden were winding paths, a wooded walk where only sixth-formers could go, and a steeply sloping field oddly called the cricket-pitch, even less suitable for cricket than our backyard. It was a place to lie and talk at break, chewing blades of grass, looking amongst the grass roots for scarlet pimpernels, and planning futures. The other place where I liked to lie and read was a steep green in Cwmdonkin Park. My brother and I liked the wild places of shore and sand and quarry and I looked down on the tameness of Dylan Thomas's Swansea spots, when I came to read about them. But since we lived a minute from Cwmdonkin it was our garden, happily out of reach or call. As children we played hide-and-seek there, and 'Queenie, Queenie, Who's Got the Ball?', and the groves Dylan Thomas said 'were blue with sailors' were magic islands in our games. Later it was the place to wander with a boy, or lie in the long grass, squint up at the tall cypress and meditate on love. There were no swans on the reservoir then. It was a mysterious expanse of water, railed, hedged round with trees, glinting beyond dark bushes. I walked round and round, thinking of past and future, loves and hopes, and running through the factory acts for my Higher School Certificate. Once a brass band played in the elegant old bandstand while I swotted history.

The school library was a good one. So was the public library. I was a fast reader and trained myself to read even faster by going to the public library every day, staying there to read a book, and then taking another home. So I overcame the disadvantage of fast reading, getting two books instead of one. The first book I took out of the children's library was E. Nesbit's *Five Children – and It,* with its marvellous combination of fantasy and domestic realism. It also introduced me to the middle classes at home. I'd met the upper-middle and upper classes in my uncles' copies of *Gem* and *Magnet,* but even to the child's mind the Hon. Augustus d'Arcy seemed grotesque. E. Nesbit took you right inside the nurseries and kitchens of the well-off or, even more exotic, the posh poor. And at school I read Vachell's novel *The Hill,* and started on Chesterton. My great loves were Rider Haggard and Charles Morgan, Francis Brett Young, Galsworthy and Hugh Walpole. These were the authors I read all through, and reread. These were mostly upper-class novelists, or seemed so. Wells and Cronin did the world I knew. Miss Harris, the school librarian, was one of a handful of English teachers whose very voices were changing mine. I asked her if I could borrow from the senior library as I'd run through the not very extensive shelves of the junior section. She thought, then smiled, 'Tell you what. You read Priestley's book on Meredith, and tell me about it, and then you can. I must say I don't care for Meredith, but if anyone could get you to like him it would be Priestley.'

The teachers' voices were different from ours in inflection and modulation. The sentences were different in syntax and phrase. Almost as soon as I got to the High School I found there were two languages where there had been one. There was the language of home and the language of school. I'm sure this language breach must have been bigger and more shocking in other regions, since there is probably less difference between the accents of lower- and middle-class Anglo-Welsh than between similar classes in London. This was true in our time, when the language of the wireless, especially the voices of announcers and uncles of *Children's Hour*, was immaculate, upper class and vowel narrowed, as any old film and recording demonstrates. Even so, the language of school, though Anglo-Welsh, was highly Anglicized. It seemed to me totally English and middle-class. At home 'vase' rhymed with 'pause', at school with 'Mars'. At home the 'au' in 'mauve' was like that in 'pause', at school like that in 'cove', approximating to French. At home 'Auntie' rhymed with 'pantie', and 'wasp' had a short 'a'. At school nearly everyone said 'ate' while we said 'et'. One of the very English teachers said 'orf' for 'off'. It was very la-di-da, but I started to try it. Sometimes I got the class thing wrong. My grandfather sometimes dropped an 'h', so his 'otel' seemed illiterate but was an upper-class usage, perhaps picked up from the squire who sent brandy to the bakehouse. He always said visitors were 'stopping' not staying, and this too I thought low but discovered was classy. There was a deacon in Mount Pleasant whose idiolect was Dickensianly comic. He would remove the 'h' from its place, then stick it where it didn't belong, beginning the announcements, Chadbandianly called the Intimations, with 'Now we 'ave the hintimations.' I'd been giggling at poor old what's-'is-name for years and now I realized that I too got things wrong. I occasionally corrected my family, but more often consciously tolerated their error. Soon I settled down to social bilingualism, but the process was troubled. Lexis was tricky. At home it was 'the lav', elsewhere 'lavatory'. At home 'serviette', abroad 'table-napkin'. But this sort of thing was nothing to the social revolution that occurred after the blitz, when I went to stay with the Sumners in West Cross, for three months. You ate pudding, which was called pudding, neither 'afters' nor 'dessert', with a fork. You actually got a spoon and fork, facing opposite ways, but only ever used the fork. You had side-plates, and ate not drank, soup, elegantly moving your spoon forwards, to sip soup from its side. That was all quickly learnt, even to using a fork for floppy jelly. Everyone politely passed bread, salt and pepper. Nobody grabbed. The only criticism of the food was Mr Sumner's distaste for the meatlessness of Lord Woolton pie, a delicious mix of potatoes, carrots, cauliflower and onion in white sauce, covered with pastry. The beautiful cycle of middle-class domestic routine unfolded itself. There was a proper bathroom, of course. Everyone had a bath every other day, as a war-time economy (saving fuel), instead of every day. Rooms were dusted every day, and I helped, wiping the top of the door and its panels, in a way I've never done before or since. Beds were made exquisitely, with hospital corners, and I was initiated into the rotation of sheets, in which the upper sheet becomes the lower and the lower goes to the wash. I adopted this cycle until they invented the fitted sheet. There were no slops to empty, because there was an indoor lavatory.

When I moved back it was to better things. The new house, 28 The Grove, Uplands, also had indoor sanitation, which Ron declared to be unhealthy. I was climbing. I began to have more frequent baths and to lay forks as well as spoons for our afters, though no one took any notice of them. I couldn't bring myself to say pudding, but settled for sweet, with gentility. My grandfather's awful manners, exaggerated by his robust, or crude, humour, made it difficult for me to ask posh friends back, but I did, once or twice, and to my amazement they didn't tease or ostracize me. I discovered that Margaret Hartshorne called her grandmother Nana, like us, even though her father was a university lecturer. She got teased about it by a superior friend, because she was honest and used the term at school, while I knew better and spoke about my grandmother, evasively and with a schooled enunciation. I could have placed all my friends and their families in the right class, though I didn't use the terms. Sheila and Glenys and Dilys and even Valerie, despite big house and bathroom, were lower-middle, fringing on working-class. Hilary, Dora, Christine, Margaret Hartshorne and Margaret Kydd, and Gwenhwyfr and Dwynwen Davies, the daughters of the Director of Education – whose hands were hairy but smelt of eau-de-Cologne as he spread them on my desk during a visit – were middle-class.

It wasn't all shame and affectation. I fell in love with the comfort and the culture as well as the forks and rotation of sheets. Mrs Sumner was quietly elegant, informal and allusive, a bit like Peggy Ashcroft as Glenda Jackson's mother in *Sunday, Bloody Sunday*. She referred to T.S. Eliot casually, saying she found him difficult. How marvellous to have a mother who not only read him but could say, easily, with a shrug, 'I'm afraid he's a bit obscure for my taste.' She took *Time and Tide*, read book reviews, subscribed to Boots Lending Library. Bob Sumner, red-faced, genial, coarser-grained but socially less daunting, was teaching himself the piano and when I stayed with them I used to follow his halting, patient renderings of Brahms and Chopin. The Sumners had family jokes about things I was ashamed to mention, like the water-marks on the bath. And there were books everywhere, modern poetry, modern novels, stories by Saki, magazines, books on science, books on current affairs, books by D.H. Lawrence, Katherine Mansfield, E.M. Forster, lying about in piles, picked up, glanced at, thrown down, talked about. It was all taken for granted. That wonderful casualness and unself-consciousness was what I most admired and longed for.

Chapter 9
A Pact with the Devil

I must have been sixteen when I made my pact with the Devil. I'd like to put it earlier, but when I check memories against facts, I have to date it in the summer of 1941. I summoned up the Devil in a lavatory with red-papered walls, in the Uplands house we moved to after the three-night Swansea blitz. It was the first time we'd had an indoor lavatory. In Cradock Street the lavatory was at the bottom of the garden, with a big plank seat and a rambling rose to screen the door. There was a nail on the whitewashed stone wall, and a string of torn-up newspaper. When my grandmother died, my mother asked the doctor about causes of cancer, and he said using newspaper was insanitary, so we changed to real toilet-paper on a roll. I loved the old lavatory. It was my sanctuary, the room of my own. A seat for dreams and meditations. One of my private games was 'Him and His Brother', played with my two hands. Thumb and little finger were arms, first and third finger legs, and the middle finger not a penis, as you might suppose, but tucked up out of the way. The hands used to walk, dance, fly and have long conversations. Every now and then someone coming up to the lavatory would hear dialogue and wonder if I was 'all there' or 'quite right in the head', but my mother was reassured when I told her that it was only 'Him and His Brother', my companions and characters. I continued the habit of plays and stories when we moved, so it seemed natural to call up the Devil in the lavatory, though I had thought I'd finished with God a few months before we moved, on the third night of the raids in February 1941.

We used to take shelter in the coal-cellar, reluctantly getting out of bed when the wail of the warning sounded. I remember extreme fatigue, not fear. We would sit on the cellar steps until we heard Jerry planes, distinguishable even to a child's ear by their steady, unrhythmical drone, and then we'd go down into the cellar space. This was normally used for the gas meters, the crates of pop, ginger ale, and dandelion-and-burdock sent every week by Manny Thomas, my grandfather's oldest customer, to be swigged from the bottle from time to time, and unhygienically for my grandfather's yeast, scales and slicing-board. And the coal. As the bombs came down, my mother would keep nipping into the back garden to look at the Messerschmitts and the Spitfires and the searchlights and the glow of burning buildings. I decided to tell God I no longer believed in him, much as I wanted to in the middle of an air raid. So I did, silently but defiantly.

We'd heard Lord Haw-Haw on the wireless earlier that evening, drawling in his simulated posh English voice that Swansea was going to get it for the third night running. We didn't know then that the posh voice was phoney. When I discovered this, in Rebecca West's book, *The Meaning of Treason*, I was indignant that her clever narrative ignored the horror and power of his broadcasts, as if she had never talked to any of his victim listeners. My little brother Bill looked at the clock, as the hands came round to the time of the warning the night before, and the night before that, and he started to cry. It was the only time anyone in the family had shown any emotion, except for tiredness and curiosity. My mother exclaimed in love and fear. I cried too. We were all upset. Lord Haw-Haw's horrid gloating had toppled our morale. He was a foul herald. It was not a good time to declare disbelief, but I was brave. 'I no longer believe in God,' I announced, to the void.

I had a nasty feeling after my announcement that God might have his knife into us. We might be blown up and it would all be my fault for suggesting that he didn't exist. To my relief, he made no sign. We were not amongst the victims of direct hits by high explosives or land-mines or incendiary bombs. But the roof and windows and walls took a battering. Dynevor and Delabache Schools, at the bottom of our street, were destroyed. A bomb fell on the chapel at the top of the street, Mount Zion (since hideously rebuilt), and my mother decided to look for another house to rent a bit further away from the flattened town centre. All the big stores were gone, Ben Evans, David Evans, Lewis Lewis, Woolworths and the rest. They were more than shops. Every Christmas Grandpa would come in from his yeast round, or a visit to his favourite pub, Number Ten, saying, in awed tones, 'What d'you think? Who'd you think I met in Oxford Street asking if you were good? Well... there was Mr Lewis Lewis, Mr Ben Evans, Mr Edward the Eagle, Mr MacCoward', a long list of all the big kind Swansea shop-owners who might have toys for us.

That address to God in the cellar seemed truly final, but faith's a funny thing. I was too old to be dithering about religion, but my belief kept coming and going even after the decision in the blitz. Even after the move, another turning-point. Having an indoor lavatory, and a bathroom with a real, if scabby, bath, was a big move up the social scale, and I'd be able to have Christine Palmer and Margaret Hartshorne to tea without praying that they would never want to go to the lavatory. But I still believed in God, on and off, when I decided to talk to the Devil, with the old feelings of doubt and courage. I couldn't have done it if I really believed, or if I really disbelieved. It was silly, but solemn too.

There were so many things I wanted. I never thought of asking the Devil to stop the war, or bring about the Good Society. These requests were too huge. I wanted more personal changes, I wanted to get away from Wales, and my relations, and religion. To have fitted carpets instead of oilcloth, and hundreds of books in white-painted shelves all round the walls, like Hilary and Margaret, and a bedroom of my own. To be a writer of plays, perhaps a poet. To have a boy-friend as handsome and sexy as Rob, but intellectual, musical and a communist. I invented a lover called Angus, who had green eyes, a Scots accent, a career as a novelist and a cottage in Gower. He was the hero of a romance I used to tell my friend Sheila Norman. She was not especially gullible, but she had a large family of cousins who lived in Cromer, and used to tell me their family saga, which I thought contained many improbable and exotic details, so I knew she wouldn't doubt the existence of Angus. I felt guilty about making up a fantasy lover when I actually had a satisfactory boy-friend, having heard of Freud and knowing that only deprivation could justify such lies. I didn't feel repressed, but I longed to meet a real writer. If the Devil accepted my offer I would go to London where the streets were thick with poets. I had met one, Peter Hellings, son of my mother's friend Dorry. He wore a green pork-pie hat and had had a poem accepted by *Life and Letters*. And there was Mother's legend about her hymn-writing grandfather, and Uncle Jim's belief that we were descended from Richard Blackmore, author of *Lorna Doone*. My grandfather's father had come across the Bristol Channel from Devon to get a job in the tin-plate or copper works in the Hafod, so that sounded plausible. Jim was the family intellectual, dead now, my grandfather's clever brother who had perfected his French by going on holiday to Normandy and making friends with a Frenchman and his wife who came to stay and speak French with him. He had been the French master in the old Dynevor School (Mun. Sec.), though he never went to college. His son Leslie, also a teacher, was said to have gone to one of the Welsh colleges, but I never met any of them, though Mother was given a paper-knife with a Moor's head belonging to Leslie, which I still have. There is a family legend that Leslie was so brilliant that Alfred Mond, MP for Swansea (and later Lord Melchett), wanted him to be his private secretary. Leslie was the first person I heard of being cremated, and his ashes were scattered into the sea at Three Cliffs or Tor Bay. I didn't know any writers, and I didn't know anyone who'd been to college, and I didn't know the way.

So I said to the Devil: 'If you're there, if you really exist, I'm willing to make a pact with you. Give me all the things I want, now and later on, and when I die you can have my soul.' No answer. I had not spoken out loud to God in the cellar because my grandfather and brother were down there with me, but this time I spoke the words, though I kept my voice down. It seemed more formal to speak. It showed I meant it and wasn't just thinking. It was quiet. The sun was shining through the transparent blue paper peeling off the high-up lavatory window as I waited. I hadn't expected a manifestation with horns and a tail and flames, of course. His non-appearance and his silence didn't prove anything. He'd be a modern devil, my devil, nice and stealthy. It was very quiet. I couldn't hear Uncle Ron singing 'The Isle of Capri' or 'Oh Play to me, Gypsy', or my brother practising Rubinstein's Minuet in G on the piano, or my grandfather listening to *Workers' Playtime* or the cricket, or the dog barking. I waited a bit longer. I didn't believe in the soul anyway. It was much harder to imagine than the Devil.

As I have said, we were Baptists, but contrary to what most people think, we were never taught much about hell and the Devil. From the age of three to the age of sixteen I went three times every Sunday, morning, afternoon, and evening, to Mount Pleasant Chapel. There was a children's service, Sunday School, and proper chapel services. I grew up thinking everyone went to chapel, though I discovered that not everybody got baptized when they were adolescent, or older, like us. Uncle Walter played the organ in Argyll Chapel, and they were Calvinistic Methodists, it said on the poster outside. He had also been the assistant organist in our chapel, where the organist was Arthur Easter Evans. But I didn't know what the differences were, nor about any other denominations and beliefs, until Uncle Ron got engaged, or nearly engaged, to the beautiful, glamorous, peroxide blonde called Rose. They broke it off because she was Roman Catholic and he wouldn't sign a paper saying their children would all be brought up Roman Catholics. (He postponed his marriage, to Kitty, until he was well over forty, very old for a Welshman to marry, and ended up the only one of the Abraham children not to have any children.) When I grew up and read about the Anabaptists, or when people asked me about my strict upbringing and what Baptists believed, I realized we had heard nothing at all about dogmas and doctrines from any of our ministers. Once a year or so there was a baptism ceremony, when the floorboards under the choir were taken up, to reveal the big tile-lined tank. Adult baptism was taken for granted. When I found out that Anglicans baptized little babies, in a ceremony called christening, it seemed very peculiar, positively perverted. There was a certain amount about heaven and hell in our hymns and prayers and sermons but no details. We had very long prayers and very long sermons, but lovely tuneful hymns, with the men and women singing different parts – wonderful in 'Bread of Heaven... Feed me till I want no more'. And we had all the thrilling Old Testament stories. My favourite was Joseph's coat of many colours, his parents' romantic love, jealous brothers, brilliant Egyptian career, Potiphar's seductive wife, good and bad dreams, and family reunion. Everything was there, long before the Victorian novel, family relations, sex, work and visions. Then there was lucky baby Moses in the bulrushes, the devoted and persistent young Samuel, clever Gideon, David and Goliath, Ruth the model daughter-in-law. They were all interesting, mostly successful, and lots of them were children, to be loved along with Robinson Crusoe, Maggie Tulliver, Uncle Tom, Jo March, David Copperfield and Anne of Green Gables. There was Jesus, too, but not a lot about God. I read Marlowe, but never saw his so-modern Devil on the stage till I was quite old. The Devil was there, though, in the family sayings. There was Leah, his stirring-stick, and anyone told 'Don't stir', knew the rest. Naughty children, usually boys, were addressed as 'Devilskin'. When the potatoes were squashy or hard, the meat tough or the cake burnt, my grandfather or one of my uncles would nod rudely at my grandmother or my mother, with 'God sent the food and the Devil sent the cook'. If somebody was promoted to bank manager or headmaster or left a pile of money, the knowing would affirm 'The Devil looks after his own'. He was there, round the corner of every day. When I stole from Bill's money-box I had qualms about eternal punishment and hell-fire, though the prospects of torment were remote compared with money for sweets.

There was one occasion when nemesis struck, though I framed the event in terms of biblical not Greek moral significance. I was performing my criminal routine of lying back on my mother's blue silk eiderdown and sliding a broad kitchen knife into the mouth of Bill's well-filled money-box, expecting a penny or two, when I was amazed by a rush of coin, several pennies and a silver half-crown. My haul was usually copper though I occasionally slipped one of the threepenny or sixpenny bits my grandmother left on the mantelpiece under a brass candlestick, to be retrieved if it was still there after a day or two, in what I thought of as a sporting spirit. And I had once taken a half-crown from Iris's handbag, to be mortally stricken when she found the loss and lamented her carelessness. But generally speaking, I stuck to small coin, which seemed, like small slaughtered animals, to reduce the sin. I knew I should return the big silver coin but it winked temptingly and I fell. I took the money to our nearest sweetshop and blued the lot on a chocolate miscellany. I carried this off to the attic and devoured it all, leaving to the last a new untasted delicacy, Cadbury's – or perhaps Rowntree's – peppermint crisp. Already full of stolen sweets, I took a bite. It was disgusting. But I was stuck with the bitten bar, its green honeycomb revoltingly exposed. If I took it through the house up to the lavatory at the end of the garden, somebody might intercept me and find the booty. The outside dustbin would be too risky. So I had to eat it, hateful though the taste was. I spent an evening feeling, but not being, sick. 'Are you sickening for something?' my mother wondered. To this day I have a qualm when I eat After Eights. The combination of chocolate and mint is unhallowed. I'd had a message from God, who sees everything.

I was baptized after my rejection of God in the cellar and my pact with the Devil in the lavatory. Total immersion was a last gamble, a daregod-daredevil throw of the dice, kill or cure. We threw dice only for Monopoly or Ludo or snakes and ladders, but my uncles and grandfather gambled, playing nap and solo, smoking Woodbines and Players and Kensitas, talking about unemployment and war, till the war came. Bill and I would hang around, watching the game, slowly unscrambling the language, discovering that 'muzair' was *Misère* and 'muzairavair' was *Misère ouvert,* hoping for pennies from the winners, gazing at the kitty, a growing pile of copper and silver. It might go to anybody. I knew about gambling.

Another reason for getting baptized was the sexy minister, the Reverend Something Pollock, MA Cantab. He preached in a black gown with a white hood, and was dark, handsome, sharp-featured, keen-eyed and English. Mount Pleasant went in for somewhat classy intellectuals from across the border. Pollock's predecessor had been a mild Scot, the Reverend Something Maclaren Cook, who preached dullish sermons, in an appealing burr, and was declared by the congregation to be a really good man. Pollock was nervy, quick and eloquent. Not everyone liked him. There was an old man who used to sit in the front row of the gallery, groaning or rhapsodizing, as the spirit and the preacher moved him. 'Praise the Lord,' he'd shout, 'Yea, yea', or 'Amen'. It was the nearest we got to shouting or audience participation in the middle-class chapel. The Hwyl was something you read about in books, or met in tales of Welsh-speaking chapels. Pollock would hesitate in his flow, looking sharply up at the enthusiast. And as soon as the new minister had settled down, the old man stopped coming. The enthusiasm had been officially discouraged. I was sorry but I still fancied Pollock.

We went to Pollock's baptism class once a week, about six of us, all between fifteen and eighteen. He told us he had been trained to perform the immersion, using a special hold, dipping and lifting weights up to twenty stone. I loved asking questions in the classes, and looked forward, ecstatically, to submission and submersion in a long white robe. The girls wore white, the boys black. But on the night it was disappointing. I was embarrassed because I hadn't brought any collection money, having no purse and no pockets in the angelic garment, and when I was lifted out of the waters and the congregation cried 'Hallelujah' three times, I was humiliated. But not excited. I hadn't expected tepid water. And what was I doing this for, after I'd told God he didn't exist? I was led solemnly and slow-ly down the aisle, dripping, into the vestry, by Sister Phoebe, the deaconess. She was a tiny woman in a navy-blue, nunlike veil and long dress, who always looked sad and spoke in a thin, quavering, holy voice. I stood foolishly in a zinc tub, to be dried by my mother, then go home with straight damp hair, in a sulky mood.

I went to chapel only once after that, to a service held about a month later when the recently baptized took communion and had their names read out, with a special text allocated. My text was 'Let this mind be in you which is also in Christ Jesus'. Though I was leaving for ever I felt a slight gratification that Pollock had chosen a text with the word 'mind' in it, for me. But when I left the fold, quietly, without a word of farewell, just staying away from chapel, he never made a move to reclaim me. Once at a Revivalist meeting – a rare event in Mount Pleasant – after a visiting Evangelist had spoken with fire and faith and fury, and we had all been asked to come forward and witness, declaring our faith, I stood up and said bossily that I didn't see the point of making a special declaration in a highly emotional state and wouldn't it be better to wait till we'd cooled down? Pollock gave me a dirty look as I subsided after my priggish speech, and I'm proud to relate that none of the younger set rushed to bear witness. So perhaps he was too sensible to try to persuade me back. And perhaps his own faith was a bit tottery.

Long afterwards we heard he'd left the Baptist Church, had a nervous breakdown, a divorce, and a job with some MP. This four-act drama may have been an expansion or a variation of the truth. He was an attractive, talented and intelligent man, a type they won't be getting in the Baptists these days, and some of my problems were no doubt close to his own. He left the remonstrances and pleas to Sister Phoebe, who showed up one evening on our front doorstep. I'm afraid I kept her there, afraid that once I let her in we'd be all night praying. 'What will you do, Barbara?' she asked in that little high voice, every 'r' in my name given a full trill in her plaintive, un-Welsh voice. 'What will support and help you to lead the moral life?' It wasn't a bad question. I was less confident than I sounded as I assured her of the strength of my humanist ethic, and belief in the fellowship of the human race.

I used to mimic Sister Phoebe, but when Pollock had pleaded a previous engagement and couldn't officiate at my grandmother's funeral, Sister Phoebe, whom Nana loved, did it instead. My mother said angrily that she was a better Christian than that old Pollock. She told me that Phoebe came from a small village in Cornwall, and had told her that when she was a little girl she always wore a red cloak and had a big dog. But I couldn't believe in her childhood. In her dark deaconess's garb she seemed one of the oldest people I knew.

I looked down on Sister Phoebe, and on my Sunday School teacher, Dilys Griffiths, a kind, plain woman, with hair screwed into a mousy bun, and a sweet, anxious expression. She told my mother that she dreaded my questions, so I worked harder at them. I particularly liked spotting the discrepancies between the Gospels, and worrying at the textual cruces. Intellectual and sexual snob that I was, I preferred Pollock to the worthy dull women. He and his good-looking wife were important role-models, as I suffered and struggled with social discontents and cultural deprivation.

The Pollocks held a discussion group for the Youth Club in their comfortable Sketty semi-detached house, providing talk, milky coffee, and scones or biscuits in a cream-carpeted lounge with thick folk-weave curtains and pale linen-covered chairs and sofa. Mrs Pollock was as dark and attractive and glamorous as her husband. She opened my eyes to nuances of social behaviour, telling me that women didn't get up as men came into a room, when I eagerly scrambled to my feet to greet the boys. I learnt that in some circles men got up for women, an eye-opener. In our family my grandfather usually occupied the only comfortable chair in the kitchen, and my uncles would make a dash for any empty chair and only get up to eat or go to bed or wash noisily in the back kitchen, or later on in the bathroom. When they brought their girls or wives home, I never noticed anyone opening a door or offering a seat. Women bobbed up and down all the time to wait on the men, who got the best seats and the biggest helping, and in peace and war, most of the meat. Perhaps my mother owed her long life to her wartime sacrifices of meat rations to the men and children. Lower-middle-class family life was warm, noisy and rough-mannered. My grandmother and mother would criticize people (usually men) for bad manners. 'Ignorant', they would say, or 'the pig', or 'Greenhill manners' or 'He was dragged up', or '*Ach-y-fi*'. Children were taught to say please and thank you ('What do you say?'), not to put their elbows on the table and not to take food in their fingers, though Grandpa or Ron might defy the rules and say: 'Fingers were made before knives and forks.' The Pollocks offered middle-class manners, mixed company, religion and conversation. Four wonders of the world in a posh house. This was life. Its greatest wonder was conversation.

Everyone talked at home, but this was different. This was discussion. This was like the arguments in Aldous Huxley's novels. The first time I spoke in public was in the Pollocks' sitting-room. The naming of rooms was so important that I can't believe I've forgotten what they called it. Perhaps it was the drawing-room. We said 'front room' or 'front parlour'. Nana and Grandpa said 'the parlour'. Iris and Gilbert had a 'lounge'. I still call my sitting-room by several names. In whatever the room was called we sat round, Swansea boys and girls, high on ideas and talk, especially talk. A raffish boy called Don, who seemed to me straight out of Noel Coward, though dressed in the uniform of Swansea boys, sports coat (tweed) and grey trousers (flannel), posed some shocking question about the effect of alcohol on belief, or perhaps on prayer. My first contribution to public discussion was the priggish proposition that a Christian might not get drunk in the first place. At the time it seemed the perfect answer. Whatever my words were, they did not slip out quick as a flash and witty too. The gap between Don's sentence and mine must have been brief, but seemed endless. I contemplated my reply, rehearsed it silently, and heard my heart beating so loud that I looked round to see the reaction of my friends. Everyone must hear that thunderous pounding. As I opened my mouth, slowly, I expected to faint, or become speechless. But I said it, the heartbeat slowly quietened down, and the hot blushes cooled. I began to recognize the sensation of triumph. Pollock nodded approval. Don shrugged. From now on I could speak in a group, put in my word, reply, disagree or go one better. I had crossed a boundary.

Sometimes sitting in the group seemed unreal. I found you could wind up that unreality feeling until you were on the verge of extinction. You kept repeating to yourself that the present wasn't happening, and the feeling grew and grew. But you always stopped just in time. I can still repeat the exercise, a kind of meditation, in meetings or talks or parties. It is not experienced alone. It is asserting yourself, when other people are strongly present, but it is also a withdrawing. The other psychic trick I acquired in the group was familiar and crude. It took the form of imagining violent interruption, swearing or blaspheming or saying something obscene. Again, you said it over and over until it almost happened. Almost but not quite.

We looked at each other, up and down. It was conversation with sex present. Don was the young-man-about-Swansea. There was a fat, cynical character called Percy. Then there was Dudley Leeker, exempt from National Service because of polio, then called infantile paralysis. He was tall, handsome, intelligent, with a leg in irons for a while. He had a tall, handsome, intelligent girl-friend, and he was the first young man I found attractive but not desirable, object of a friendly warmth. He said he'd get baptized with me, but he stayed a believer much longer, for ever for all I know. I remember trying to explain to him and his girl that I was losing my faith because I'd fallen in love, and found love much stronger than any religious emotion. They seemed interested in the idea, which developed as I spoke. It was only partly true. I was improvising. I had no idea how to explain the loss of God. I hadn't gone through a crisis of science or scholarship, like a Victorian agnostic. Faith had always been weak, something you felt you were feeling because you said your prayers and sang hymns about it. Of course love was more interesting. Not to mention sex.

One member of our group was my friend and mentor, Glenys James, authority on sex, culture and life in London. It was she who told me that we were all flocking round the minister because of his sex appeal. She had a cousin who wrote a column for the *Daily Mirror*, and from time to time he'd come to stay with her and her grandfather in their house in Cromwell Street. One day she announced she'd been to bed with him. It was for experience. She added, mysteriously, that they'd decided she should keep her virginity. It was all so far beyond anything I'd thought, felt, read or been told that I couldn't begin to frame my questions. Another time I was talking about a boy I rather liked. He was my first date. We went to see *The Boys from Syracuse*, which I found boring, then walked home with Alan holding my upper arm and elbow in a strange grip. No kiss, and no further date. I said he was rather nice, and Glenys said, at random, or to introduce another sexual subject I wouldn't know about, 'Yes, he wouldn't practise masturbation.' I rose: 'What's that?' 'Sometimes it's called onanism.' I dashed straight home to Uncle Ron's red fake-leather *Modern English Dictionary* which he used, with *Roget's Thesaurus*, for doing 'Bullets', a witty-word competition run by *John Bull*, in which they supplied the first phrase, as it might be, 'Peace in Our Time', and the competitor the punch-line, strictly limited to six: or eight words, as it might be, 'but a time bomb for Hitler'. Ron and my mother used to do 'Bullets' and sometimes won small cash prizes. There were even experts who would do them for you, at a price. I found 'masturbation' and the entry indeed said 'onanism'. But when I turned to 'onanism' I was sent back to 'masturbation'. Consulting another dictionary in our form library at school, I found 'self-abuse', but was none the wiser. Then someone directed me to Onan, hero of onanism and of Genesis, Chapter 38, which I turned up expectantly, to find an obscure story about a man who spilt his seeds before going in to see a girl, because he didn't want to raise up seeds to his father. Another dead end.

I went on drinking in Glenys's words. She patronized me, using hard words that hid sexual mysteries, giving me low marks for 'sensuousness' in the *Weekend Book*'s game of 'Qualities', then explaining the difference between sensuousness and sensuality, which did little to soften the blow. She advised me not to cross my legs so high, at the thigh, because Don had asked her if I was a virgin. She also patronized Don, telling me he was trying to present himself as a rake, which I dare say was true, and looking down on the whole gang as provincial and dowdy. She was the one who lent me Huxley and Lawrence, and told me about Freud. She was a clever girl, and like so many clever girls at the time, even in educationally ambitious Wales, had no one to push her into higher education. She left school at sixteen to go into an office. I met her only once afterwards, just when I'd decided to get married, in the gap between being called up for work of National Importance, in my case, death duties, and going back to finish my degree. She was still one up on me, despite my university experience and my engagement. Sophisticated as ever, she didn't congratulate me, as provincial girls always did, but smiled faintly: 'You do sound a bit doubtful.' Her presence must have bred irony or plain uncertainty in my announcement. 'I wouldn't rush into anything, if I were you.' I had the advantage of a deprived and ambitious mother. Glenys was an orphan, living with her grandfather, who had brought her up. Like me, she seemed shy of inviting friends home, but once when I called for her to go for a walk, her grandfather asked me if I liked poetry. I fell into the trap, and we sat down in their front room to listen to a recitation of Edgar Allan Poe's 'The Raven', which lost nothing of its gloom, length and monotony in Mr James's slow, sonorous rendering. Glenys was never dull, always on to some new idea or writer or fact. A plain girl with a rather pink long nose, a slim figure, and long legs which she told me were good legs, she said, 'Of course I'm not pretty, but my cousin says I've got sex appeal, and that's what matters.' Another grown-up mystery, like masturbation.

I'd been masturbating for years but had no idea that what I did had a name, let alone several illustrious ones. One night I'd been unnerved by a strong little spasm as I sleepily explored cracks and crevices. For years I used to concentrate on my eyes, trying the effects of squeezing the eyeball, looking at light and after-images, rolling the eye round to see the red flashes of retina. Moving to the other end of the body didn't seem very different, until I got that little shock. I thought I'd damaged something, but after a couple of weeks with no after-effects I tried again, to find the sensation repeatable and pleasurable. Nobody told me about it, or warned me about what used to be called forbidden pleasure, so I didn't think I'd go mad or fall into a decline. It did seem furtive, and in some way not quite right, especially when it eventually got joined up with the masochistic fantasies I'd had as long as I can remember, since I was an infant. Vampire stories, nightmares about killing monsters that kept on resurrecting, unexpected spasms in places you didn't show in public, cruel guardians fattening or starving children in cages and pigsties, and nasty, big boys pulling down your knickers – all that was sex. Sex had nothing to do with falling in love. Not for years and years. When Glenys asked, 'Do you know what you're doing when you cross your thighs?' I said coolly, 'Of course', to show off. I hadn't known I was crossing my legs high up, why anyone should notice, or what that had to do with being a virgin. 'What is a virgin?' I asked Miss Mountford in a history class, when we were doing the reign of Queen Elizabeth, not yet called the first. 'An unmarried woman,' she said briskly, and got on with the lesson. I used to wonder what it would be like to lose one's virginity, both before and after I thought I knew what it meant, but it was a few years before I found out that I'd lost it without knowing, all on my own.

I may not have known about virginity, but I knew about love. When I was five or six, Auntie Leah told me that her husband's nephew Walter, Betty's cousin but not mine, was my little sweetheart. He was dark, brown-eyed and handsome. He and his sister Enid both had polio, and wore leg-irons for years. I was happy to receive his verses, 'Roses are red, violets blue, / Carnations are sweet and so are you', which I thought he had cleverly composed. A year or two later I was pursued by another good-looker, a little boy in my class called Reggie Cooper. I

liked his curly hair and bold declarations of love, but I was terrified as he followed me home from school every afternoon,
and decided to make myself unattractive. I spent my pocket-
money on a sixpenny pair of empty spectacle frames from
Woolworths, putting them on next time he came after me down
Primrose Hill. It worked only too well. He turned to his friend
and shouted disgustedly, 'She's got glasses!' I took them off,
laughed loudly, and kicked the frames along the pavement.
Then I was terrified again, chiefly of someone in the family seeing Reggie and his friend, when they followed me all the way
home and sat down on our railings, outside 22 Cradock Street.
I crept into my grandparents' front bedroom at intervals during the late afternoon to see if they'd gone, but the boys stayed
for an hour or two before giving up and going home. Of course
they wouldn't have dared to ring the bell.

I loved Reggie Cooper at a safe distance, and fantasized
about our future as I sat in the lavatory, in peace and quiet.
When I grew up I would have a red sports car and immortalize
my love for Reggie, whose exact place in the story was vague
even then, by having RC as a registration number. (A knowl-
edgeable friend told me you couldn't choose, but I was
anticipating vanity plates, as I realized long afterwards when
shown them on a car in New England.) My love for Reggie
would always be unspoken, but I would have lots of affairs. I
would wear a lot of black and drive very fast. The Devil would
look after his own. I'd be rich, sophisticated, independent and
successful. I hadn't decided whether to be an actress, a drama-
tist or a politician. I had drafted the beginning of a play about
a clever Welsh girl who was ashamed of her family. It was written in a highly coloured South Welsh dialect and modelled on
Emlyn Williams's *The Corn Is Green*, which I'd seen at the
Grand Theatre. If I went in for politics, it would be communist
or pacifist, or both. The reason I hung on to Jesus Christ, after
losing my faith permanently, was political. Jesus was more solid,
more alive and more individual than God or the Devil, who were
only abstract ideas. That was why you could talk to them,
whether you believed in them or not. Jesus was too much of a

character for such roles. He was my hero, because I was a pacifist and a socialist, and he was on our side. We enjoyed those Old Testament stories which were as good as fairy-tales and novels, but we studied the life of Jesus, with the particulars of each miracle and parable and disciple, in great detail, for the annual scripture examination, run by the Sunday School Union. This was a great boon to a book-lover, because if you did well you got one prize from the Sunday School Union, and another from your own Sunday School. That's how I started my library. 'Buy a classic,' my mother advised as I hankered after *The Best Bat in the School*, choosing the prize in Wayne's Bookshop.

My only bad mark for English – really bad, it might have been as low as C minus – was for an impassioned essay written on the set theme, 'To Love Nothing Better than Your Country Is to Make It Unworthy to Be Loved'. My essay combined pacifism and militant Welsh nationalism. I went to pacifist meetings and read pacifist literature, but I had never met any Welsh nationalists. I don't know how I brought together the Peace Pledge Union and Plaid Cymru, but I did my best. In one terrific paragraph I mocked the Christian warmongers in a derisive image of Christ driving an armoured tank. After one burst of high style, I abused my history teachers for telling us all about past national heroes, like Owain Glyndwr, while never mentioning modern times and the name of Saunders Lewis. Nansi Evans, our revered English teacher, a more reticent and less right-wing Miss Brodie, disfigured my rhetorical sincerities with her slashing red pencil. I was summoned to see her outside the staff-room, after school. I was cheap, journalistic, self-indulgent, guilty of clichés and purple patches. I was unfair to Miss Stewart and Miss Lewis, who would be delighted to talk to me about Welsh nationalism, if only I asked. I discovered, as I picked up the pieces of a writer's pride from the dust of the High School corridor, that strong passions might lead to bad rhetoric. There was even sin in style. So I returned to more orthodox writing, and got As again. We hardly ever wrote general essays any more, being diverted by examination goals into literary criticism, which I detested for a month, then adopted with enthusiasm.

The Devil was beckoning me along that rough track that leads to high honour, and closely resembles the primrose path.

There was no place for the Devil in my school essays. I'd met him in all those family sayings and wise tags, once or twice in more gruesome appearances. I'd seen a copy of a famous religious picture, showing a pious woman praying in chapel, with checked flannel shawl and high black hat, like the costume worn by the girls from really Welsh families on St David's Day. When you looked hard at the folds of her shawl and the arm bent to hold the Bible, you could make out the features of the Devil. Another nasty religious shock was in store when you looked at a photograph given to all the Sunday School children by a missionary. It was a black-and-white picture of a garden, mostly hedge, and after a bit the face of Jesus would emerge from the foliage. I hated them both, dreamt about them, but couldn't resist taking the Jesus photograph out of the drawer.

But I couldn't believe in hell-fire, in spite of the fires of the blitz, part of the changed sky, lurid after bombs or raked with searchlight rays. I had seen a real fire when Archie Jenkins's artificial-limb warehouse caught alight, just opposite our house in Cradock Street, and my mother or an uncle held me up, wrapped in a blanket, to look and listen, a stone's throw from the blaze. All the arms and legs we used to gape at in his glass showcase must have burnt to crisps, we said afterwards. But it had been beautiful, pure spectacle, taking the fear out of hell-fire.

Other supernatural images, feared and desired, were in my grandfather's stories about his adventures in Pembrokeshire as a young baker. My favourite story was about his father, on his way home one dark night, on horseback. Tired, he stopped for a glass of ale at a country inn. He was invited to take a hand of whist with two men of his acquaintance, playing cards by the fireside with a stranger. After they'd been playing for half an hour or so – 'and drinking', my mother would insert – a card slipped from my great-grandfather's fingers as he was putting his hand in order. He leant down to pick it up, but as he did so he caught sight of the stranger's foot, just by his chair-leg, on the quarry-tiled floor. The stranger wasn't wearing a boot. And his foot wasn't a foot. It was a hoof. When I first heard the story I expected the dropped card to be the ace of spades, dreaded as the Death card by my mother and my grandmother, who hated to get it even though it meant a trick at whist. But Grandpa never said what card it was. His father put it back in its place, played out the hand, took out his watch, made his excuses, said goodbye, went out, untied the horse and rode away as fast as he could. As he set off he thought he heard the door slam again, and soon there were hoofbeats following, always at the same distance, never catching up with him. He galloped hard, got home and dismounted, to find the mare covered with foam. He dashed in, slamming the back door and collapsing into his chair – 'This very one I'm sitting in now.' My mother would look at my terrified expression, and inquire, 'And how much had he had to drink, then, I wonder?' I was always afraid to go to bed after the story, and even when I was safe under the sheets I would pray not to dream about the Devil. My mother eventually prohibited the story, but that simply lent a forbidden thrill to the secret telling and listening. When I heard it first I was so young I couldn't understand why the horse was covered in foam. And I was puzzled about the way the Devil kept his distance and was shut out of the house so easily. Why hadn't he overtaken my great-grandfather? Why hadn't he broken in the back door? Much older, I learnt that the Devil, like vampires and the Little People, must be invited over the threshold. That explained another of our family sayings, 'Come in, if you're good-looking', which I used to think was a joke about handsome visitors. It was a way of covering yourself, making an exception to the hospitable general invitation, questioning the anonymous knock at the door, barring the Devil's free entrance. Not much consolation to me. I hadn't even been sure I believed in the Devil when I invited him over the threshold. As I certainly had.

Chapter 10
Je Vous Aime

My first love was Haydn Watkins. Our love was sudden, intense, pure, then lost. When we met I was ten or eleven, either just before or after my first year in Swansea High School. Throughout the affair, I proudly wore my green blazer with that legend on its pocket, *The Journey of High Honour Lies Not in Smooth Ways*. Lightning struck at our annual Mount Pleasant Sunday School treat, in the little village of Penllegaer, a few miles outside the town and then very green and rural. Some time during that afternoon of sack races, flat races, relay races, egg-and-spoon races, obstacle races, and tea with potted meat, egg-and-cress sandwiches, seedcake, fruitcake, and of course bread and butter, one of my friends, Thelma Richards, brought me the message that Haydn wanted to be my boy. Many years later someone told me that what turned me on was being fallen in love with. That was certainly true the first time. Where there had been nothing there was pleasure, excitement and charm. My vacant virgin heart was occupied. We sat together in a pink cloud.

After the treat came the return to Swansea in the charabanc. Haydn and I sat on a back seat upstairs. We did not touch, and we were never to touch during the period of our love. We talked together while the tiny far-off others sang the songs that had been so mirthful and melodious on the road from Swansea to Penllegaer, 'One Man Went to Mow', 'Ten Green Bottles' and 'There Is a Tavern in the Town'. That tavern was to become a tragic image after our parting, but on the first journey it was mere distant music. As we drove through the Hafod, we passed an undertaker's glittering black-and-silver window with the best

200

coffin on display. Haydn, who was sitting next to the window, pointed and said: 'Before we've finished, you'll be getting them for me.' His meaning sank in. I was speechless with bliss. Love at first sight, then my first proposal, romantic, original, morbid, oblique and Welsh.

As I said, we never touched. It was true love. It stretched easily and sadly into that imagined death, which alone could part us. I don't think we were ever more alone together than on that road from Penllegaer to Mount Pleasant Chapel, where the coach stopped.

We started going together, as it was called. For us that meant going out for walks or to the park with a little gang of other eleven-year-olds, including one other couple who had become ßattached at the treat, Thelma and Bernard Smith. There was a girl from Sunday School called Barbara Nener, and one or two others. In the late summer and early autumn we flirted and joked and held off, hanging round the swings and roundabouts in Mayhill Park, half-way between Townhill, where Haydn lived, and our house in Cradock Street. Bernard lived on Mount Pleasant Hill and Thelma somewhere near Mayhill. Some snob said nastily that Haydn's family was common, and that his mother called him 'our 'Aydn'. My grandfather's aitches (called haitches by the illiterate Welshy poor) were erratic, and our family was just as lowly, but I felt a sense of social condescension as I forgave my beloved his humble origins. I loved his name. I had never heard of the composer and, when I first came across him, I simply thought he was Welsh and the boy and the musician shared common names. I didn't generalize the Welsh love of musical names for many years, until I was enlightened by a big beefy Welshman who played Rugby and was called Handel Jones.

I adored my Haydn. He was thin and pale, with chiselled features, as some book had taught me to call them, and an especially fine nose. One of his speech habits was to say 'Properly, now' instead of 'Really and truly' or 'Honest', and I enjoyed the first savouring of the beloved's mannerism. 'Properly, now' was his phrase, with his flavour. I would repeat it over and over in those sweet baskings in love in love's absence. I thought about him night and day, meditating on everything we'd said (not much) and done (even less) since the first meeting. Love thoughts woke me in the morning, sent me to sleep at night, and delighted me when I sat in my favourite seat, on Nana's fender in the kitchen, while the family chatted and argued and listened to the wireless, far away. I started to look forward to the meditations more than to the meetings, and years later when I read Proust's marvellous account of developing the images of love in the dark-room of imagination, I knew exactly what he meant. I had felt it all during that early unreal affection.

I thought about Haydn night and day, especially when he wasn't there. Slowly and surely I became bored with his presence. Our meetings were tainted with anti-climax, paling before the strength of retrospects and prospects. I began to be offhand and even rude. Then I began even to tire of those passionate pleasures of amorous reflection. One night I realized that my mother wasn't having to ask me four times if I'd like a banana or if I was enjoying my book. I was laughing at my brother's funny faces, and listening to the wireless instead of wrapping myself cosily and blissfully in the image of the loved one. Love was dying of malnutrition, at an alarming rate.

It died, to be cruelly resurrected. I discovered that other great truth about the shallowness of the heart's affections, and felt the futile nostalgia for what's gone and had to go, the intensity of remorse's renewal of love. When I read Thomas Hardy's elegies for his once-loved, once-hated, loved-again dead wife I knew all the symptoms. I had known them from the age of eleven.

One afternoon I forgot our date in the park. My mother had been invited to tea in Tycoch, with Renee, and I said I'd love to come, having refused all such family treats for weeks past in favour of Haydn. I was back to easy distraction. Love faded before the prospects of one of Renee's heavenly teas. She was an excellent cook, but her cuisine was chiefly valued by Bill and me for its one invariable feature, a glass cake-stand heaped with Eynon's pastries, cream slices, Viennese pastries and chocolate eclairs. Bill and I used to quarrel over them, because there was always only one of each, chosen in the shop from the window display, extracted by the girl with a pair of elegant silver tongs, then packed in a square white box, tied with silvery tape. My mother was ashamed of our rudeness, and we always promised not to argue about cakes again. We were famous for our quarrels, and deserved our reputation, fighting at every opportunity, with tooth and nail, open hands, fists, feet, swords, bayonets and a pair of carved African spears brought back from Kenya or the Gold Coast by Father. We were very quarrelsome children, they said. People quickly labelled children, like Jonsonian humours. I was greedy and selfish. Bill was a tease and sometimes mischievous. I was domestically idle. The labels were approving as well as disapproving. Bill was unselfish. That meant he never grabbed or snatched. I was honest. That meant I was never found out in a lie or a theft. I was a good liar, poker-faced. My mother told me that liars could never look you in the eye as they lied, so I practised hard, and proved her wrong. Nor did anybody discover that I was a chronic and cunning thief. But my notorious greed was my undoing. The Tycoch cream cakes swallowed up all recollections of our gang, Mayhill Park, love and Haydn.

Next day, either in Sunday School or on the road to High School, Thelma informed me that Haydn was finished with me. He was now going with Barbara Nener instead. It had been decided in the park while I was eating the chocolate eclair. The messenger added a cruel touch: 'And they sealed it with a kiss.' Rejection turned ennui into heart-break, in the twinkling of an eye. Lightning struck again, darkening the world. I was astonished to find that I was jilted, but more astonished to find that I was in love again. My rival was not only another Barbara, with another two-syllable surname beginning with N, but physically my opposite, a dark beauty with raven hair and brown eyes. At once she took her place in the song, which became, tragically, our song:

> He left me for a damsel dark, damsel dark,
> On Friday nights they used to spark, used to spark,

And now my love once true to me,
Takes that dark damsel on his knee.

This was heart-break, as famous as love at first sight. It last-
ed on and off, in calm and storm, for a couple of years, till I fell
in love again. The pang of rejection was sharpened by the sting
of remorse. If only I hadn't gone to tea with Auntie Renee. If
only I hadn't turned flirtation into rude banter. If only I hadn't
forgotten all about our date, and Haydn, for the whole
Saturday. And how could I have thought love was weakening?
It had never been stronger. A couple of days later I saw Haydn
walking towards me in Walter Road as I was coming home from
school. He passed, saying nothing, and pushed into my hand
the love-favour I had given him. It was the small, silvery heart
out of my lucky packet, with a hole for a chain, and the words,
'Who keeps this, keeps love always'. I dashed home, opened
and closed the front door quietly, and went straight into the
front room, to sob as silently as I could into the bristly leopard-
skin on the sofa, another of my father's trophies. I still have it,
and the silver heart.

My affection for Haydn led to another great lesson of sentimental education. Never go back. Trite but true. Haydn went
on after our pure, platonic friendship to become a small-town
Casanova. One of my friends told me he had acquired a reputation for being fast. In those days of course you could earn this
reputation for what came to be called, though not by us, heavy
petting. We called anything from holding hands to mutual masturbation 'necking', though usually we didn't call it anything,
and namelessness made it even more sweet and sinful and dangerous. Haydn was one of those fast boys. He had a string of
girl-friends, shot up in height, and grew even handsomer. We
never spoke if we passed in the street. Whenever I saw him I felt
a pang or two. My friend Glenys James told me a girl had told
her he'd taken her aside, on a walk with several others, and said:
'Let's forget the present and be happy.' I pondered on the
words and sighed jealously over the neat if obscurely worded
proposition. A few years later Haydn was going with a well-
dressed, well-off girl called Della Morgan, whom he eventually

married, and I had a steady boy-friend, Rob Sumner. One evening, Haydn asked me to go to the pictures. We'd been chatting with a group of friends after chapel, Della was on holiday, and Rob was away, having joined the Royal Engineers. Haydn and I went to a cinema called the Castle, and groped and kissed in the back row, as our past pure loving selves had never dared or desired to do. I refused to let him pay for my seat, as boys always did, saying coolly that it had been 'a convenient arrangement, not a real date'. I felt experienced, world-weary, complacent. That was the nail in the coffin.

Rob was my first proper boy-friend, though after Haydn I had several crushes on remote heroes. Rob was the first one who held my hand, the first one who kissed me, the first one who woke my desire, the first one who said 'I love you'. He said it in French, one night when we were hugging and kissing, in the guest-room in his house in West Cross, where I was staying. I had fancied him for some time. He had been Thelma Richards's boy-friend for a while, and used to come to Sunday evening chapel, all the way from West Cross, to go for a walk with her afterwards. His sister Hilary told me about it. Thelma was in the choir, and Rob sat in a pew downstairs. I would look at him looking at her, from my seat in the gallery. I applied the language of divine love, in our hymns, to profane love. 'Loved ones far away' expressed my sorrow about Haydn who was lost, then my interest in Rob who was another's. There was a lot about love in our hymn-book, plenty of longing, and hearts, and bosoms, and parting, and union. The double meanings made hymn-singing much more interesting. I discovered that if my eyes filled with tears, sensitized by some especially poignant hymn, its words of love and longing intensified by the organ and the mingle of male and female voices, my short-sighted vision was briefly improved, and I got a better view of Rob in his far-off pew.

Our first kiss took place one night after I had been to tea with Hilary. She had offered to walk down West Cross lane with me, to the Mumbles train stop, but erotic premonition stirred and I said I'd be all right on my own. I wasn't surprised when

Rob joined me just outside their house, Lanivet, and walked down the lane, taking my arm. We didn't speak. We waited for the train, standing by a shed or shelter, till he led me round the corner, took me in his arms, and we kissed. The journey back beside the sea, and the walk home to the Uplands by Brynmill lane was ecstatic. The kiss was isolated, and none the worse for that. A few months later when I went to stay in Lanivet after the blitz, I hoped for the best, though I had been a bit daunted when Hilary, from whom I'd kept the kiss a secret, told me Rob's current girl-friend worked in their father's office as a secretary, and was very smart. Her name was Joan. That meant she was grown-up, probably the same age as Rob, who was an articled surveyor's pupil, working in his father's firm until going into the Army.

At first nothing happened. I enjoyed sitting at the same table, and tried not to blush when his brother (Nick) and sisters (Hilary and Jean) teased him about his girl-friend. She had unusually large eyes, or some feature they found a proper subject of family banter. But one day he waylaid me on the landing and we kissed again. At first I shared a room with Hilary, because the spare room was needed for her grandmother. The grandmother, either Grannie, the maternal grandparent, or Grandma, the paternal one – enviably posh forms of address compared with the working-class 'Nana' – took her leave, and I had a room to myself. Rob would visit me when the house was quiet and everyone was asleep. They were a family who went to bed early and rose early, but before Rob dared turn my doorknob, an hour or so would pass. Bob Sumner, local estate agent and auctioneer, a red-faced, jovial, generous man, was teaching himself to play the piano. The last sounds of the evening were his slow, careful, gradually improving renderings of Chopin or Brahms. I remember 'Liebestraum' and 'Rustle of Spring'. I liked the melodies, but longed for them to stop and night to come.

It was a turret room, with an extra window in the corner, looking over the long garden. It was the first time I had ever had a room of my own, and the first time I had been sexually in love. Holding hands was arousing, embracing and kissing were amazing, I couldn't believe my luck. Rob told me he had stopped seeing the girl in the office. Then one night he said the words '*Je vous aime*'. I said nothing. We didn't talk much, and our exchanges were shyly confined to 'darlings'. I don't know why he said it in French, certainly not because either of us was linguistically proficient. It may have seemed more discreet, or more indiscreet. (I did wonder about the *vous*.) He may have been shy – I never asked him. I did worry a bit about the significance of its foreignness and asked Hilary, who still didn't know about us, if she thought it meant the same if someone said something to you in French instead of English.

'What sort of thing?'

'Well, *chérie* instead of darling, for instance.'

'Well, that's exactly the same.'

'Well, it wasn't that. Just something like that.'

'Like "*Je vous aime?*"'

'How did you know?'

'It was pretty obvious.'

And soon it was obvious that her best friend and her brother were a couple. But I wasn't certain if it would go on after I left. It had the gratuitous feel of an *amour de voyage*, even though it was the opposite, an *amour de la maison*.

Just before I left for the new house in the Uplands, Rob said 'Can I hope for some dates?' and I said 'Yes'. Hilary brought a note to school, and our three-year romance began. It soon went public, with visits to each other's houses. I don't think Rob's mother altogether approved, perhaps because he once took me back to tea in her absence. Once, Hilary told her that I'd gone to see a Will Hay film because Rob liked Will Hay, though I didn't, and Mrs Sumner had said, 'So she must care about him.' Incipient mother-in-law trouble, I reflected. I vaguely thought we would marry, though there was always a voice that said, to myself but also out loud, 'I'm not going to get married. I want a career.' My mother approved of this resolution, in a way, though she said she hoped I would marry some day. So every Wednesday and Friday or Saturday, Rob and I would sit and kiss on the front-room sofa, in the dark, when it was dark. It was better in the dark. We didn't talk much, our conversation being conducted mostly in loving murmurs. From time to time our dangerous games intensified. He would say 'I know what you want', and I would say 'No, I don't'. It's odd to think how your sex life is made by history. All the boys I went out with, or stayed in with, were boys who approached and solicited me. The first date, the first touch, the first declaration, were made by them. Once or twice in my life I asked a boy to dance, when I was a student, but when I did so it seemed very bold – 'brazen', as Nana would have said. If Rob and I had been born twenty years later, we'd have been lovers. Though we'd probably have ended up exactly as we did. My mother said she was a bit anxious about our spending all that time alone in the front room together. Bill occasionally looked in for his violin, accidentally or on purpose, but not often. Perhaps she sent him. I said I could take care of myself. I suppose that was true. We were dying to make love, but our class and education – and of course, to some extent, the place and circumstances – restrained us. I think it was the sense of home territory that was the sword between us. A year or two later, I slept with somebody I didn't care for at all, and wanted much less than I wanted Rob. It was half-hearted, a passive giving-in not to desire but to the pressure of several years of nearly and not quite doing it. And it happened because time and place pandered to instinct.

I was a pacifist, and Rob was called up, joining the Royal Engineers, but we never talked about war, or about any other political issues. I gave him an anthology of poetry, *Other Men's Flowers*, and he gave me book tokens, with which I bought two volumes of Housman. We were very nice to each other, held by sex and liking, so easily called love. Though it had the aphrodisiac charm of repeated stimulus and repeated fruition, our love-making couldn't support love in absence. So there was another death from malnutrition.

Rob was the boy next door, extremely nice, very attractive, in every way a good potential husband. We never talked about marriage but sometimes thought of our future together, and I was sad when I started to prefer someone else. I wrote the farewell letter, hating myself. We went on writing stiff little friendly letters, and from time to time I had that old back-swerve of feeling. When he wrote to say he was going abroad I was anxious, sorry that I was no longer the official girl-friend with a right to feel anxious. I would say to Hilary, 'I've got *hiraeth* for Rob.' The feeling was more like homesickness than love. Why couldn't you have more than one boy-friend? I wondered. When I started to go out with Peter, I wrote to Rob asking if he minded, and the friendly letter in which he said he wouldn't want to stop me was the most intimate he'd ever written. When I wrote to say it was over, he said he'd been expecting it. Saying goodbye to him had the sadness of a possible life not lived, as many later farewells did not. It was the first grown-up passion.

It's comforting to think of a love-life as a *Bildungsroman*, with relationships improving, even maturing. My pattern looks like a pattern only if I leave out the one-night and one-week stands, but the first three did mark a kind of progress. Rob brought sex to love, and Peter brought elective affinity to love and sex. I was lucky, or unconsciously wise, in my first loves.

The way to school had changed when we moved to the Uplands. I had a short, ten minutes' walk from the Grove past the shops, but the walk was long enough to allow for passings and meetings. I noticed Peter one day, and noticed him noticing me. His parents kept the post office. Like Haydn and Rob – and unlike some later loves – he was exceptionally good-looking. My first instincts were physically aesthetic. Peter was smaller than my first two loves, with a round, cherubic, sexy face, like the cupids in Botticelli's *Venus and Adonis*, and an intellectual light in his eyes. One day he put a letter in my hand as we passed. It said briefly, almost shockingly, that he had observed me looking at him and wondered if I'd go out with him. He would be at a certain place in the Uplands at a certain hour on a certain night. I boasted to a school-friend, Marian Lloyd, who also knew him by sight, about my conquest. She begged me not to break his heart. He looked so young, she said. I had talked about him as 'the little boy'. He was about a year younger than I, but after a few conventional, qualms I decided it didn't matter. Unlike Rob, he delayed touch. For weeks we went out several nights a week, enjoying the heady pleasure of sharing and swopping ideas. Once more I felt lucky. Peter was charming, handsome and an intellectual. He declared himself to be an atheist. He was left-wing but not sure about socialism. He was philosophical, literary, artistic, musical. Everything I wanted. And the platonic abstinence was powerful foreplay. Peter was the first friend I'd had, since those early days at Infants School, who was deeply interested in religion. He explained to me in great detail the difference between agnosticism and atheism. For a while I thought I was an agnostic, but decided it was too vague a term for what I thought and felt. I didn't feel tolerant enough to be an agnostic. I hated Christianity. Peter also had a violent dislike of church-going, which I found congenial and attractive. He took a rationalist journal, and introduced me to analytic, anti-Christian propaganda, and the tradition of Victorian Higher Criticism, which I'd never heard of. It was an eye-opener to analyse those weaknesses and discrepancies in the Gospels. It was marvellous to learn about comparative religion. Peter's family was Church of England, but refused to let him stop going to church. He had to go, or get no pocket-money. So he used to go, once a Sunday, ignore the responses, and read a novel. When I became interested in George Eliot's struggles with family about church attendance, and her reading of Strauss and the Higher Criticism, I realized I'd been in at the tail-end of these Victorian conflicts and critiques. Our intellectual hostility and irony brought us closer. The crude rationalist press was our Pandarus. The war raged, far and near, but the private life was dominant. They took the railings away from the Grove's front gardens but I scarcely noticed. The Battle of Britain and the Beveridge Report were bad and good news in the distance.

One night Peter kissed me. Once more it was what I wanted but was too completely schooled by the culture to initiate. Not that I minded waiting. It was thrilling. So was the first embrace. The love-making was more restrained than mine and Rob's, but

I made the great discovery that every lover has a different taste and texture. I had thought that difference was sexual difference and that it would be much the same with any man, except for differences of technique, and of course conversation. I was delighted, and unnerved, to find this was not the case. Smells and textures and bodies and movements were all new. And there was another new thing, talk about sex. This made the sex more, not less exciting. I always thought D.H. Lawrence's attack on sex in the head was stupid. Sex in the body, of course, but sex in the head is nourishing and necessary as well. I first learnt that with Peter. He startled me one night by moving back from our embrace and abruptly asking, 'What does all this love-play mean to you?' I had no idea what to say. I had no idea what I thought. I had no idea what the word 'play' meant. Weren't we just neck-ing because we fancied each other, but not going all the way because we were nicely brought-up, frightened children? I began to think about it all. This little boy was sophisticated.

Our love-making was sweet and mild. We went to midnight mass, two unbelievers holding hands on a cold night. He praised my wine-red, church-going hat, and my small hands. We used to walk up Windsor Hill from the Uplands to a stretch of undevel-oped land opposite the old Fever Hospital, on the road to Cockett. It was a lovely little opening in a built-up area. You went up a lane, climbed a couple of fences, crossed ploughland, and there was grass and privacy. We lay in a sloping meadow, talking and touching. The night before I went away to college I tore my new dog's-tooth tweed skirt on the barbed wire surrounding our trysting-place, and my mother had to mend it before I packed. Our other place was on the sea front, in a shelter overlooking the sea. We weren't especially interested in nature at the time, but nature was a good provider for us. I was ignorant about sex, and I think my boy-friends were too. Peter and I read Huxley and Lawrence, but there was a huge gap between the people in the books and Swansea boys and girls. Not for the last time, I read erotic passages in novels and envied the fictitious lovers. Every now and then, some time after the jealous, excited, first readings of Lawrence, Mailer, Roth, I'd realize, in literary recognitions that were often incongruous and distracting, that at last I was doing what Connie Chatterley and Portnoy had done. But not for a long time. Not as a girl in Swansea. Yet when Peter said 'sex-play', it was sophisticated stuff, out of the mouth of characters in Ethel Mannin and Rose Macaulay, my early authorities and examples. From them I learnt about homosexuality, male and female, and about sexual variations and deviations. Huxley had characters who were nymphomaniacs, in whom I've never believed. I read one of the best war novels, written a decade after the war, Evadne Price's *Not So Quiet*, for which she used a pseudonym. I was enjoying her Jane books, written as rivals to the great William books though not as good, but didn't know she was Helen Zenna Smith. (A few years ago I edited it for Virago.) This book introduced me to lesbianism, and abortion, but when I first read the novel I was bewildered. The allusiveness required at the time meant you could understand only what was hinted at if you already knew much more than I did. The lesbian in *Not So Quiet*, Skinny, is an unpleasant character. Price makes an allusion to her predilections, of which another woman is careful not to disapprove, and there is a hint about Skinny's not being interested in men. But it was Greek to me for many years. It didn't take so long to get a glimmering about abortion. I did understand a reference to sleeping around and not knowing which lover was the father of the child. But these parts of the story had been totally obscure when I first read it. Somebody in the family took *True Romance* and *True Confessions*. I read these at an age when I was often totally be- mused by what was happening. The characters often seemed to be only hugging and kissing but they were doing forbidden things. There was one story that really foxed me. It was about a woman who'd spent the night with a group of men, and when she was found to be pregnant one of them married her but in a spirit of self-sacrifice. Since the story made it sound as if they had all just gone to sleep after a party, I found it very odd.

My mother promised to tell me the facts of life when I was fourteen. Once I was fourteen I knew enough to dread intimate disclosures, and rejected her offers of information. Sex was never mentioned in the family, let alone discussed. One Christmas we were playing a game of Stump Speeches, and Ron said, daringly, that he'd been to a party where someone had spoken on the subject of birth control. My mother looked furious and shushed him. That was the first time I'd heard the phrase, and I had absolutely no idea what it meant. Glenys James had told me about a famous lesbian novel called *The Well of Loneliness*, and I hoped to read it when I was grown up. (When I did I was disappointed by its sentimentality.) Sex lay in the future. We were ignorant as we hugged, kissed, French-kissed, groped and masturbated. I read about fertility and pregnancy in my mother's eight-volume *Medical Encyclopedia*, and enjoyed the lurid illustrations. I read in its pages about gonorrhoea and syphilis but didn't realize people you knew could get them. I felt the little pain of a first ovulation two weeks before I menstruated but had no idea what ovulation was. I came home from school one day to be told by my mother that I'd started 'being poorly'. She'd found the stained sheet, but though I'd felt off-colour and a bit damp I'd spent a day at school not knowing what had happened. I'd played with my clitoris long before I knew its name. For years I thought penises were perpetually erect, as I had handled them only in that condition. I wasn't enlightened until some time after I'd stopped being a virgin, by a boy-friend who was a medical student and a mine of technical information. I was a university student when I technically lost my virginity. It was far less thrilling than masturbation, and a disappointing experience, not nasty or brutish but perfunctory. My first experiences of sexual intercourse were very disappointing, because of ignorance and because I was casual and self-destructive. The first affairs were risky, and followed by days or weeks of nightmare. But God is very good, as my grandmother used to say, and thanks to him, or a long streak of luck, I didn't become a teenage mother or a shot-gun wife. The best early loves were the unconsummated ones. I didn't go to bed with my first Swansea boys, but they were lovely. The pains of adolescence were nothing compared with its pleasures, and I look back at my young, fresh lovers with new affection.

In No Named Place

Summer and winter we'd be up at dawn
in the V8 or old Mercedes heading west
our earliest mapmarks an Esso sign
and a new factory's yellow pyramid
the kids singsonging as they woke
in crazy sleeptime 'Is Swansea in London?'
and 'Is that Grannie's house?'
mooing to brown cows cwching down for rain
'Are you Gower cows, mae'n bwrw glaw heddiw'
counting red cars, spring lambs or Christmas trees,
piecing an alphabet from the signposts
unriddling Cirencester and Cloucester
savouring chips and the view from Birdlip
counting green bottles and men gone to mow
passing old mines in the Forest of Dean
to find the Brecon Beacons darkening
sun still brilliant on the English side
shimmying along the head of valleys' road
up and down Merthyr's black streets
by the slagheap and pits
swopping our childhood's bad thirties
in South Wales and South Shields
on the high narrow road by Senni Bridge
stopping to hear the flat cracked Sunday bells
of drowned towns deep down in the reservoir
always mapping some new crossing place
until they slung a silver road up high
a wiry tightrope over the fierce tide

and 'I won't go on that' one child declared
'No, just look at the waves' her sister cried
'the river's swirling and terribly wide
I'll keep my eyes tight shut till we're across'
so they sat hunched unmoving and wordless
until we reached the Welsh side and I said
'See, all safe now on the dry land
the new bridge held us and we're nearly home.'

On the way back I saw my mirrored frown
I had to cross the airy bridge on foot
on my own

stop somewhere in the middle
to look down at the quick brown tide
from the narrow footway or a dream
in no named country.

Funny things, bridges,
stone, wicker, wood, iron, steel, Roman, Victorian, modern,
humpbacked, roofed, suspended, pile-driven
over the Connecticut, Cothi, Thames, Tawe and Severn.

About the Author

Barbara Hardy is an internationally-renowned critic. She has
written on lyric, narrative, Shakespeare, Austen, Dickens,
Thackeray, George Eliot, Hardy and Dylan Thomas. She has
published a novel, *London Lovers*, and a volume of poetry,
Severn Bridge: New and Selected Poems.